Gilbert Odd

Boxing
The Great Champions

Hamlyn

London New York Sydney Toronto

Published by
The Hamlyn Publishing Group Limited
London   New York   Sydney   Toronto
Astronaut House, Feltham, Middlesex, England

© Copyright the Hamlyn Publishing Group Limited 1974
ISBN 0 600 31302 6

Text set in 10/11 point Gill Light Monotype 362

Printed in England by
Jarrold and Sons Limited, Norwich

'The Champs'

Introduction

Boxing as a professional sport began in England at the start of the 18th century and has grown into a vast world-wide business ever since, especially with the coming of films, radio and television. From the days of the comparative few that were happy to stand around the ropes in all weathers to watch the bare-fist battlers, to the present, when millions have the colourful atmosphere of the prize-ring brought to within a few feet of their fireside armchairs, the sport has gained increased popularity. Great champions have paraded and gone, leaving behind vivid memories that have been passed down from one generation to another. During that time the financial side of boxing has developed with the changing pattern of life; from the guineas thrown on to the turf by the so-styled Corinthians, through the 'hungry fighter' era, to the ultimate unbelievable electronic age when, due to televising rights, a promoter can guarantee each fighter a million dollars for participating in a world's heavyweight title contest.

This work is a collection of the truly outstanding exponents of the Noble Art of Self Defence, to give boxing its originally intended title, and my task has been made both pleasurable and easy because so many of the outstanding fighting men were ring idols in their day and have picked themselves for inclusion. In fact, because my boundaries had to be fixed, the most difficult part has been to decide who among the many who reached the pinnacle of fame, would of necessity have to be omitted. The heavyweight champions, who always command the greatest public interest, have been included en bloc, because to achieve the richest prize in sport is a recognized sign of greatness, therefore the big boys take up the bigger share of the contents. But there have been many famous fighting men in the lower weighted divisions, from light-heavies to speedy flys, and the cream of these have been incorporated. So here they are, the fistic greats from James Figg in 1719 to the present time, following in chronological sequence from the bare-knuckle bruisers to warring with gloves, all through the weight classes to such heroes as little Jimmy Wilde, the first of the recognized flyweight kings. Of equal

Muhammad Ali v. Al 'Blue' Lewis, 1972

importance, appropriate reference is made to the back-room boys, the big promoters, such as Tex Rickard, who created the first million-dollar gate and who capitalized on the prowess of the great Jack Dempsey; Mike Jacobs, who controlled the fistic fortunes of Joe Louis, the famous Brown Bomber; manager Al Weill, who moulded Rocky Marciano into an unbeatable fighting machine; and Angelo Dundee, who contributed largely to the fabulous success of eloquent Cassius Clay, to mention only a few of those behind the boxing scene who have helped to maintain the attractiveness of this exciting and colourful sport. Adding to these must be the referees, some of whom have caused never-ending controversies, as in the case of the 'long count' in the second Dempsey

v. Tunney fight, and the way the world title was won by Max Schmeling when on the canvas claiming that he had been fouled.

All the information and statistics included herein have come from a lifetime of study, an instinctive and unexplainable obsession for watching the fights, writing about them, meeting the fighting men and rubbing shoulders with all the colourful characters associated with the Fight Game throughout the world – promoters, managers, trainers and the like – during which an amazing collection of pictures, newspapers reports (mostly my own) and records have been accumulated. An engrossing and almost singular devotion has made my task simple and

satisfying, much of it coming from sheer memory, with all data checked carefully to make the result a standard work of reference for students and avid followers of the sport and a lasting tribute to all those who have trod the turf or the canvas-covered boards to battle for belts, purses and individual glory.

Space has not allowed provision for the 'junior' or in-between weight divisions, most of which have come into being since the Second World War, although the junior-welter is of longer standing and provided a memorable occasion when gallant Jack (Kid) Berg won this championship in 1930, causing Lord Lonsdale to rise from his ring-side seat and declare, in righteous indignation, that no such title existed.

James Figg

taught. Figg enjoyed the patronage of the aristocracy, including royalty, one of the frequent visitors to his tournaments being the Prince of Wales, father of George III, who came accompanied by courtiers and noblemen.

Winning several battles with cudgels and fists, notably against Timothy Buck, Tom Stokes, Bill Flanders and Chris Clarkson, permitted Figg to claim the championship of England, a title which was disputed by Ned Sutton, a pipe-maker from Gravesend. But Figg beat him on three occasions to receive

public acclaim as the best at his profession. In 1720 Figg moved into Oxford Road, now Oxford Street, and his original place was taken over by George Taylor, one of his pupils. Several other similar arenas sprang up as the sport of prize-fighting became more and more popular, and in 1723 George I had a 'Ring' formed in Hyde Park, encircled by a fence, for the purpose of staging impromptu conflicts. Figg remained in business until his death at the age of 38. He is universally recognized as the Father of Boxing.

Although recognized as the first of England's prize-ring champions, James Figg (1695–1734) was by no means the first bare-knuckle fighter, there being records to show of men of fistic fame who preceded him dating back to 1681; 38 years before he came into prominence. His rise to public recognition and fame was due to two reasons – his friendship with William Hogarth, the celebrated artist, who portrayed him in his famous picture, *Southwark Fair*, and drew up a business card for him that was widely circulated, and the setting up by Figg of an academy on the outskirts of the London of those days, in the vicinity of what is now known as Tottenham Court Road.

Born at Thame in Oxfordshire, Figg took up all forms of athletics in his youth and by the time he reached London he was proficient in cudgelling, single-sticks and backsword, as well as pugilism. By giving exhibitions of his skill, he became so popular at the city's centres of amusement, the fairs and playing fields, that he was able to find the money to build his own amphitheatre, where bare-fist battles were fought and the art of self-defence

Above: Sir James Thornhill's 1732 portrait of James Figg. *Right:* **Figg's business card, designed by Hogarth.**

James Figg

Master of y Noble Science of Defence on y right hand in Oxford Road near Adam & Eve court. teaches Gentle -men y use of y small. backsword & Quarterstaff. at home & abroad

John Broughton

One of the most prominent performers at both Figg's and Taylor's establishments was John Broughton (1704–1789). Born at Cirencester, he made his way to London to become a Thames waterman, and being particularly well built, at 5 ft 11 in and about 14 stone, he was soon competing in all the strenuous sports of the day. After he had defeated Taylor, who had claimed the championship on the death of Figg, Broughton found an enthusiastic sponsor in the Duke of Cumberland, who lent him £300 to open an academy of his own. It became the most popular place in London and aroused the jealousy of Taylor, who set out to find a man capable of defeating Broughton. Tom Pipes and George Gretting were produced, but were beaten in turn, then George Stevenson, a Yorkshire coachman, challenged the champion.

It was a match that excited the whole country. The Prince of Wales backed Stevenson; his younger brother, the Duke of Cumberland, wagered on Broughton and won handsomely when the coachman was battered into an unconscious state at the end of 35 minutes of fierce fighting. Stevenson died as a result of the fearful punishment he had taken and this tragedy induced Broughton to draw up a set of Rules in

The only memorial stone to a boxer in Westminster Abbey, that of John Broughton.

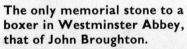

an effort to prevent a similar mishap in the future. He called a meeting of several of his most influential patrons at his academy on 16 August 1745, when the Rules were adopted and remained in force for nearly 100 years.

Broughton was challenged by Jack Slack, from Bristol, and was induced to defend his championship by the Duke of Cumberland, who backed him to the tune of £50,000. John was 46 then and past his best, yet he looked like having the beating of his opponent until a terrific punch to the face closed both his eyes and he was rendered defenceless. A heavy right to his unguarded jaw floored the champion, whereupon the Duke became very agitated and shouted: 'What are you at,

Broughton. You can't fight and we shall lose our money,' to which the champion replied: 'I am blinded, your Highness. Let me see my opponent and we shall still win the day.' But in the next round Slack battered him into subjection, whereupon the infuriated Duke walked out in disgust saying that he was finished with prize-fighting. He had Broughton's place closed by order of the Legislature and the beaten champion never fought again. He turned his academy into an antiques shop and did so well that when he died, at the age of 85, he left the sum of £7,000. In his late years he was made a Yeoman of the Guard and there is a stone in the floor of Westminster Abbey that commemorates his name.

Daniel Mendoza

Outstanding among the prize-ring champions was the Aldgate Jew, Daniel Mendoza (1764–1836), who although standing only 5 ft 7 in and weighing a little over 11 stone, was remarkably quick and, by making full use of the ring, introduced a lot more science into bare-fist fighting.

His greatest rival was Richard Humphries, known as the 'Gentleman Boxer' because he came of well-to-do parents. They had three famous battles, the first taking place at Odiham in Hampshire, which Humphries won in 29 minutes, after which he sent a message to his backer saying that he had 'done the Jew', while a black pigeon sped to London's East End to inform Mendoza's friends that they had lost their bets amounting to thousands of pounds. In a return contest Mendoza gained revenge by beating Humphries in 52 minutes at Stilton, in Huntingdonshire. Their third meeting, in 1790, in the yard of the Rose and Crown Inn near Doncaster, commanded such attention that the arena was filled to overflowing and touts reaped a rich harvest by selling ten-shilling tickets for as much as ten pounds. This time Mendoza was

all over his old enemy and won the contest in 15 minutes.

He claimed the championship after this victory and was twice challenged by Bill Warr, from Bristol, but won on each

Below: Mendoza (*right*) fighting Humphries at Odiham.

occasion, first at Croydon in 23 rounds, then at Bexley Common, in five rounds that lasted 15 minutes. Mendoza remained undefeated from 1789 until 1795 when he accepted a challenge from John Jackson. They met at Hornchurch in Essex and the champion was doing very well against a bigger and far heavier opponent, when Jackson seized him by his long hair with one hand and punched him into insensibility with the other while holding his head in chancery.

Mendoza retired from the ring to become an expert instructor in boxing and self-defence; he also wrote his memoirs which give an excellent account of his days as a prize-fighter. He made a comeback in 1806, defeating Harry Lee at Grinsted Green, near Bromley in Kent, and returned to the ring again in 1820, at the age of 56, when, not surprisingly, he lost in 12 rounds to Tom Owen on Banstead Downs in Surrey. He spent a lot of time touring the country and giving exhibitions before settling down as a publican, keeping the Admiral Nelson in Whitechapel, as well as a wife and 11 children. He died at the age of 72.

John Jackson

Taking prize-fighting a stage further in its development was London-born 'Gentleman' John Jackson (1769–1845), so named because of his well-dressed appearance and gentlemanly manners. An athlete as well as a boxer, he excelled at running and jumping, and was a magnificent figure of a man, standing 5 ft 11 in and weighing 14 st 6 lb. A skilful boxer and correct hitter, he engaged in only three contests, winning the first by beating William Fewterell in 67 minutes, but losing the second to George Ingelston when he had the misfortune to break his leg after 20 minutes. His third contest, with Daniel Mendoza, gained him the championship of England, after which he retired from the ring to open a boxing academy at No. 13 Old Bond Street, in London.

This establishment became the sporting centre of the day and its proprietor enjoyed the patronage of many notable people, including Lord Byron who frequently sparred with the champion and mentions the fact in his diaries. Others who sought Jackson's company were the Dukes of York and Clarence.

Jackson tidied up the Rules and formed the Pugilistic Club. When Queen Caroline was barred from attending the coronation of her husband, George IV, at Westminster Abbey, Jackson supplied a bodyguard of 18 prize-fighters to keep order in the event of rioting by the Queen's admirers. All went well, however, and the boxers were rewarded with a royal letter of thanks and a gold medal to *share*. This was raffled and won by Tom Belcher, from Bristol.

While Broughton had first introduced the 'mufflers' to protect the aristocratic faces of his pupils, it was Jackson who further encouraged their use by insisting that his patrons should wear gloves exclusively in his rooms when sparring together. He remained a favoured sporting celebrity throughout his life and when he died, at the age of 76, a magnificent memorial to his memory, sculptured by Thomas Butler, showing his magnificent physique with the tomb surmounted by a crouching lion, was erected in Brompton Cemetery, where he was buried.

Tom Cribb

Like so many famous prize-fighters before him, Tom Cribb (1781–1848) came from the West Country, being born at Hanham, a village about five miles from Bristol. A powerful, thick-set man, weighing nearly 14 stone at a height of 5 ft 10 in, he carried a heavy punch in each hand.

In 1805 he engaged in five strenuous contests, losing only one, to George Nicholls, when he dropped from sheer exhaustion in the 52nd round. It was his one and only defeat. After beating coloured Bill Richmond in 90 minutes at Hailsham in Sussex, Cribb stayed out of the ring for 18 months, then took on Jem Belcher, a former champion, who was anxious to win back the title. Belcher had only one eye, having lost the other in a game of rackets. For all

that he gave Cribb a tremendous battle, but had to give in to his stronger opponent in the 41st round. Cribb next defeated George Horton in 25 rounds and was recognized as champion after stopping Bob Gregson in 23 rounds. Later he defeated Belcher in 31 rounds.

Cribb might not have fought again but for the advent of Tom Molineaux, a freed slave from Virginia, whom the aforementioned Bill Richmond had brought to England, having heard that he was more than useful with his fists. A fight was arranged to take place at Copthall Common, near East Grinstead, on 18 December 1810. It was the first black versus white contest for the championship and was fought in pouring rain. The exchanges were so savage that by the end of the 28th

Belcher staggers Cribb with a left in their first fight.

round Cribb was too far gone to come up for the next, whereupon Joe Ward, one of his seconds, darted across the ring and accused Molineaux of carrying a bullet in each fist. By the time it had been proved that the coloured man was innocent of this illegality, Cribb had recovered, while the Negro was shivering with the cold. The fight was continued, but in the 33rd round Molineaux could take no more and had to give in. In a return contest nine months later, Cribb was successful in 11 rounds, mainly because the Negro had eaten a boiled chicken and an apple pie, washed down with a half-gallon of porter, for his breakfast.

Tom Sayers

One of the smallest of the prize-ring champions, yet one of the most famous, was Tom Sayers (1826–1907) who stood but 5 ft 8½ in and weighed less than 11 stone. Born in the London district of Pimlico, he became a bricklayer by trade, but his keen interest in boxing saw him spending so much time in sparring with his work-mates that the foreman sacked Tom and advised him to concentrate on a fighting career.

Sayers was 23 then and in the next ten years he took part in 15 bare-knuckle contests, some of them of marathon distance, one with Harry Poulson at Appledore in Kent in 1856 lasting 109 rounds. Sayers won and his victory gave him the right to style himself champion of England. A bout with Don Collins at Edenbridge was interrupted by the police after nine rounds had been fought, so they moved to Redhill to continue the battle for a further 39 rounds before darkness caused the referee to declare a 'draw'. There was a solitary loss to Nat Langham prior to this, but subsequently Sayers defeated Aaron Jones in 85 rounds, William Perry, the 'Tipton Slasher', in ten rounds, Tom Paddock, who stayed 21 rounds, and Bill Benjamin (twice).

Sayers's last battle and his most important, was an international affair with John C. Heenan, who claimed the championship of America. He was a giant compared to the Englishman, topping him by five and a half inches and outweighing him by over three stone. They fought at Farnborough on 17 April 1860 and the match attracted 12,000 spectators, among them Members of Parliament, including Lord Palmerston. Sayers trained at New-market and, to avoid the police, travelled in a horse-box to London on his way to the fight. Heenan, however, was arrested after fleeing from his headquarters at Bedford, but was released on bail of £50. He, too, had to be smuggled to the scene of battle.

Heenan forced the fighting, while Sayers defended and countered well, but had the misfortune to break his right arm in the sixth round. The loss of his 'Auctioneer', which he had named his knockdown weapon, put the Englishman at a great disadvantage, but

he fought on valiantly until the 42nd round, by which time the American was partially blinded and on the point of defeat. In desperation, he seized hold of Sayers by the throat and bending him over the ropes almost throttled him. At this moment someone cut the ropes and a riot ensued, but the arrival of the police caused the multitude to scatter in all directions. The bout was declared to have been 'drawn', but each man received a silver belt to commemorate the event.

When he retired from the ring, Sayers lived in Camden Town. He died on 8 November 1865 at the age of 39½.

Jem Mace

The last of England's prize-ring champions was Jem Mace (1831–1910) who was not only a superlative boxer, but also had the gift of being able to impart his knowledge to others. In fact, it can be claimed that he taught the world to box and he has rightly been named the 'Father of Modern Boxing'. Born at Beeston in Norfolk, the son of a blacksmith, he developed a fine physique by working at the anvil. But he had a restless spirit and in his early twenties he left home to roam the country with the travelling fairs, working for the showmen and earning his keep by boxing in the booths. As an additional accomplishment, he taught himself to play the violin.

There was nothing wild about the way he boxed. His blows were well timed and delivered with such accuracy that although he was only a middleweight and stood 5 ft 9½ in he was able to beat the biggest of his opponents, and won the championship by defeating Sam Hurst, ironically named the 'Stalybridge Infant', although he weighed over 15 stone and was 6 ft 2½ in tall. Mace won in eight rounds that lasted 50 minutes and then accounted for Tom King, an ex-sailor, in 42 rounds, during which both men were badly punished.

In a return match ten months later, Mace was caught by a terrific right to the chin in the 19th round that dropped him heavily. He never recovered from the knockdown and two rounds later, after being battered into helplessness, his seconds threw in the sponge. King did not want a third contest, so Mace reclaimed the title and after beating off a challenge from Joe Goss, of Northampton, he went to America. Here he defeated Tom Allen in ten rounds and then fought Joe Coburn, who claimed the American championship. He was no match for Mace, however, and was so reluctant to exchange punches that after 12 rounds that had lasted 3 hr 48 min the referee declared the bout to have been drawn, a decision that so disgusted Mace that he went to the Antipodes.

At Timaru in New Zealand he staged a novices' competition which was won by Bob Fitzsimmons, whose parents had brought him to New Zealand when he was a child. Fitzsimmons won another of Mace's competitions a year later, then decided to turn professional and joined Jem in Sydney for further tuition. Mace taught such fine boxers as Peter Jackson, Frank Slavin, Dan Creedon, Jim Hall and other notable Australian boxers, all of whom went to America where their style was copied and perfected, so that to say Mace taught the world to box is no exaggeration. At 59 he was still boxing and defended his English title against Charley Mitchell, but lost in three rounds to a man 30 years younger than himself. Mace took a travelling boxing booth all over England until just before his death in 1910 at the age of 79.

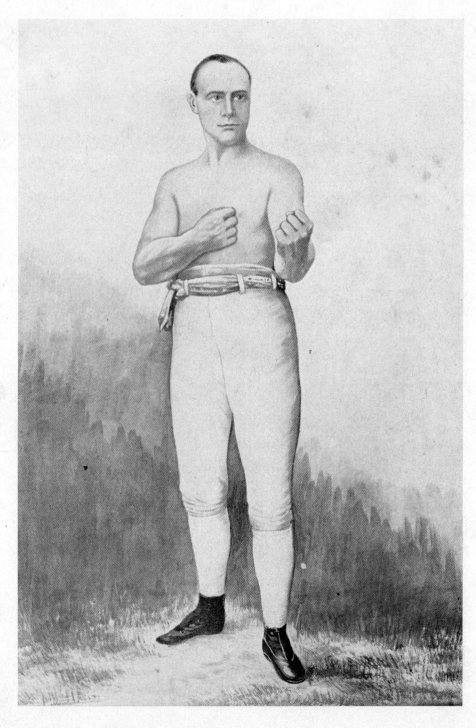

John L. Sullivan

They called John Lawrence Sullivan (1858–1918) the 'Boston Strong Boy' because as a youth he delighted in feats of strength and is credited with once having lifted a streetcar back on its rails. As a fighter he proved to be a powerful hitter, especially with his right and few could stand up to him for many rounds. Something of a braggart,

he let it be known that he could 'lick any mother's son in the world' – soon he had the American public believing it. He became a national idol and it was a proud man who could say he had shaken the hand of the mighty John L.

His first famous victory was against Paddy Ryan, from Tipperary, who was battered into submission in 10 min 30

sec for 5,000 dollars and the championship of America. He next issued a challenge to anyone who could stay four rounds with him and only one man achieved this distinction, Tug Collins, who ran round the ring, fell down whenever Sullivan got within striking range, or hugged him tightly until broken by the referee.

Sullivan continued his winning way and in 1887 was presented with a diamond belt valued at 10,000 dollars by his Boston admirers. He then went to England, where he boxed an exhibition bout before the Prince of Wales (afterwards Edward VII) at St James's Barracks. From there he went to France where he defended his title against Charley Mitchell, the only man to have knocked him down. They fought in pouring rain for 39 rounds and over three hours, and then agreed on a 'draw'.

The following year Sullivan had a fight that created nationwide interest when he accepted a challenge from Jake Kilrain, who had been specially imported from Ireland to beat him. They fought for 75 rounds until Kilrain was knocked unconscious and now Sullivan claimed the championship of the world. Success went to his head, however. He acquired a taste for champagne and soon got out of condition. For two years he toured the States in a melodrama entitled *Honest Hearts and Willing Hands*. John L. could not act, but his mere presence brought in the crowds. Sullivan became pot-bellied and was in no shape to defend his title when challenged by James J. Corbett, a man eight years his junior, who knocked him out in the 21st round after outboxing him from the start. They fought with gloves, Sullivan having declared after the Kilrain battle that he would never again box with bare fists. Although he is usually regarded as the first heavyweight champion of the world, it is more correct to style Sullivan as the last of the bare-knuckle champions.

Although defeated, Sullivan remained the idol of the American public until his death at Abingdon, Mass., 26 years later. He became an Evangelist and toured the States preaching against evils of strong drink.

John L. Sullivan

James J. Corbett

The first man to win the heavyweight championship of the world under the Marquess of Queensberry Rules was James John Corbett (1866–1933) who put science before brawn and was a bank clerk before his usefulness as an amateur boxer encouraged him to turn professional at the age of 19. Born in San Francisco, he topped six feet by an inch and was light for a heavyweight at 13 st 2 lb. Corbett specialized in a straight left lead and a right cross and he cultivated footwork to a fine degree. They called him 'Gentleman Jim' because he dressed in the height of fashion, could hold his own in any company and had handsome features.

One of his earliest opponents was a local rival named Joe Choynski with whom he had several bitter battles, the last on a barge when Jim won by a knockout in the 27th round. Corbett rose to fame, however, when he elected to fight Peter Jackson, a coloured West Indian, whom champion John L. Sullivan had refused to meet. They fought for a purse of 10,000 dollars and stubbornly contested 61 rounds, by which time the referee wanted to go to bed so he stopped the bout and declared it 'no contest'. It was afterwards recorded as a 'draw'.

This gave Corbett the opportunity to challenge Sullivan for the heavyweight title, but the champion kept him waiting for 15 months before agreeing to meet his challenger at the Olympic Club in New Orleans for a purse of 25,000 dollars with 20,000 dollars stake money. They boxed with five-ounce gloves and Sullivan outweighed Corbett by 34 pounds and was favourite to win at four to one. Sullivan tried desperately to keep his title, but Corbett was too fast for him and midway through the 21st round, knocked him out with a clean right-hand punch to the jaw.

Corbett's first defence of his title was against the veteran Englishman, Charley Mitchell, who could last only three rounds, then more than three years elapsed before Gentleman Jim was ready to face another contender. This time it was British-born Bob Fitzsimmons, the reigning world middleweight champion.

Eventually they met at Carson City, Nevada, on 17 March 1897, in a specially constructed outdoor arena. There were about 5,000 spectators and for the first time in boxing history moving pictures were taken of the contest. The champion had all the best of the early rounds, but was knocked out in the 14th by a left swing to the body. Corbett made two attempts to regain the heavyweight title, both against burly Jim Jeffries who had succeeded Fitzsimmons. He seemed like winning the first time when, with only two more rounds to go he was knocked out in the 23rd, but the second time Corbett was beaten in ten rounds.

Corbett (*right*) losing his title in the grudge fight with Fitzsimmons.

Bob Fitzsimmons

The first man to win three world championship titles was Bob Fitzsimmons (1862–1917) who was a physical freak as well as a fistic phenomenon. Born at Helston in Cornwall, he was taken to New Zealand as a child and brought up at Timaru where his father conducted a blacksmith's business. After schooldays young Bob helped in the forge and proved an expert at shoemaking. At the age of 18 he had built himself a magnificent pair of shoulders and deep chest, but as these were perched on a pair of spindly legs, he looked somewhat grotesque when stripped for action. Winning two competitions for novices organized by visiting Jem Mace, former champion of England, Fitz went to Australia where his boxing was perfected and where he developed astonishing punching power.

In 1890, when he was 28 and considered too old to make any real progress, he went to America, was given a try-out in San Francisco and never looked back. He knocked out Jack Dempsey (the 'Nonpareil') in 13 exciting rounds to win the middleweight championship of the world, a title he defended successfully against Jim Hall in four rounds and Dan Creedon in two, and for which he was never beaten. A sensational 95-second victory over Peter Maher at Langtry in Texas paved the way for a title fight with James J. Corbett, and after considerable difficulty in finding a State that would permit the contest to take place, it was finally staged at Carson City, Nevada on St Patrick's Day, 1897. By that time Fitz was 35, four years older than the titleholder and he was the lighter man by about 20 pounds. The betting was two to one against the Cornishman, who had taken the precaution to become a naturalized American before the contest.

The fight was won by Bob's wife, Rose, one of the few women at the ringside. Between the rounds, in each of which her husband took very heavy punishment, she implored him to stop trying to knock Corbett out with a jaw punch, but to concentrate on the body. In the sixth round Fitzsimmons was put down and forced to take a long count. He was bleeding badly from a

lacerated lip and things looked very bad for him. Yet he survived the round and spoke to his wife in the interval, telling her not to be upset by the sight of a little blood. Once more she implored him to concentrate on the body. 'Hit him in the slats, Bob,' she urged. 'That's his weak spot.' It took him into the 14th round before he could see the right opening, then he changed quickly to a southpaw stance

and put all he knew behind a left swing to the body. The vicious blow caught Corbett in the vital nerve centre between and just below the ribs known as the 'solar plexus'. It knocked all the life out of the champion, who went down gasping, his face paralysed with pain and he was unable to gain his feet in time to beat the full count.

So Fitzsimmons became the one and only British-born boxer to win the world's heavyweight title. He remained champion for over two years without defending his laurels, then lost it to James Jackson Jeffries, a much younger and stronger man. They fought at Coney Island, the New York pleasure spot, and although Fitzsimmons broke the knuckles of both hands in trying to knock out his beefy opponent, who outweighed him by four and a half

stone, he finally succumbed to Jeffries's heavy swings and went down for the full count in the 11th round.

Although defeat came just five days after his 37th birthday, Bob was far from finished as a fighter. The following year he beat Gus Ruhlin and Tom Sharkey, both leading contenders, in six and two rounds respectively, and defeated three other men to put himself in the role of leading challenger again. He had to wait two further years, however, before Jeffries could find the time to meet him, but when they met in San Francisco in a return match for the title, Bob could only stand up for eight rounds to the champion's lusty punching, which wasn't surprising seeing that Jeffries was junior to Fitzsimmons by no less than 13 years.

Most people imagined that Fitzsimmons would now retire, but boxing was his life and in 1903, at the age of 41, he challenged George Gardner for the light-heavyweight championship of the world, and walked off with his third title with an undisputed points verdict. When Jeffries retired two years later, Fitzsimmons fancied he could regain the heavyweight crown and to prove his right to challenge for the vacant throne, he put his 12 st 7 lb championship at stake against Philadelphia Jack O'Brien, a widely experienced boxer, 16 years younger than himself, who also had ambitions towards becoming heavyweight champion.

Alas, Fitzsimmons was knocked out in the fatal 13th round and once more the public relegated him to the scrap-heap. But he kept bobbing up in fights here and there, although one boxing commission after another revoked his licence to fight. His last contest was in 1914, and he died of pneumonia three years later in Chicago.

One man who defeated Fitzsimmons before he became champion was Tom Sharkey. They met at San Francisco and the notorious gunman, Wyatt Earp, was appointed to referee. He disqualified Bob for an alleged foul, and was forced to quieten the irate crowd by letting them see that he was carrying a revolver.

James J. Jeffries

Tommy Burns

James J. Jeffries (1875–1953) was the strongest of all the heavyweight champions, both in build and hitting power. Born at Carroll, Ohio, he was apprenticed to a boilermaker, and this arduous work fully developed his natural physical resources until when he came of age he stood 6 ft 2½ in and scaled 15 st 10 lb. He first came into boxing as a sparring-partner to Jim Corbett, the champion, who used him as an animated punching-bag.

Jeffries started his professional career with five knockout victories in a row. Two drawn 20-round contests followed, against Gus Ruhlin and Joe Choynski, who were leading heavies, then five more victories, including a 25-round points verdict over Tom Sharkey, which was notable for the heavy punishment handed out on either side, and Jeffries was elevated to the role of leading challenger.

He was such an open target for a straight puncher that he was encouraged to adopt a pronounced crouch when attacking, which made him far less easy to hit. When he met Bob Fitzsimmons for the championship at the age of 27, these tactics caused the titleholder to break both hands on Jeffries's hard head, whereupon Big Jim beat him down with savage body blows and eventually won by a knockout in the 11th round.

Jeffries got his own back for the ill-treatment he had suffered in the training sessions with Corbett, because he gave Gentleman Jim two opportunities to win back his crown, but knocked him out on each occasion. He left it rather late the first time, because the talented ex-champion was a mile ahead on points up to the 23rd round. Then Jeffries bundled him into the ropes and as he rebounded off them, Corbett was caught by a mighty right to the chin that knocked him cold. When Corbett made his second attempt three years later, he skilfully outboxed Jeffries for several rounds, but the burly boilermaker proved too vigorous and strong and 'Gentleman Jim' took the full count in round ten.

Jeffries retired undefeated as a professional boxer after 22 contests, 16 of which he had won inside the scheduled distance. Six years later, by public demand, he came back to fight coloured Jack Johnson in an attempt to return the heavyweight title to the white race. He was 35 then, a mere shell of his former physical excellence, yet he stayed 15 rounds with the talented champion, before his remaining strength deserted him and he was put down and counted out while endeavouring to regain his feet.

The smallest man ever to win the heavyweight championship, Tommy Burns (1881–1955) stood but 5 ft 7 in and weighed only 12 st 7 lb. In reality he was only a light-heavy, but his great courage, plus a high degree of confidence and a long reach of 74½ inches, enabled him to take on the biggest and defeat them decisively, because he had taught himself to punch correctly and to concentrate on the most vulnerable parts of the body for his targets.

He was born Noah Brusso at Hanover in Canada, becoming an all-round competitor in a variety of sports, including baseball and boxing. He began fighting professionally at 19 and was outpointed only three times in 38 contests, 23 of which had ended inside the distance. When Jim Jeffries relinquished the heavyweight title, it was won by Marvin Hart who defeated Jack Root, and seven months later Burns outpointed Hart over 20 rounds to claim the crown.

A shrewd business man, Tommy did not need a manager to look after his fistic affairs and in the next two years defended his championship most lucratively no less than 11 times. He beat the outstanding contenders in America, with the exception of Jack Johnson, who was too dangerous to

tackle at so early a stage in his reign as heavyweight king, then came to Europe where he defeated the champion of England, Gunner James Moir; the champion of Ireland, Jem Roche; and the champion of Australia, Bill Squires. All were knockout wins and Burns had proved that he was champion of the world in every sense of the term.

Johnson had followed him to England, so Tommy popped off to Australia where an enterprising sports promoter named Hugh D. McIntosh put a tempting proposition to him.

'You'll never be able to avoid Johnson for ever and they won't let you fight him in America, because of the fear of race riots. Why not fight him here?' 'I'll want £6,000 win, lose or draw', came the reply. This was an extra-ordinary amount in those days, but McIntosh told Burns he would do better than that, promising him £15,000 for three bouts, the first two to take place in Sydney and Melbourne, to get him known to the Australian sporting public, the third to be for the title with Johnson. Burns agreed, beat Bill Squires

Jeffries (*left*) in his losing come-back fight with Johnson. *Opposite page:* Above, Jeffries. Below, Burns.

and Bill Lang by knockouts within nine days of each other, then stepped into the ring on Boxing Day 1908 to face his nemesis. For 14 rounds he fought courageously against a man his superior in every department of the game, then the police intervened to save him from an assured knockout defeat. The first coloured heavyweight champion had been crowned.

Jack Johnson

In order to fully appreciate the true position of Jack Johnson (1878–1946) among the great heavyweight champions, it is necessary to understand the difficulties encountered by Negro boxers in his day. In America particularly, they were regarded as inferior both mentally and physically to white fighters, who could 'draw the colour line' if they wished to avoid meeting a dangerous black man. Coloured boxers were forced to meet one another over and over again, and if they wanted to earn money with their fists, were thrown into a ring, a dozen at a time, and left to eliminate themselves to the amusement of the white spectators. These multiple bouts were known as 'battle royals'.

John Arthur Johnson, born in Galveston, Texas, began his career in this way, but his all-round cleverness allowed him to emerge as the winner so frequently that before long he was able to forge a reputation for himself as a formidable ring proposition. It took him ten years, however, to reach the status of leading challenger for the heavyweight title and another full year before Tommy Burns could be coaxed into the same ring. Jack, who liked to style him-self 'Little Arthur', chased Burns all over America, then to England and finally caught up with him in Sydney, Australia, where, in a specially constructed ring at Rushcutters' Bay, he hammered the champion to defeat in 14 rounds. From that moment he became the most hated man in his own country and there was a world-wide search for a 'white hope' to beat him.

They even brought out Stanley Ketchel, the hard-punching middleweight champion, to bring Johnson down and the spectators went mad with delight when the well-named 'Michigan Assassin' caught the coloured champion with a roundhouse right to the chin that knocked him off his feet. Their joy was short-lived, however, because Jack got up almost immediately and as Ketchel charged in for the 'kill', Johnson caught him with a beautifully timed right uppercut to the chin that spilt a number of his teeth and spread

Below and right: **Two views of Jack Johnson winning the title from Tommy Burns at Rushcutters' Bay, Sydney on Boxing Day 1908.**

BURNS–JOHNSON CONTEST.
Kerry. Copyright.
37.

him on the canvas for the full count. Fostered by the newspapers, there was now a public demand that Jeffries should come out of retirement and wipe the golden smile from Johnson's ebony face. This referred to the fact that most of the champion's teeth had been stopped with gold that gleamed whenever he smiled at his opponent's unavailing efforts to conquer him. The old undefeated champion was 35 and living on a ranch in wealthy ease; he had no desire to go through the training mill again, or fight anyone. But the Press and the promoters would not let him alone and when Tex Rickard offered 101,000 dollars for the contest, Jeffries could not refuse.

They fought at Reno in Nevada on Independence Day (4 July) 1910 before 15,760 spectators who paid 270,775 dollars. Both fighters shared in the motion-picture rights. Jeffries received 192,066 dollars, which was more than Johnson got by 46,466 dollars. He earned every cent of it, for the coloured champion skilfully evaded áll Big Jim's attempts to land a decisive punch for round after round, then battered him into helplessness in the 15th round, finally putting him down for the first time in his life and causing the referee to call a halt. The result inflamed race riots throughout America and the showing of the film of the fight was prohibited.

Two years went by before Johnson could coax another challenger into the ring, then Jim Flynn, a railway fireman of great pluck, but little skill, met the coloured menace at Las Vegas and managed to stay nine rounds before the police stopped the bout when the white man was taking a scientific battering. Johnson came out of the ring without a mark to show that he had been fighting and was paid 30,000 dollars for his trouble.

The hatred against Johnson was intensified and he did not help matters by ridding himself of his coloured wife and marrying a white woman who committed suicide. He then married a teenage white woman and further jeopardized his career by infringing the Mann Act, which forbade the transportation of a white woman for 'immoral purposes'. Johnson was charged and given a sentence of a year and a dày, but he broke bail and headed for Europe where he remained in exile for nearly three years, living expensively from the money he obtained from music-hall engagements in London and Paris and other continental capitals.

There were few fights to be had in Europe. He had been barred from

fighting in London in 1911, when his match with the British champion, Bombardier Billy Wells, was vetoed by the Home Office, because of the adverse effect that a coloured victory might have in the Colonies. In Paris, however, he went through the motions for ten

Johnson easily stops a rush by former champion James J. Jeffries, who was brought out of retirement to challenge him.

rounds with Jim Johnson, another Negro, which was termed a 'draw', and in June 1914 he outpointed Frank Moran, a white American, who had been imported for a title contest. Then war broke out, Johnson fled to London and there he might have remained for the rest of his life, but for the arrival of Jack Curley, an American promoter, who persuaded the champion to defend his championship against Jess Willard, a giant in size, but no great shakes as a fighter.

The fight would take place on Mexican soil, where there would be no interference, and Curley hinted that in the event of losing, Johnson would be able to re-enter the United States unmolested and that his sentence would be quashed. Actually the contest took place on the racecourse at Havana and after outboxing his big opponent for 25 rounds, the coloured man went down and out in the 26th and the heavyweight title had been restored to the white race. For the rest of his life Johnson declared that he had been forced to 'lie down' to Willard, but this was emphatically denied by all the others concerned and remains a doubt to this day.

Johnson continued to box and give exhibitions for the next dozen years, but he was never allowed to get anywhere near a title fight. He served his prison sentence and the old animosity died down until in his latter years he became quite a popular figure and was given credit for being one of the great boxers of all time. Jack's skill at leading, picking his punches and whipping in precision blows was unequalled, so too was his uncanny ability to deflect punches aimed at him, or to make an opponent miss by a fraction of an inch as he drew back his head, or smilingly side-stepped to have his rival floundering and very often at his mercy. His left jab was straight and true, his right cross sheer artistry, while his uppercuts were devastating. He was expert at drawing an opponent into his punches and, of course, as they advanced so they met his blows with double impact. 'They just knock themselves out', he was fond of saying.

Of 113 listed contests, Johnson won 78, 48 of these inside the distance. He drew 14 bouts and another 14 were of the 'no-decision' variety. He was beaten only seven times and two of those defeats were when he was an old man of 50. He never suffered a cut eye or any other facial injury, and right up to his death in a car crash in 1946, he was giving ball-punching displays in an amusement arcade.

Jess Willard

Apart from the fact that he was the tallest man at 6 ft 6¼ in to hold the world's heavyweight title, Jess Willard (1881–1968) gained fame for being the best of the 'white hopes' by taking the title from coloured Jack Johnson, who had reigned for nearly seven years. As Willard weighed 17 st 12 lb, he was a formidable opponent to face in the ring and because he had worked on a horse ranch and liked wearing the typical Western costume, they named him the 'Giant Cowboy'.

With a fantastic reach of 83 inches, Willard could extend a prop-like left to keep his opponents out of striking range, while his right-hand blows, delivered downwards by necessity, were hammer-like in the way they landed on a recipient. A third of his bouts went the full distance for the simple reason that Big Jess did not possess the 'killer' instinct and was not a natural 'finisher' when he had a rival in trouble.

When promoter Jack Curley selected him as the one man who might beat Jack Johnson, Willard was 34 and at the peak of his physical powers. They made the fight for 45 rounds, so that the longer it went the more tired and weary the 37-year-old, out-of-condition champion would become. The giant survived all Johnson's efforts to knock him out and in the 26th round, when Jack was tottering, Willard put over a hard right to the chin that dropped the titleholder on his back for the full count. There was a good deal of speculation about the result, and whether Johnson had 'taken a dive' under pressure, but the general delight at having a white champion again overshadowed all else.

Willard made a solitary defence of his title in New York a year later when he condescended to meet Frank Moran, known as the 'Pittsburgh Dentist', in a no-decision bout of ten rounds, no verdicts being permitted in New York

at that time. Moran could have won the title by stopping the champion, but was unable to get near enough to land a knockdown punch and the giant kept his title.

For the next two years he occupied his time with a travelling circus. It was a profitable business, and there were no challengers in sight, until a hustling young miner from Manassa in Colorado, piled up an astonishing list of quick victories and steadily eliminated the other contenders one after the other. He was 24-year-old Jack Dempsey. Though Dempsey knocked out Fred Fulton, who stood 6 ft 5½ in and weighed 16 st 3 lb in the lightning-like time of 18 seconds, Willard did not demur when promoter Tex Rickard guaranteed him 100,000 dollars to defend his title against Dempsey at Toledo in Ohio, on 4 July 1919.

Willard leaves the ring after beating Johnson in 1915.

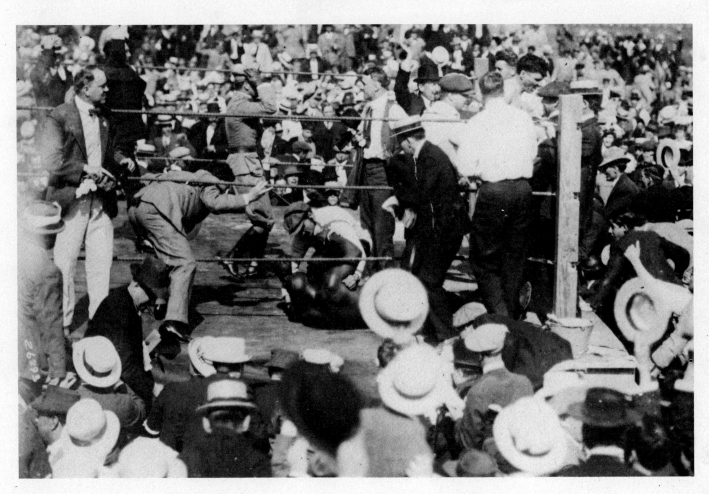

24   The gamblers made the champion a slight favourite to win and 19,650 fans cheerfully paid 452,224 dollars to take a look at the 'Giant Cowboy', interested to see how the smaller Dempsey would cope with the champion's great physical advantages. They were not left long in doubt. Dempsey had bet the whole of his purse of 27,500 dollars at odds of ten to one that he would win in the first round. He thus stood a chance of making a fortune or fighting for nothing, and his gamble almost paid off. At the sound of the starting-bell the challenger tore into the champion and soon had him bewildered with savage blows under the heart, his chin sagging into

Right: **Willard, at 6 ft 6¼ in, towers over challenger Frank Moran.** *Below:* **'Doc' Kearns, Dempsey's manager, climbs into the ring as Willard goes down in the title fight.**

range of left and right hooks that put him down seven times and left him sitting helpless on the canvas when the opening round came to an end. Dempsey thought he had been counted out and left the ring triumphantly, but had to be brought back to resume the contest. The knowledge that now he had only the title to win and no financial reward for his labours, made Jack fight with even greater ferocity and he battered the giant so effectively that Big Jess could not come out for the fourth round.

   Willard afterwards complained that Dempsey had used 'hard' bandages (impregnated with powder that had solidified with the sweat of his hands), but this could never be proved. He made a comeback in 1923, at the age of 42, but after being beaten by Luis Firpo, retired for good. He died within 14 days of his 87th birthday.

Jack Dempsey

To name Jack Dempsey as the most exciting of all the heavyweight champions is no exaggeration, for he packed more thrills and drama into his ring battles than any other and carried a knockdown punch in each fist to the delight of the onlookers. To be a consistent attacking fighter, one has to be game and durable. Dempsey possessed both qualities, and these assets, together with his dedication to physical fitness, made him a terrifying opponent for anyone. The fact that his record boasts of 49 wins inside the distance from 81 fights, speaks for itself.

Born at Manassa in Colorado in 1895 of farming stock, his real name was William Harrison Dempsey, but he took the name of Jack because of his admiration of a former middleweight champion who was his boyhood idol. At 19 he was working in the local lead mines and lumber camps, places where plenty of fighting, bare-fist and otherwise, could be had for the asking. Young Dempsey proved tough enough to stand up to the best, although he lost one or two decisions when he elected to turn professional and was even knocked out in a single round by

Jim Flynn, who suffered a similar indignity a year later to give Jack ample revenge.

The turning-point in his fighting career came when he teamed up with Jack 'Doc' Kearns, a smart young manager, who skilfully steered Dempsey to fame and fortune. A keen publicist, Kearns built up his ring warrior as a ruthless 'killer', and used the sporting

Following page: Boxing's most famous count. Tunney down for 14 seconds in his second win over Dempsey.

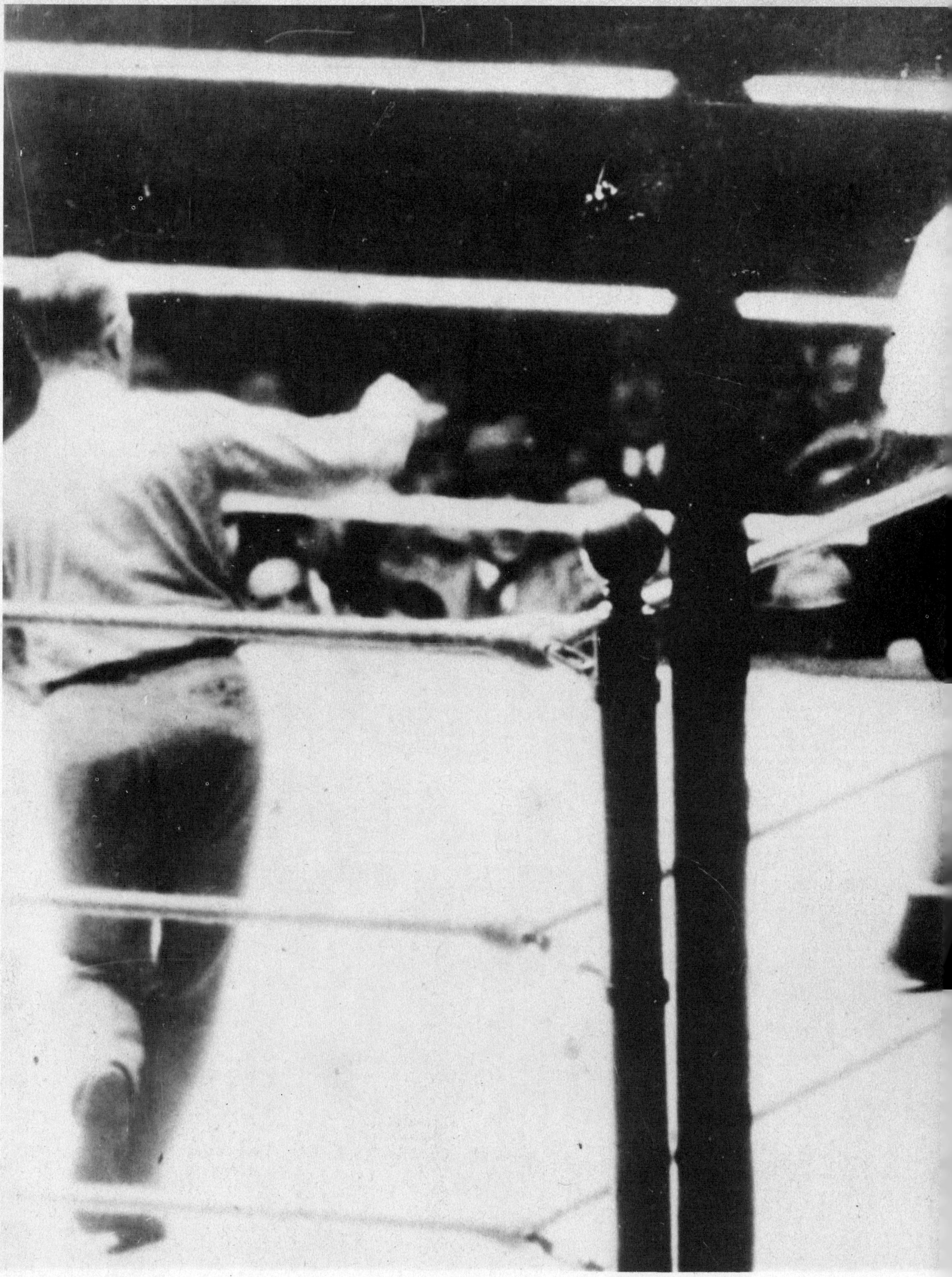

pages of the newspapers to the widest extent, so that when his approach to promoter Tex Rickard for a title fight with Jess Willard had been turned down on the grounds that Dempsey was too small, he used his powers to have all the boxing writers clamouring for the 'Manassa Mauler' to be given his rightful chance.

At 6 ft 1 in and weighing 13½ stone, Dempsey was at every physical disadvantage against Willard, but mere size never bothered Jack who reckoned that the bigger they were the harder they fell. He demolished his giant opponent in three rounds, providing the fans with a massacre that has rarely been repeated in the ring. Then he retained his crown by knocking out Billy Miske in three rounds and Bill Brennan in 12, to bereft himself of American challengers.

Rickard had to look elsewhere to keep his money-spinner employed. In France there was Georges Carpentier, who had beaten every European heavyweight conclusively, although he was only a light-heavyweight. One look at him convinced the big promoter that he would be hard put to stand up to the rough-and-ready methods of the champion, so he had the Frenchman train in private while working up his ballyhoo so well that the outdoor arena at Jersey City, built specially for the occasion, was filled to its capacity of 80,000 when Dempsey and his challenger climbed into the ring on 2 July 1921. The cash receipts amounted to 1,179,238 dollars, making a record in gate money, and Rickard styled it 'The Battle of the Century'.

It did not last long. Carpentier's pet punch, the one that had destroyed so many European heavyweights, was a fast straight right to the chin, following a dazzling left measure. He tried it repeatedly on Dempsey's unshaven jaw, even to the extent of breaking his thumb in the process. But the Manassa Mauler never took a backward step and in the fourth round Carpentier lay curled up at his feet, out for the count.

Dempsey now took a year off, but defended his title twice in 1923, first against Tom Gibbons, who surprisingly took him the full distance of 15 rounds at Selby in Montana. Meanwhile, Rickard was scheming up another million-dollar gate, having found a large Argentinean, Luis Angel Firpo, a man of immense strength, even if limited boxing skill. For this one the promoter used the vast Polo Grounds in New York. Good publicity and the fact that Firpo had scored a number of victories on American soil, drew 82,000

spectators through the turnstiles to the tune of 1,188,603 dollars.

If ever a fight crowd got value for money it was this one. It was fireworks from the start. Within half a minute Dempsey had floored the 6 ft 3 in, 15 st 6 lb, Firpo and the thrills had begun. Jack had no trouble in crashing

Top: **Dempsey knocked from the ring in the first round by Firpo.** *Bottom:* **Firpo knocked out in the second.**

his dynamite-laden punches into the bulk of the big Argentinean, but his challenger kept getting up to fight back until put down again. Seven times Firpo hit the canvas, yet got up to slug back at Dempsey, first, to drop him momentarily and finally, to knock him clean through the ropes and out of the ring on to the Press benches, with a clubbing right to the head. Had this blow struck the champion's chin it is doubtful if he would have got back in time to beat to beat the count, but aided by the boxing scribes, who wanted his weight off their necks, Dempsey managed to return to the ring and stand, dazed but defiant as the challenger came at him to finish off the fight. The crowd made a tremendous noise as the champion managed to keep out of trouble until the bell sounded to end this amazing round.

It was all over in the second. Again

they tossed punches at each other, but Dempsey's were more accurate, better timed and carried more zip, and after dropping Firpo again he finished off the big Argentinean with a short right to the chin that knocked him unconscious before he hit the boards.

Dempsey did not fight again for three years because no worthy challenger could be found. Much to his manager's disgust, he had married Estelle Taylor, a film actress, and her influence caused a tragic split between the two Jacks. Dempsey was bothered with lawsuits and domestic worries, so when in 1926 Rickard wanted to match him with Gene Tunney, the one-time 'Mauler' was sadly out of fighting trim and had to request that the fight should be limited to ten rounds.

It took place at the Sesquicentennial Stadium in Philadelphia, before an amazing audience of 120,757, who paid nearly 2,000,000 dollars for the privilege of sitting in the pouring rain to watch the fleet-footed challenger outbox the ring-rusty champion and receive a well-earned decision together with the heavyweight title. Dempsey wanted a chance to redeem himself, and a year later almost to the day, they again met over ten rounds, this time at Soldier's Field, Chicago, when the attendance was 104,943, the gate receipts reaching the hitherto unprecedented total of 2,658,660 dollars.

To prove to the public that he was more than ready to take back his title, Dempsey had knocked out Jack Sharkey, a high-ranking contender, a victory that caused the crowds to flock in to see if the old 'Mauler' could do what no heavyweight had ever done and twice win the championship. He almost succeeded. For round after round he chased after Tunney and in the seventh he trapped him against the ropes and let loose four punches at the champion's chin in such rapid succession that Tunney's knees were buckling as he was going down. At this supreme moment in his career, Dempsey tossed his chance away by hesitating to obey the referee's order to retire to a neutral corner. Meanwhile the champion was struggling to regain his feet and by the time he had done so, it is estimated that he had been on the canvas for 14 seconds – thus the 'Battle of the Long Count'. In the last three rounds Tunney not only kept out of trouble but boxed Dempsey to a standstill to remain champion, but it was Dempsey who was cheered from the ring and he has remained a national hero ever since. Rickard wanted a third match, but Dempsey declined.

Gene Tunney

Many famous boxers have related that their advent into the fight game came as the result of being given a set of boxing gloves for a birthday present. Not so with Gene Tunney, who *demanded* them when he reached the age of 11, because by that time he had made up his mind to become the heavyweight champion of the world one day. Born in Greenwich Village, a suburb of New York, in 1898, of comfortably-off parents, he had no need to become a professional fighter, indeed, his family tried hard to persuade him out of the idea. They did not mind him joining a boxing club and competing as an amateur and pointed out that if he stayed as he was there was no danger of getting hurt. 'Punches hurt just as much whether they are thrown by an amateur or a professional,' he told them.

He engaged in a number of minor bouts, then enlisted in the US Marines where he found plenty of opportunities for developing his fistic talents. James Joseph Tunney had brains, as well as a well-modelled physique, and he made a study of every move in boxing, from the

The referee making his long count over Tunney in the second title fight with Dempsey.

42

Tunney never became a massive heavyweight, but at 13 st 8 lb he considered himself big enough to go after the championship, bringing himself into the role of leading challenger by efficiently disposing of Georges Carpentier in 15 rounds and Tommy Gibbons in 12. When he learned that he had been matched to fight Jack Dempsey in Philadelphia on 23 September 1926, he practised running backwards and boxing on the retreat so that he could cope with the champion's well-known non-stop attacking style. It paid off because he took a ten-round undisputed decision to become what he had set out to accomplish 17 years earlier and was now the heavyweight champion of the world.

For the return fight which Dempsey demanded, Tunney was paid the all-time record purse of 990,445 dollars for a single fight in the days before boxers could earn fantastic fortunes because of radio and television rights. Again he defeated Dempsey on points, but this time was the fortunate receiver of a 14-second count in the seventh round when, after being smashed down by a dynamic fusillade of deadly punches, he was able to take his time in rising, because of his rival's reluctance to go to a neutral corner as ordered by the referee. Gene always maintained, however, that he could have been up before ten seconds had expired had it been required of him, and no one has been able to prove otherwise.

Promoter Rickard's failure to induce Dempsey into a third match with Tunney, caused him to make his one and only mistake as a boxing impresario. Now that Tunney had achieved his ambition and was a very wealthy man, he was not interested in prolonging a ring career. But Tex wanted to exploit him once again and brought in Tom Heeney, a tough New Zealander, as challenger for a championship battle at the Yankee Stadium in New York on 26 July 1928. But without the glamour of Jack Dempsey the fans showed such apathy that the show lost over 150,000 dollars. Heeney was stopped in 11 rounds and Tunney retired undefeated as world heavyweight champion and did not make the mistake of trying a comeback, his marriage to an heiress making this doubly certain.

feet upwards, putting the avoidance of a blow as more important than the delivery of one. In France, at the end of the First World War, he became light-heavyweight champion of the American Expeditionary Force and brought even more notice to himself by defeating the heavyweight champion, Bob Martin.

On his return to civilian life, Tunney threw himself wholeheartedly into a professional boxing career, being undefeated in 27 contests that included winning the American light-heavyweight championship from Battling Levinsky. More wins followed, but when he defended his title for the first time, against a rough and tough middleweight named Harry Greb, he was subjected to a fearful battering that would have broken the heart of most young boxers. Greb broke his nose in

the first round and plastered him with punches for the remaining 14 to take Gene's title. Tunney gamely stuck it out to the finish, but had been so badly mauled that he had to stay in bed for a week. Then he sent for his manager and asked him to secure a return fight with Greb. 'Are you mad?' exclaimed his mentor. 'Greb half killed you – he'll finish off the job completely if he gets you in the ring again. You'll not fight him all the time I'm your manager.' 'Then I must get myself another one,' replied Gene. And he did. What's more, he took the title back from Greb and decisively licked him on three more occasions. After their fifth meeting the 'Human Windmill' came into Tunney's dressing-room and growled: 'I never want to fight you again.' Brain had demonstrated its superiority over brawn.

Max Schmeling

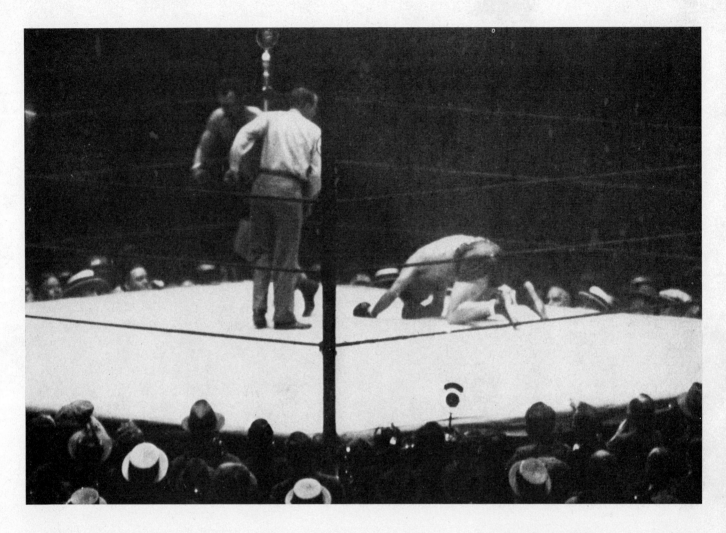

Apart from English-born Bob Fitzsimmons and Canadian-born Tommy Burns, America had maintained a stranglehold on the heavyweight championship since the introduction of gloves. Now the major crown in boxing was to pass into the hands of a European. With the retirement of Tunney, Jack Sharkey had become a leading contender as the result of a dubious low-punch victory over Phil Scott, the British champion, and on 12 June 1930, he was matched with Max Schmeling, of Germany. Schmeling was born at Klein Luckaw, Brandenburg in 1905. Beetle-browed and looking astonishingly like Jack Dempsey, the German had been boxing professionally for six years, and had enjoyed a run of five victories in American rings. Yet he was not fancied to win when he faced Sharkey at the Yankee Stadium in New York, with nearly 80,000 fans there to

see who would be the next world champion.

They were in for a disappointing evening, not only because Sharkey lost, but because Schmeling was crowned as titleholder when writhing on the canvas, holding his lower abdomen, while his American manager, Joe Jacobs was screaming at the referee that the German had been fouled. It was the first and only time that the heavyweight championship had been decided in this manner and Schmeling gained no popularity for his win, despite the fact that all the evidence showed that he had been well and truly fouled by the erratic-hitting Sharkey.

A year later Schmeling returned to America to defend his title against Young Stribling, the 'Pride of Georgia', who had been carrying all before him and seemed smart enough to cope with the somewhat plodding champion.

Schmeling (on the canvas) winning the title. Sharkey put him there with a foul blow.

Schmeling's biggest asset was a straight right and he toppled over his challenger with this punch in the final round to keep his crown. But when he was again matched with Sharkey, in Long Island, New York, on 21 June 1932, he failed to land this potent weapon with any effect on the cagey American and was adjudged a points loser. It was a disputed decision, however, one of the two judges voting for Schmeling.

Max was too strong for Mickey Walker, former middleweight champion, but was surprisingly beaten by heavy-hitting Max Baer, who stopped the German in ten rounds. It now seemed that at the age of 28, Schmeling was out of the reckoning as a championship proposition, but after scoring several convincing wins in Europe, he was recalled to America by promoter Mike Jacobs to provide a stepping-stone for the fast up-and-coming Joe Louis, who was unbeaten in 27 contests and was already being called the 'Brown Bomber'.

No one gave Schmeling a chance, although he told pressmen before the contest that he knew how to beat Louis. Obviously, he did, because despite being outpointed at the start, he produced his knockdown right in round four to send the young Negro flat on his back for the first time in his all-conquering career. Joe never really recovered from that well-tossed punch and although he came back into the picture in the next seven rounds, he was caught again by that tremendous right in the 12th session and took the full count. It was the upset of the century and put the German right back as the leading challenger to Jimmy Braddock, the current champion.

It was a situation not at all to the liking of the American fight fraternity. The Hitler regime in Germany was in full flood and there was a great deal of animosity directed against Schmeling. Moreover, Mike Jacobs was not going to risk the championship going back to Europe when he wanted control of it through the medium of his Brown Bomber. So, although the New York State Boxing Commission matched Max with Braddock for the title, and Schmeling even weighed-in for such a contest, it never took place. Jacobs bribed the champion to make a voluntary defence of his title against Louis in Chicago and James J. was beaten in eight rounds.

By rights Schmeling deserved first crack at Louis, but he did not get it and it was not until 1938, by which time he was nearing 33, that he came back to America determined to regain his title. But he met a totally different Brown Bomber this time. Not the green ex-amateur, but now a perfect fighting machine, who set about the German challenger with such a spirited attack that he had Schmeling down and out in 2 min 4 sec of the opening round before an ecstatic crowd of over 70,000, who paid more than 1,000,000 dollars to see Joe Louis wreak revenge over his former conqueror.

During the war Schmeling served as a paratrooper and made a comeback in 1947 that lasted a year, after which he retired, a comparatively wealthy man, to run a mink farm and other business interests.

Jack Sharkey

There is something enigmatical about the career of Jack Sharkey, a Lithuanian whose real name was Joseph Paul Zukauskas. Known as the 'Boston Gob' because he had seen service in the US Navy, he was an exceptionally good boxer, who met with few defeats. He was also very temperamental, almost all his most important contests having something controversial about them. Born at Binghampton in New York State in 1902, he launched out as a professional in Boston while still a sailor and made such progress that Tex Rickard matched him with Jack Dempsey, when the famous 'Manassa Mauler' was

endeavouring to get himself into fighting shape for a return match with Gene Tunney.

Here was an opportunity for Sharkey to put himself forward as the leading challenger for the championship, but in the seventh round, after receiving a powerful punch to the body, he made the error of turning his head to complain to the refereee and was promptly knocked out by a left hook to the chin. That temporarily disposed of Sharkey's title ambitions, but three years later, he was matched with Phil Scott, the British titleholder in a semi-final eliminator for the championship left vacant by Tunney's

retirement. Sharkey was a great advocate of body punching, it being his contention, and rightly so, that if you concentrated on the midsection sufficiently, your opponent's guard would automatically be brought down, whereupon you could transfer your attention to his chin.

He overdid it against Scott and should have been disqualified after hitting the Englishman on the sciatic nerve in the third round of their Miami contest. He got away with it via the ineptitude of the referee, but came a cropper when he fought Max Schmeling for the title, being ruled out in the fourth round for hitting below the belt.

He might have got away with it had not Schmeling possessed a most voluble manager in the person of Joe (Yussel) Jacobs, who leapt into the ring screaming 'Foul' as soon as his fighter went down. He yelled the word persistently at the bewildered referee, eventually escorting him to the ringside where he demanded that the judge should confirm that Schmeling had been hit low. When the surprised official nodded, Jacobs hauled the third man across the ring to the other judge who was also questioned. This man refused to answer, so Jacobs returned the referee to the first judge, who again agreed that the German had been fouled. 'That's two to one,' roared Yussel, whereupon the referee indicated that Sharkey had been disqualified.

Next time out, he could only get a 'draw' against Mickey Walker, a blown-up ex-middleweight champion, but then made the headlines by outboxing Primo Carnera, who was being groomed for titular honours. That surprising victory gave Sharkey a return championship match with Schmeling, which he won on a split decision, but his reign as world champion was restricted to a year and eight days when he went down some-what gracefully to Carnera and took the full count in the sixth round. Sharkey did not do a lot of boxing after that, but three years later, at the age of 34, he was brought back to fight Joe Louis, who forced him into retirement with a clean-cut knockout win in round three.

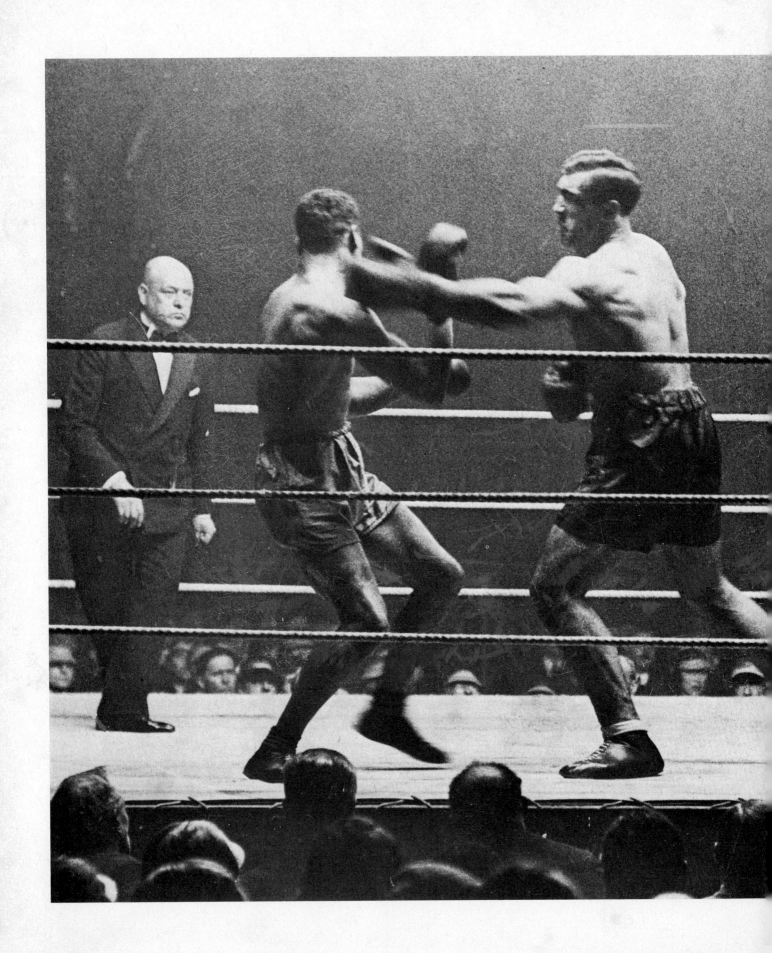

Primo Carnera

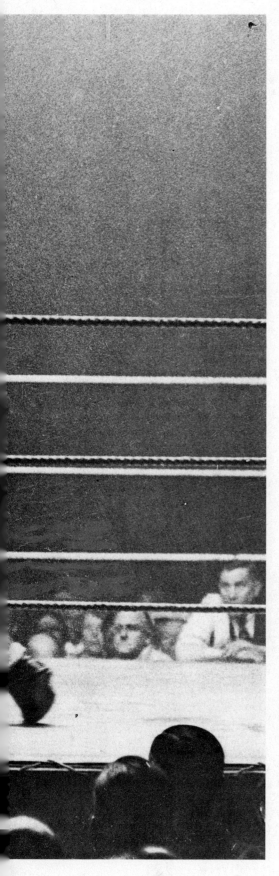

There was something quite pathetic about the boxing career of Primo Carnera (1906–1967), the Italian giant, who stood 6 ft 5¾ in and at 18 st 8 lb was the heaviest of all the world heavyweight champions. Simple and amiable, he had a fighting career thrust upon him and was easy prey for those who managed his affairs in America where he was exploited, robbed and finally ditched. Born at Sequals, the first son in a large family, hence Primo, he left home when he had grown to such a size that they could no longer afford to feed him. Carnera got work in a circus, where his size and strength were useful in setting up and dismantling the show, while he was later put into the programme as a strongman and wrestler. It was in this latter capacity that he was spotted by Paul Journée, a former French heavyweight, who introduced him to Leon See, his former manager. Between them they set out to convert Carnera into a boxer, being convinced that he could be developed into a star attraction in the ring if a modicum of skill could be added to his size.

To their great pleasure they found him most assimilative. To his reach of 85½ inches and immense bulk that could absorb plenty of punishment, they added the rudiments of the noble art, so that when at the age of 22 he made his pro début in Paris, his great size caused a sensation and his undoubted boxing ability was equally astonishing. Primo boxed in London, Spain, Germany and Italy without defeat and was then whisked off to America. Here he was speedily parted from his manager and fell into the hands of a racketeering group who took him on a barnstorming tour of the fight towns where he built up an impressive record of quick wins over mediocre opposition.

The showdown came when he was neatly outpointed by the much smaller Jack Sharkey, who raised the roof by knocking the giant off his feet for a count of 'six' in the fourth round. So Primo returned to Europe, where he re-established himself, then went back to America to run up another long tally of victories, mostly gained by the knockout route. Then came an incident that had a marked effect on Carnera's

future. He knocked out Ernie Schaaf, a 24-year-old New Jersey heavyweight, in the 13th round. His victim hit the boards with such a crash that he could not be restored to consciousness and had to be removed to hospital where he died. The tragedy had a deep-rooted effect on Primo, especially when a boxing commissioner stated that because of his giant bulk, Carnera should be barred from fighting ordinary-sized heavies.

This did not prevent the big Italian from challenging Jack Sharkey for the title four months later, or from winning by a clean-cut kayo in round six from a punch that many observers considered to be of the lightest.

Both Paolino Uzcudun in Rome and former light-heavyweight champion, Tommy Loughran, at Miami, stayed the full 15 rounds with Primo in successful title defences, but he came a terrible cropper when he put his crown at stake against Max Baer at the Long Island Bowl in New York, on 14 June 1934. By this time it must have dawned on the easy-going Italian giant that his fighting career wasn't as lucrative as he thought. He now had so many managers and his expenses were always so high, that on paper he finished up owing them money after a contest. He was due to draw 135,000 dollars for the Baer fight, plus 17,000 dollars from the film rights. Yet before he entered the ring he knew he was on the verge of bankruptcy and this after six years of fighting. Any wonder, therefore, that he put up a miserable exhibition against the swashbuckling Maxie, who floored him 11 times, with Primo being saved by the referee in the 11th.

They sacrificed the fading giant to Joe Louis a year later and he gamely took a merciless beating before the bout was stopped in round six. After that, Primo turned his attention to his first love, wrestling, at which he became a great favourite, recouping much of his lost earnings as a boxer. After retiring from the mat, he took a liquor store in Los Angeles, but returned home to die in his birthplace of Sequals at the age of 60.

Carnera (*right*) beating Reggie Meen by a knockout, London, 1930.

Max Baer

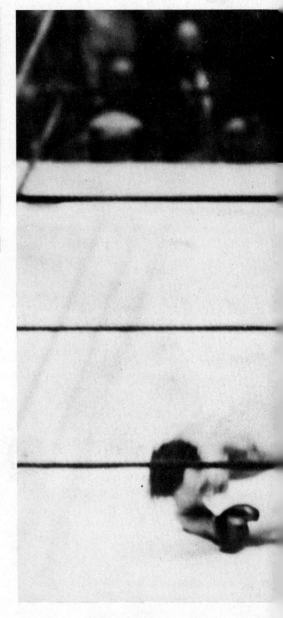

When the boisterous Max Baer (1909–1959) burst on the fistic scene, he appeared to be a welcome throwback to such exciting great ones as John L. Sullivan, James J. Jeffries and Jack Dempsey. Born at Omaha, Nebraska, Baer at full maturity had everything that goes to the making of a ring hero. His height was 6 ft 2½ in and he weighed 15 st 10 lb of solid bone and muscle. He could take a punch and carried a big right hand capable of knocking anyone out when it connected on a vulnerable spot. As Baer swung it with frequency during a contest, he piled up a most impressive record, although, of course, he sometimes came up against a skilful opponent, who dodged his big swings, and then he was outpointed. But 50 of his 65 wins in a total of 79 bouts saved the referee from adding up his score-card.

Son of a cattle-dealer, Max helped in the business in his youth, riding and living a range life that toughened and developed him into the superman he came to be. He had extreme confidence in his physical powers and tremendous courage. He also had a great sense of humour, a large streak of gaiety and a playboy attitude towards life – three qualities that were to prove his undoing as a champion boxer.

He made his start in the local boxing booths, enjoying the atmosphere of a Saturday night in town when he was in his element among the bright lights, noise and bustle, and delighted in the roar of the crowd when he bowled over an opponent with one of his mighty swings. Soon he was being sought after by promoters, particularly in California, where he built up a reputation that was to take him to New York. One night he knocked Frankie Campbell helpless into the the ropes, then battered him to the canvas. When they came to pick up the unconscious boxer they found he was dead. Baer was exonerated from all blame, but did not fight again for four months and then had to be persuaded into returning to the ring.

Gradually he eliminated the rated contenders, giving Ernie Schaaf a fearful beating, stopping Tuffy Griffith in seven tempestuous rounds, then staking an indisputable claim to a title chance by defeating former champion Max Schmeling, with a sensational ten-round display of heavy hitting. The championship fight with Primo Carnera was a shambles. Baer's playful arrogance, his quipping and his strutting, gave him a psychological advantage over the quiet-minded giant when they met at the weighing-in ceremony, adding to the inferiority complex that had been built up in Carnera when the pair had acted together in a film entitled *Every Woman's Man*. With a long reach of 81 inches Baer swarmed over the giant, catching him repeatedly with his big right and knocking him off his feet no less than 11 times in the 11 rounds the fight lasted. The champion was down three times in the first round and three times in the second, but Baer could not finish off the big Italian. In fact, he put so much behind his punches that twice he fell to the floor with his opponent and they had to wrestle themselves free of each other before getting to their feet. When Max tired in the middle rounds, Carnera outboxed him with ease, but Baer got his second wind in the tenth and after smashing Primo down several more times, had him in such a bad way that the referee called a halt.

A year later, when an opponent for Baer had to be found, the best available was 30-year-old James J. Braddock,

classed as a has-been, with a very meagre record and no great puncher. Max came into the ring a favourite to win at the long odds of ten to one, and very few of the 35,000 fans who crowded into the Long Island Bowl, on 13 June 1935 could have anticipated a victory for the colourless challenger. In fact, most people felt sorry for Braddock. They might not have had they known that Baer had not trained for the fight and had engaged in only a few frivolous exhibition bouts during the past year, even if he had lost his temper and belted out King Levinsky in two rounds, whom he

accused of taking a liberty while they were sparring. So the crowd sat silently spellbound as Braddock gave Baer a boxing lesson for the full 15 rounds and walked off with the verdict and the championship with barely a bruise to show that he had been in the ring with one of the hardest hitters of all time.

Baer laughed off his defeat. He had been champion for a year to the day, he was only 26 and thought he had all the time in the world to win back his lost laurels. Three months later he was persuaded to justify his claim for another title chance by taking on young

Joe Louis, the unbeaten coloured boxer from Detroit. This was one fight that Max was really serious about, even to the extent of having Jack Dempsey in his corner. But he did not stand a chance against the Brown Bomber, who cut him to ribbons with his mechanical jabbing and had Baer kneeling in the centre of the ring, unwilling to get up for any more midway through the fourth round. Baer continued for several years after that disaster, but never again reached his former greatness, and after twice being stopped by Lou Nova, he finally retired in 1941.

Jack Petersen

From 1907, when Gunner James Moir, the British heavyweight champion had failed to take the world title from Tommy Burns in London, Great Britain had not been able to produce a worthy challenger for the world championship. There had been bright hopes about Bombardier Billy Wells and Joe Beckett, while Phil Scott had proved too vulnerable. But in the early 1930s Jack Petersen appeared on the scene and at once he was regarded as a likely aspirant for the highest honours.

Born in Cardiff in 1911, the son of a former amateur boxer, young Petersen was raised in his father's well-equipped gymnasium and as soon as he showed a natural aptitude for boxing, he was groomed accordingly. Before he was 20 he had won the ABA light-heavyweight title and soon afterwards turned professional, being sponsored by the members of the Stadium Club in Holborn, London. Inside a year he had run up a string of 18 wins and garnered three titles – the Welsh heavyweight crown and the British light-heavy and heavyweight championships, most of his wins being scored inside the scheduled distance.

Jack was a fine left-hand leader and possessed a right of speed and power. But he was very impetuous and wasted a lot of punches by flinging them wildly when more controlled hitting would have gained him quicker and more decisive results. Also, to the dismay of his admirers, he did not gain sufficient weight to enable him to compete among the best heavyweights in the world, while he cut easily around the eyes, a handicap that ultimately put him out of the fight game at the age of 26.

For all that he became the idol of British fans, who were assured of thrills and excitement whenever he performed. There was a two-rounds free-for-all with Jack Doyle at the White City; a cliff-hanging 15-rounder with Charlie Smith that Petersen pulled out of the fire with a knockout win within seconds of the finish; a coming-from-behind win against giant Jack Pettifer, and a surprising loss of his title to talented Len Harvey, whom he twice defeated subsequently. But the bouts that fans remember most were his torrid scraps with Walter Neusel.

They met first at Wembley Arena when Petersen exhausted himself in trying to knock out the big blond German, then had to retire with eye injuries in the 11th round. Four months later they filled Wembley Stadium in a return match that was even more hard fought, when the handsome young Welshman, spurred on by the multitude, had Neusel wanting to retire in his corner at the end of the ninth. Persuaded to come out for just one more, Neusel was able to inflict an eye wound on Petersen that caused his surrender at the end of the round. When Jack lost his British and Empire crowns to Ben Foord of South Africa in three rounds, one more British 'Hope' had fallen by the wayside.

Petersen (*right*) in one of his great battles with Neusel.

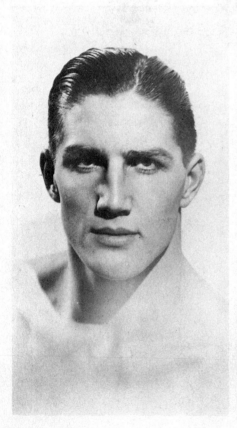

James J. Braddock

They called Jim Braddock the 'Cinderella Man' and not without good reason, because in his prime as a fighter he failed to make the big time and received almost a fairy-tale opportunity when he was thoroughly discouraged and had virtually retired from active fighting. At that time he was in his 29th year, had not fought for nine months and had won only 46 of his 79 contests. Six of his defeats had taken place in his last 11 bouts, in one of which he had been stopped, while another had seen him and his opponent thrown out by the referee who declared 'no contest'. Not an impressive record after eight years of pro fighting for a man destined to become world heavyweight champion.

Born in New York City in 1905, James Joseph Braddock had a liking for boxing as a youth, but did not turn professional until he was 21 and then as a middleweight. His first years in the ring were fruitful without being sensational, but he gained pace as he grew into a light-heavyweight and was thought good enough to pit against Tommy Loughran for the championship. Braddock was a good upstanding boxer who fought on orthodox lines, a smart mover and a precise puncher. He found himself outboxed by the talented titleholder and after 15 copybook rounds had been outpointed. A bad streak followed, in which he lost six of his next nine bouts, and he was no more successful when added weight made it necessary for him to mingle with the heavies.

By the depression years of the early 1930s, he found promoters becoming more and more reluctant to feature him on their programmes and by 1934, with a spell as a dock hand coming to an end, he was forced to stand in the bread-line to feed his wife and family. Then they wanted a stepping-stone for a promising youngster named Corn Griffin and someone thought of old Jim Braddock. Willingly James J. accepted the 200 dollars for a preliminary bout on the Carnera versus Baer championship contest, and having disposed of his rival in two rounds, Braddock came out to watch the title change hands. What he saw of the winner induced him to think that he

knew how to beat him, and he resolved to put himself into the role of leading challenger. A win over John Henry Lewis, followed by an 'eliminator' victory over highly fancied Art Lasky, saw Braddock climbing into the same ring in which he had watched Baer and Carnera a year earlier, and he astounded the fistic world by winning the championship by a comfortable points margin.

Alas, Braddock's tenure of the title was limited to one defence. Had his

challenger been the rightful Max Schmeling, he might have secured a points victory, but against Joe Louis he had no chance, even though he dropped the vaunted Brown Bomber in the first round. But for taking Louis as an opponent he was guaranteed ten per cent of the new champion's future earnings as titleholder, and that, when it is considered that Joe made 25 defences, was worth all the pain and suffering he had to take for the six rounds the fight lasted.

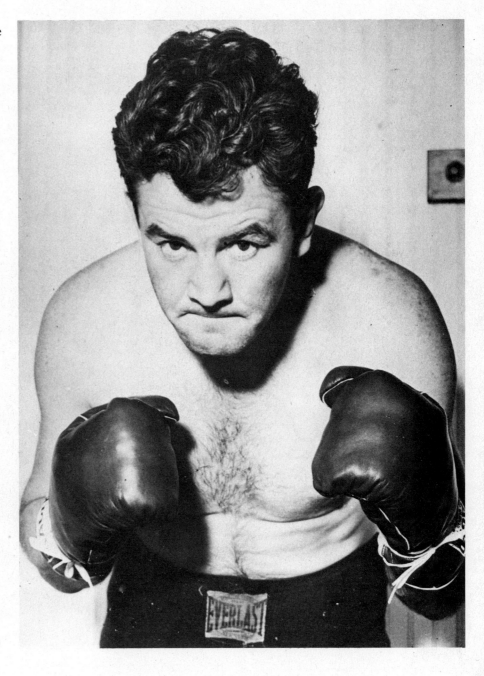

Joe Louis

Undoubtedly the finest fighting machine ever to step into a ring, Joe Louis would have been a musician if his mother had had her way. She gave him a violin for a birthday present and provided him with money each week to pay for his tuition. But her boxing-crazy son hid the instrument behind a dustbin, while he handed over the cash for the privilege of using the local gymnasium, where he became one of the most ardent members. His deception was discovered in due course, whereupon he told his mother that he did not wish to play in an orchestra, but would rather be a boxer. 'If that's want you want, Joe,' she said, 'make sure you are a good one.'

Louis was a good one. His record is unsurpassed. Up to the time he became champion he lost only once in 36 bouts and he was only 22 at the time. He remained champion for 12 years and defended the title 25 times, never dodging a challenger. He served in the US Army during the Second World War when he was at the peak of his powers, yet returned to keep his crown against all comers, finally retiring undefeated as champion, with the single blot on his record put there by the far more experienced Max Schmeling, who stopped him in 12 punishing rounds, but over whom he gained more than ample revenge two years later. He was the second coloured fighter to become heavyweight champion of the world, and while Jack Johnson did much to discredit his race, Louis raised their prestige to its rightful level.

Born Joseph Louis Barrow, at Lafayette, Alabama, in 1914, the seventh child of an impoverished sharecropper, he grew up in a shanty town. In due course the family moved to Detroit, where his father obtained work in the Ford factory. At school-leaving age, Joe followed suit, spending his leisure in learning the art of boxing and becoming such an accomplished amateur that he won a number of titles, including the National AAU championships in the light-heavyweight class. In 54 amateur bouts, he lost only four decisions, while 41 of his wins were scored inside the distance.

Soon after his 20th birthday, two coloured business men, Julian Black and John Roxborough, sponsored his entry into the paid ranks. They appointed Jack Blackburn, an old Negro fighter, to coach young Louis and in the first six months of his pro career, Joe scored 12 wins in an aggregate of 52 rounds. Ten more victories followed, then ticket-speculator, Mike Jacobs, recognized his potential and persuaded those behind Louis to let him groom their prospect into the big time.

Blackburn had developed Louis into a poker-faced, deliberate attacking fighter, who came forward in a shuffle behind an almost mechanical left jab, that travelled the shortest distance between any two points, was straight, true and deadly. It would snap a man's head back with sickening monotony until he wavered under the steady punishment, when he was speedily polished off with swift and accurate hooks from both hands, or a finely timed right cross that carried such knockdown force that few who took it could survive. Louis was ice-cold in action, rarely wasted a punch and had an uncanny way of anticipating and

avoiding a blow by the merest move of the head.

Jacobs gave Joe the stepping-stones that the public would recognize as important moves up the championship ladder. First ex-champion Primo Carnera, who had barely recovered from his battering at the hands of Max Baer. Joe disposed of him in six rounds; knocked out King Levinsky in one; former titleholder Max Baer, in four; tough Paolino Uzcudun in four and Charley Retzlaff, a fancied contender, in one. Next on the list was Max Schmeling, another former champion, but if Jacobs expected his protégé to score a hat-trick over kings of the past, he was in for a rude shock. The strong German took Joe's jabs unflinchingly and whenever he saw an opening, banged over his big right. The first of these floored Louis so completely that he fought on by sheer instinct until Schmeling caught him again in the 12th round and the man the boxing scribes had named the 'Brown Bomber' had been bombed out of the contest.

Some people in Mike Jacobs's position would have rested his beaten boxer or given him some easy opponents to restore his confidence. But Jacobs did nothing of the kind. In two months he had Louis back in the ring to oppose yet another ex-champion, this time Jack Sharkey, who was put away in three rounds. Ten months afterwards he had Louis fighting for the world title and winning by a knockout over Jimmy Braddock in eight rounds at Comiskey Park in Chicago, before a crowd of 45,500. By all the rules of the ring Schmeling should have had the fight with Braddock, but 'Uncle Mike', who wanted the sole ownership of the heavyweight title, bribed the champion out of his obligation, and incidentally, out of the championship.

Holding the biggest prize in sport, Jacobs moved into Madison Square Garden and formed the 20th Century Sporting Club with Joe Louis as the principal asset. He outsmarted London promoter Sydney Hulls, who planned to match Schmeling with Tommy Farr, by bringing the young Welshman to New York and giving him a title fight only 69 days after Louis had won it.

Without a doubt, Farr gave the Brown Bomber plenty to think about and lost only by the narrowest margin of points. It was the stiffest competition encountered by Louis up to the time he met Billy Conn 17 title fights later, because after sleepy-eyed Joe had blasted out Schmeling in a single round of their return contest, the famous 'Bum of the Month' parade started and, apart from one or two anxious moments, such as when Tony Galento put him down and Buddy Baer toppled him out of the ring, Louis successfully defended his crown both comfortably and competently. As for Conn, he had Louis on the way to a points licking, when he became over-confident and

Left: Louis down in the first round of his title challenge against Braddock. *Below:* **Braddock's turn to hit the canvas.**

42

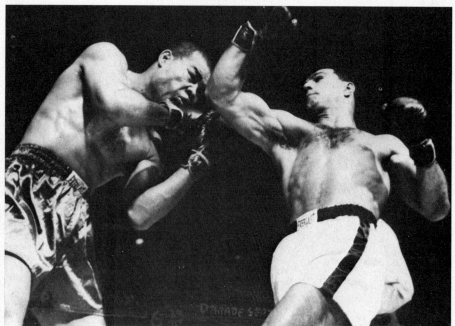

Joe Louis in action. *Top left:* Sharkey knocked out in the third round. *Above:* Schmeling's head resting on the ropes as Louis batters him to a first-round defeat. *Left:* The ageing Louis in his last fight takes an uppercut from Marciano on his way to an eighth-round defeat. *Right:* Louis knocks Mauriello off his feet in the first round.

paid the full penalty for his rashness, being knocked out in round 13.

In the early part of 1942, Louis donated his purse for a fight with Buddy Baer to a naval relief fund, and his earnings from a contest with Abe Simon to an army relief fund. Joe then became a sergeant instructor and did not resume his professional career until June 1946, when he repeated his victory over Conn and whipped Tami Mauriello in a single round. There wasn't another challenger in sight, so Jacobs engaged old Jersey Joe Walcott to box a ten-round exhibition with the champion in Madison Square Garden. No one wanted to see it, so the promoter extended the distance to 15 rounds and labelled it as a championship contest. What had he to lose?

Almost everything as it turned out! Louis had grown a lot bigger and

heavier with army food and as a consequence was a lot slower. Realizing that he had a golden opportunity to find fame and fortune, the veteran Walcott, who had been boxing four years before Louis started, took the play away from the titleholder and dropped him for counts in the first and again in the fourth rounds. The result was a split decision in favour of the champion, who was so convinced that he had lost that he crossed over to Walcott, held out his hand and said he was sorry.

So was Jersey Joe six months later when he secured a return title fight only to find himself up against a far sharper champion, who had him on the defensive for most of the fight and then knocked him out in the 11th round before 42,667 fans who paid 841,739 dollars to get into the Yankee

Stadium to watch it. On 1 March 1949 Louis announced his retirement as unbeaten for the world heavyweight title. His had been a glorious reign in which he reached the heights of popularity and everyone hoped he would not be induced into making a return to the ring.

But heavy income-tax demands forced him to make a comeback within two years, only to be outpointed by Ezzard Charles, who had succeeded him as champion. Louis was nearly 37 then, but the preparation for Charles made him think he could still win back his title. Alas, Rocky Marciano ruined any such dreams by pounding the old warrior out of the ring in eight rounds, and reluctantly Louis hung up his fighting gloves for good. It is estimated that his ring earnings totalled over 4,500,000 dollars.

Tommy Farr

No man tried harder than Tommy Farr to win the heavyweight championship of the world. He got his opportunity with a certain degree of good fortune and made the most of it. His determined fight with Joe Louis, when the Brown Bomber was approaching the height of his powers, was lost by only a narrow margin of points. Had the fight taken place in England, it is conceivable that the young Welshman would have got the verdict. But he was a stranger in a strange land, boxing under a different points system from home, his destiny in the hands of American officials. The champion was credited with winning eight rounds to Farr's six, with one even, while referee Arthur Donovan, who had officiated at every Louis fight in New York, showed his partisanship by awarding only one round to the Welshman.

Born at Clydach Vale, South Wales, in 1914, Tommy was working in the local pits as soon as he was old enough to be sent down. Wales was a hotbed of boxing in those days and like many other boys, Farr became engrossed in fisticuffs, especially if there were a few extra shillings to be picked up. His first recorded contest took place three months before his 13th birthday when he outpointed a certain Jack Jones over six rounds. After that they could not keep him out of the ring, and as his skill improved, so his tally of wins lengthened until he came to the conclusion that to get into the real money it would be necessary to go to London. He walked most of the way.

There he met a sad reception, losing to Eddie Steele in seven rounds, so he came back, won the Welsh light-heavyweight title from Randy Jones, then returned to London to be outpointed by Eddie Phillips. By sheer perseverance, he forced his way into another fight with Phillips, this time with the British title at stake, but again he was outpointed. It was a set-back to his ambitions, but his zeal for scrapping had not gone unnoticed. Ted Broadribb, a very experienced manager, shrewdly recognized that, with careful guidance, Farr could be manipulated into a top-line fighter. They formed a partnership that almost took them to the heights.

Tommy was what the trade calls a 'cagey scrapper'. He came in, bobbing and weaving, presenting a difficult target to hit, could use a straight left with the best and sling over a right that, while not lethal, contained considerable stopping power. In his next 20 contests he was unbeaten and after taking the Welsh heavyweight title from Jim Wilde in seven rounds, he went ahead like a forest fire. He surprised the fans when he outpointed Ben Foord at Harringay Arena to win the British and Empire heavyweight titles, and astonished them when he outboxed the renowned Max Baer in the same ring a month later. Delighted at these upsets, promoter Sydney Hulls gave Tommy a third testing, this time against Walter Neusel, who was unbeaten in five London fights, three times over Jack Petersen. Most of the critics fancied that the burly blond German would prove too tough and too hard a puncher for Farr, who would be outweighed by a couple of stone, but Tonypandy Tommy, now a great popular favourite, caused a sensation by putting Neusel down for the full count in the third round.

This victory caused Hulls to do some rapid thinking. Max Schmeling had been gypped out of a title fight with Jim Braddock, through some skulduggery on the part of American promoter, Mike Jacobs; the British Boxing Board of Control upheld the German's claims, and the Harringay promoter lost no time in announcing that Schmeling would meet Farr for the world title. It was a bold stroke and one that frightened the life out of 'Uncle Mike'. Swiftly he dispatched an envoy to Britain with a blank cheque-book, a contract and a lot of promises. Farr and his manager decided that a bird in the hand, etc., and sailed for America where, in the Yankee Stadium before 32,000 fans, Farr put up the fight of his life, listened to with rapture by thousands of Britishers who sat glued to their radio sets into the early hours of the morning.

Farr had four other fights in America, dropping points decisions to Max Baer, Lou Nova, Red Burman and Jimmy Braddock. Then he came home to see about regaining his British and Empire titles, which he had forfeited in his absence abroad. But the Second World War started before he and Len Harvey, the new champion, could be brought together.

It seemed that Tommy was lost to the ring, but once again he astonished everyone by making a comeback in 1950 when in his 37th year and winning his way into an eliminating contest for the heavyweight title. That was as far as he could get. Don Cockell proved too young and too strong, causing Tommy to retire in his corner after seven courageous rounds and leave the glove game for good but never to be forgotten for his gallant stand against Joe Louis.

Farr leads with a left in his great battle with Joe Louis for the world title.

Ezzard Charles

heavyweight by stopping the redoubtable Joe Baksi in 11 rounds at the end of 1948.

Then Joe Louis retired and Charles was matched with Jersey Joe Walcott for the vacant crown by the National Boxing Association. Ezzard won on points and although he defended this title against Gus Lesnevich, Pat Valentino and Freddie Beshore in the next two months, he was not given full recognition as world champion until he had outpointed Joe Louis, who had decided to make a comeback. Four more successful defences followed, including one against Walcott, but the third time he tangled with Jersey Joe he came unstuck, being caught by a flashing left hook that put him flat on his back for the full count. There was a return with Walcott the following year which he lost on points, then most of the critics were prepared to regard Charles as a has-been.
He was turned 30 and the

championship had passed into the hands of boisterous Rocky Marciano, who was knocking out his challengers, left, right and centre. Yet Charles did not hesitate when offered a title fight with the 'Brockton Blockbuster' and stayed 15 rounds with him in the Yankee Stadium ring. He lost on points, but had not been knocked off his feet, furthermore the champion left the ring bleeding badly from a laceration over his left eye. A return fight was a 'natural'. It took place two months later in the same ring. This time Charles was knocked out in the eighth round of a terrific battle, but not before he had inflicted a nose injury on Marciano that was to be a major cause of Marciano's retirement two fights later. It was not quite the finish for Charles. His experience enabled him to carry on for a few more years, but when he found himself being beaten by men he could have lost in his hey-day, he hung up the gloves, aged 38.

Georgia-born Ezzard Charles was not one of the world heavyweight champions that the fans talked about with bated breath, but the fact that he reigned as titleholder for two active years and participated in 13 championship contests, and came very close to winning the title for the second time, puts him among the fistic greats, irrespective of his artistic boxing skill that saw him the loser of only 25 of his 122 bouts, 13 of his defeats coming at the tail end of his career when he was well into his thirties.

A native of Lawrenceville, he had a natural aptitude for boxing, so much so, that he was undefeated as an amateur in 42 bouts and won every tournament he entered – State titles, National titles, Golden and Diamond Gloves. He became a professional four months before his 19th birthday and raced ahead as a light-heavyweight, beating Joey Maxim and Archie Moore, three times each, both of whom became kings of the 12 st 7 lb division. In spite of this he was never given an opportunity to win the title, but came into fame as a

Charles (*right*) in his third and title-losing fight with Walcott.

Jersey Joe Walcott

Born at Merchantville, New Jersey, in 1914, Jersey Joe Walcott was the oldest man ever to win the world's heavyweight championship, being $37\frac{1}{2}$ and the father of six children, when he produced a pay-off punch to knock out Ezzard Charles in seven rounds. It was his fifth attempt to become titleholder and after he had seen his rival counted out, Jersey Joe dropped to his knees in the centre of the ring and gave thanks to God. Real name Arnold Raymond Cream, he changed it to Joe Walcott, which he fancied was a far more suitable name for a fighter, also because his boyhood hero had been Joe Walcott, one-time welterweight champion, known as the 'Barbadoes Demon'. He added the word 'Jersey' to denote the State of his origin.

Walcott was boxing professionally at 16 for the same reason that made any well-built, under-privileged, coloured youngster get into a business that offered a higher rate of pay than ordinary labouring. Jersey Joe had a great respect for the noble art of self-defence, especially the latter half of the term. He believed that avoiding punishment was just as important as handing it out, consequently he became a somewhat negative boxer, with no great box-office appeal, and by the time he was 30 had got exactly nowhere. Much to his wife's relief, he put his kit in the cupboard under the stairs and employed his muscular physique in a steady job that would bring in the rent and pay the family food bill.

Then, at the start of 1945, a local promoter who had reopened a small hall, asked Walcott to give his new venture a start-off by appearing in the main event. Jersey Joe obliged and pleased the fans so much that he became a regular performer. Other promoters hired his services, including Madison Square Garden in New York, where he scored a decision over Lee Oma and stopped Tommy Gomez in three rounds. These wins induced promoter Mike Jacobs to put Walcott in with Joe Louis for a ten-round exhibition bout, this to be the main attraction for a Milk Fund charity show sponsored by Mrs Randolph Hearst.

So few were interested, however, that 'Uncle Mike' had to make it a

15-round contest with the Brown Bomber's heavyweight title at stake, a change that brought in a near-capacity attendance of over 18,000 who sat entranced as Jersey Joe boxed the ears off the champion. At the finish practically everyone, including Louis, thought the title had changed hands, even the referee, Ruby Goldstein, indicating that Jersey Joe was the winner. But the two judges decided otherwise and all Walcott's hard work had been in vain.

It had been a good pay-day for Walcott, however, and the disputed verdict entitled him to another chance. This time, however, Jersey Joe forgot to duck in the 11th round and was put down and out by a vastly better-conditioned champion. A year later, Louis having retired, Walcott was back fighting for the vacant crown with Ezzard Charles, to whom he dropped a points verdict, being outspeeded by the sophisticated 'Cincinatti Flash'. They fought again with a similar result and Charles saw no harm when a third match was suggested. In their two previous encounters, Charles had become aware that Walcott's pet punch was a sharp countering right to the head, which he had become used to

Walcott out in the 13th round to lose his title after outpointing challenger Marciano for most of the fight.

avoiding. In the third fight Ezzard was doing nicely and keeping a watchful eye on Jersey Joe's dexter mitt until Walcott switched to a left hook that landed with explosive force on the champion's chin and after five attempts Walcott at last was champion.

The following year he kept his crown by outscoring Charles, and three months later ducked through the ropes at the Municipal Stadium in Philadelphia, to face the unbeaten 'Brockton Blockbuster', Rocky Marciano. The challenger was rugged but raw. His iron fists and slugging tactics had gained him a run of 42 victories, all but five of them inside the distance. But Walcott had been in the ring for 22 years and there wasn't a boxing move he did not know or had not invented.

Right from the start Walcott showed his superior boxing skill. The challenger charged into the attack, his own method being a non-stop forward assault. Jersey Joe glided round, waited for the right opening, then let Rocky have it. A picture-punch left hook that travelled

a matter of inches thudded against The Rock's jaw to send him down into the resin for the first time in his life. It looked like the end, or the beginning of the end, but miraculously Marciano got straight up as if he had been pulled into the upright like a puppet on a string. Jersey Joe was horrified. Now he knew he would have to pull out all the stops if he was going to hold on to the championship.

It went into the 13th round with Marciano bulldozing in with his hooks and swings and Walcott boxing superbly, minimizing the knocks he could not wholly avoid, picking up the points and lasting well under the hurricane attack. Afterwards it was proved that one of the judges had him eight rounds ahead, the other and the referee, were crediting him with seven apiece. There was little more than two rounds to go when the relentless challenger forced Walcott into the ropes. Jersey Joe sidled along them to get clear, made the orthodox move and was caught by a short right that came from nowhere to collide with his chin. Down went Jersey Joe and he had lost his title. And when they met in a return match eight months later, the memory of that mighty punch was so strong in Walcott's mind that he was put down and out inside 2 min 25 sec of the first round.

The astonishing thing about Jersey Joe is that although he was fighting professionally for 23 years, he took part in only 67 recorded bouts. Of these he won 49 (30 inside the distance), while one was drawn. When he retired he became a parole officer for juvenile delinquents. He was also a referee, but made rather a hash of the second bout between Sonny Liston and Cassius Clay, there being a doubt as to how it ended and in what time.

Walcott's long-delayed moment of triumph. Charles out in the seventh round of their world title fight.

Rocky Marciano

There is a legend that the fighting career of renowned Rocky Marciano (1923–1956) started in a Cardiff pub as the result of an altercation with a large Australian soldier. Rocky, in the uniform of the US Army, swung a punch from his boot-tops that flattened his rival and resulted in Marciano's immediate entry into the company's boxing team. When he reached his home in Brockton, Massachusetts, at the end of the war, his best pal persuaded him to find out what it felt like to be paid for punching noses, and Rocky did so well that after his first 22 bouts, all of which he won in an aggregate of 62 rounds, it was decided that he should apply for a contest at Madison Square Garden in New York, the Mecca for all aspiring boxers.

Matchmaker Al Weill, naturally interested in heavyweight prospects, sent him a one-way ticket, but was disappointed when he confronted the stockily built New Englander. Marciano was only 5 ft 10½ in and weighed about 13 stone, while his short arms suggested a reach appropriate to his height. But he was given a try-out in a near-by gym. One look at Rocky's crude idea of boxing and the greedy way he absorbed punishment, caused Weill to walk away, but he turned back when he heard a crash – and there was the sparring-partner on the floor, so the boy from Brockton was given a pre-liminary bout which he won in a brace of rounds. His non-stop, swarming tactics and the way he marched in regardless of what an opponent tossed at him, was all to the liking of the fans. This resulted in more Garden engage-ments, with the matchmaker taking over the management of this astonish-ingly strong Italian, whose real name was Rocco Francis Marchegiano.

Marciano's brand of belligerent destructiveness had to be seen to be believed. There was no art or finesse about his work, he just bulldozed in and took his opponents apart with his hooks, swings and uppercuts, not taking any aim or placing his shots, merely saturating the other man with leather until he had been battered into submission. In his eagerness to plaster an opponent with as many punches as could be got into every round,

Marciano had no time for discretion. He hit them anywhere above the belt line, but if he went below it, he hadn't a moment to spare in apology. Knuckles, wrists, forearms, even elbows, and the inevitable shove, all came into play and it was a good man who could survive the scheduled distance with such a human tank. Some did, and six of Rocky's 49 pro contests went all the way; the rest either called for the timekeeper's services or the referee's charity.

An eight-round win over Joe Louis, nine years his senior and making a comeback, put Marciano firmly on the title trail. This was followed by a six-round win over another veteran, Lee Savold, then Rocky was ready for an eliminating bout with Harry Matthews, from Seattle, who had built up such an impressive record that his followers were convinced that with his academic boxing he could bring the fistic juggernaut to a full stop. Totally ignoring his rival's classy reputation, Rocky sailed in and beat Matthews into pulp inside two rounds, so now, at the age of 29, with a mere 42 contests under his belt, albeit all victories, he climbed into the Philadelphia Stadium to do battle with Jersey Joe Walcott for the heavyweight championship.

Within the first minute Rocky was on the floor from a well-timed left hook to the chin. The fans could not believe it, nor could Rocky. It was the first time he had visited the canvas and he obeyed his instincts and got up without taking a count, although the timekeeper had reached 'three' by the time he had got into a fighting stance again. Walcott, too, was perturbed at this display of toughness, but proceeded to give Marciano a boxing lesson, in spite of the fact that he was on the retreat for most of the succeeding 12 rounds. The intense pressure must have weakened old Jersey Joe, for in the 13th he made a mis-move, ducked into a short right swing, sagged down clutching the near-by ropes, and was still struggling to beat the count when the 'out' came.

Rocky came out of the fight with a nasty cut over his left eye, but he had eight months in which to get this healed before giving Walcott a return

bout. Again Marciano had Jersey Joe on the defensive from a swarming attack, with the new champion even more aggressive this time. Walcott speared him off as best he could, but it was obvious that the veteran had lost a lot of his confidence. A sweeping left to the jaw followed by a vicious short right to the other side of Walcott's sagging chin had him down and floundering. He failed to get to his feet inside the stipulated ten seconds and Rocky had won in 2 min 25 sec of the opening round.

There were five more title defences. Roland LaStarza, who had taken Rocky the distance in his third visit to New York, was pounded into submission in 11 rounds, but when Marciano accepted a challenge from former champion, Ezzard Charles, he was given the second hardest fight of his brief career, being taken the full distance of 15 rounds and only bringing off victory in the final two rounds when his rival was on the point of exhaustion from the pace and the punishment he had been forced to take while waging a punch-for-punch battle with the irrepressible Rocky. Judge Aidela gave it to Marciano by eight rounds to five with two even; Judge Barnes made it eight–six–one in the champion's favour, while the referee scored Marciano eight, Charles six and one drawn. The champion had kept his crown, but he left the ring with blood streaming down from a severe cut by

***Following pages:* Marciano leaves Cockell draped across the ropes after a typical assault.**

52 the side of his left eye and knew that he would have to meet Charles again.

When he did, things were far different. As with Walcott in his return fight with Rocky, Charles did not stand a chance. He was punched silly in a fight in which he could do little but defend himself, so intense was the stream of punches that came at him from all angles and without a moment's breathing-space. In the opening round Charles hit the champion with a straight right to the jaw and then another, shorter right on the same spot. Rocky merely blinked. From then on it was all Marciano. He put Charles down for a two-second count in round two, but Charles kept out of further trouble until the eighth when Rocky landed a power-driven left hook that made the challenger's knees wobble. A right to the jaw, another left on the chin, plus one more right smash and it was all over. Charles pitched over on to his face and was counted out.

There wasn't another American contender in sight, so they sent for Don Cockell, the British champion, who had the guts to take on the most feared man in the current fight game. They met at Kezar Field in San Francisco in a particularly small ring from which there was no escape and it is a marvel that the 'Battersea Blacksmith' lasted as long as he did. Marciano gave him the full treatment and got away with murder, and the general impression among the British pressmen was that Rocky would have been ruled out several times by an English referee. However, Cockell took it all as part of the business and traded punches all the time he was on his feet. There were knockdowns and shovedowns, with Cockell pushed through the ropes, even struck when down. Rocky did not deliberately foul Don, but in his eagerness to win decisively, he ignored the rules and had won in the ninth round when the over-tolerant referee came to Cockell's rescue.

The final title defence came against Archie Moore, light-heavyweight champion and another veteran of vast experience. He fancied himself to win the title and looked like doing so when, in the second round, he made Marciano miss with a left hook and countered him with a short right to the chin that sent the champion down on his hands and knees. The sight brought a roar from the 61,574 fans packed into the Yankee Stadium in New York, but as in the first fight with Walcott, Rocky was up inside three seconds and then proceeded to punch the living daylights out of 'Ancient Archie'. Down from a blistering attack in the sixth round for counts of 'four' and 'eight', Moore managed to stay half-way through the ninth when he took a bludgeoning near the ropes and sank down, too thoroughly spent to get to his feet, and Marciano had won yet another title fight inside the distance.

While they were conjuring up who should be the next lucky man to be brought to the slaughter, Marciano was doing a great deal of thinking. He had earned over 4,000,000 dollars with his flailing fists, but he had twice suffered severe cuts and Ezzard Charles had damaged his nose severely in their last bout. On 27 April 1956, seven months after the fight with Moore, he publicly announced his retirement – the only world heavyweight champion ever to leave the ring unbeaten in his entire career and never to make a comeback. He did appear in a computerized film with Cassius Clay some years later, but turned a deaf ear to all the fabulous financial inducements to fight again. The world learned with deep regret that this great fistic warrior had lost his life in an air crash in Iowa in 1969 at the age of 46.

Marciano beats off British challenger Don Cockell (left).

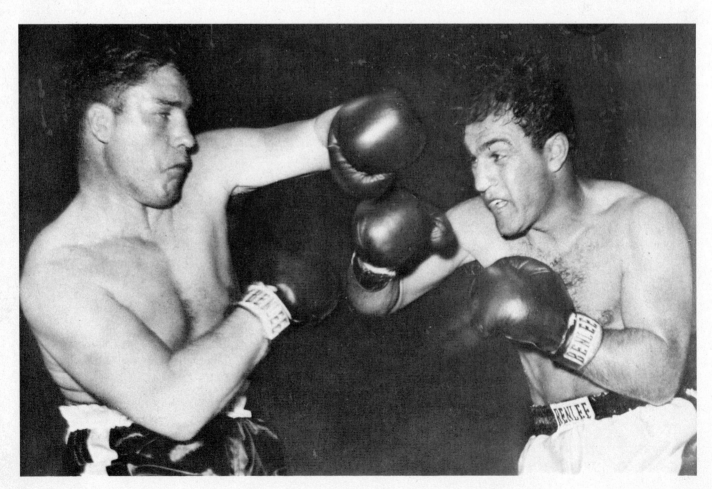

Ingemar Johansson

Apart from Bob Fitzsimmons (1897), only three other European boxers have won the world's heavyweight title: Max Schmeling (1930), Primo Carnera (1933) and Ingemar Johansson (1959). Born in Gothenburg in Sweden in 1932, he built up a fine amateur record that ended ingloriously at the 1952 Olympic Games at Helsinki, when he was ruled out of the final of the heavyweight class against Ed Sanders, of the USA, for 'not giving of his best' and forfeited the silver medal that was due to him in any case.

In December of that year he turned professional, being aided and abetted by Eddie Ahlquist, a newspaper proprietor, who became a boxing promoter as soon as it was clear that Johansson had what it takes to go places. After five paid wins, Ingemar served in the Swedish Navy for 11 months, then returned to ring activity, beating all the continental heavies that could be found to face him, including Franco Cavicchi, from whom he won the European title by a knockout in 13 rounds, and the best of Britain's big boys.

Peter Bates was disposed of in two rounds and Henry Cooper in five, while Joe Erskine, the British champion, was forced to retire in 13. Heinz Neuhaus, former champion of Germany, could stay only four rounds, giving Johansson an unbeaten run of 20 wins, then the young Swede was given his stiffest test to date, being matched with Eddie Machen, a coloured Californian, rated second only behind world champion Floyd Patterson. Those interested in the American must have imagined that there was no danger in meeting the Scandinavian fighter, otherwise they would never have taken the contest with Machen so close to a title chance. Eddie himself was full of confidence until he encountered the 'Hand of Thor', a straight right which Johansson had perfected and which he could throw with lightning speed across an opponent's guard to land stunningly on his chin. The first one of these that struck Machen sent him catapulting across the ring to land in a heap by the ropes. He got up in a daze, was dropped by another belting right, once more managed to rise, then was flattened for

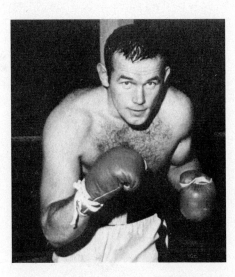

the third and last time by another Swedish thunderbolt. It was all over in 2 min 16 sec of the opening round.

Nine months later, Ingemar, his family, his fiancée and his manager were in New York for a championship fight with Patterson at the Yankee Stadium. There was a poor turn-out of 18,215 fans, because no one thought a lot of the champion, who was favourite at 8 to 5, and they were suspicious of European heavies, even though the short television film of Machen's destruction had been shown in shop windows over and over again, both at normal speed and in slow motion, as a publicity stunt for weeks before the fight. It would have been to Patterson's advantage had he broke training for a few minutes to watch the film himself. It might have saved him a lot of pain and humiliation.

Johansson had a tantalizing left flick to the face which he used to blot out an opponent's vision and mesmerize him into leaving an opening for the Hand of Thor. Patterson, who liked doing all the leading, leaping in to let loose rapid combinations of punches from each hand, found himself baffled by the long reach of the Swede. After two rounds of achieving nothing, he came out of his peek-a-boo defensive guard to take a look at what was going on. Wham! Over came 'Ingo's Bingo' and the champion was on the canvas. Seven times Patterson was floored in that sensational third round, with the champion displaying wonderful courage in getting up after each stunning

knockdown. Finally referee Ruby Goldstein decided that Floyd had taken enough and a halt was called with 57 seconds of the round remaining.

The contract called for a return contest and their second meeting was at the New York Polo Grounds, with considerably more interest aroused, 31,892 fans assembling, while a multitude looked-in on closed-circuit and theatre television. Patterson had been favourite to win the first fight, now Johansson was installed as the likely winner at the odds of 8 to 5. He was supremely confident that what he had once achieved, he could do again, while the fans anticipated that Patterson would be too gun-shy to be able to take the initiative away from the Scandinavian.

Yet that is precisely what Floyd did. Right from the start he carried the fight to the champion, successfully dodging his bombs and leaping in to rattle Johansson with swift bursts of rapid fire from both fists. By the fifth round Patterson had his man reeling and a flashing left hook, followed by another, dropped the Swede flat on his back to be counted out. Nine months later, Floyd proved that his victory was no flash in the pan by disposing of Johansson in six rounds and Ingo's world championship adventures had come to an end.

He came home to regain the European title he had been forced to relinquish while world titleholder, knocking out Dick Richardson in eight rounds, but after coming perilously close to defeat against Brian London, who had him down and saved by the bell in the final round, Johansson retired at the age of 31 to conduct his haulage business and partner his manager in the promotion of boxing tournaments.

Following page: In the top picture Johansson earns his title chance by knocking out Eddie Machen in the first round at Gothenburg in 1958. Patterson meets the same fate in the lower picture against Johansson in a title fight the next year. Referee Ruby Goldstein stops the fight on Patterson's seventh knockdown.

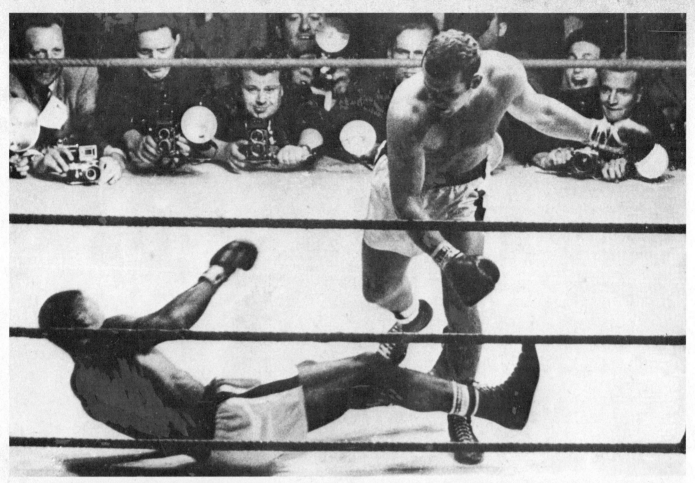

Floyd Patterson

To Floyd Patterson goes the distinction of creating two records in the heavyweight class of boxing. At 21 years, ten months and 26 days, he became the youngest man ever to win the championship, and he was the first and only man ever to twice win the heavyweight crown, breaking the age-old adage that they never come back. Add to this the fact that at the age of 38 he was still well up in the ratings and you have a dedicated fighter who qualifies to be among the great ones.

Born at Waco County in North Carolina in 1935, he was a third son of ten children born to an unskilled labourer employed on the docks. When he was quite small the family moved to Brooklyn, into a crowded, poverty-stricken area known as Bedford-Stuyvesant – another Harlem.

He had no wish to be educated and played truant from school so often and was so backward that he was sent to a special place for retarded children. Floyd thought he was going to prison, but one look at the playing fields around the place convinced him that

here he could be happy. Sport and athletics interested him more than anything else and when the physical instructor introduced him to boxing, he knew he had found his heart's delight.

Always he was first in the gymnasium and the last out and when he left

Patterson gets a right to London's chin (*left*) and London down in the tenth (*right*).

school to go home to find work, his first thoughts were to continue his boxing training. Two of his brothers were embarking on a professional career and he joined them at a grimy establishment in a rickety building kept by a man named Cus D'Amato. In a twinkling he realized that young Patterson was a natural boxer and at 16 Floyd was winning amateur titles, including Golden Gloves competitions, finally being selected to join the Olympic boxing squad for the Helsinki Games in 1952.

He came home with the middleweight gold medal and a few months later became a professional under the management of his trainer. Between them, Patterson and D'Amato travelled straight to the top to make ring history. It was a stony path, only made easier by Floyd's brilliance as a boxer, his courageous heart, physical fitness and dedication to his trade, plus complete confidence in his mentor.

They were in no hurry because of Patterson's youth; in fact, D'Amato told the boy that it would take six years for them to get within reach of the

56

Above: Patterson becomes the first world heavyweight champion to regain his crown by knocking out Johansson in the fifth round of their second fight. *Below, right:* Patterson going down in the third round of his first fight with Johansson. *Right:* Patterson going down for the third and last time in his second losing fight with Liston. *Opposite page:* Patterson winning the vacant heavyweight title for the first time by knocking out Archie Moore.

heavyweight championship. It was his belief that Floyd would grow that big, even though he would never be a giant. Actually it took only four and a half years for Patterson to get into the contender class, being aided in that direction by the unexpected retirement of Rocky Marciano. In that time Floyd had 30 bouts, dropping a solitary decision to the far more experienced Joey Maxim, but winning 21 contests inside the distance.

His defence was an exaggerated cover with both arms that became known as his 'peek-a-boo' guard. From behind this he would leap at his opponents with a rapid two-fisted fire of punches, whipping in a tattoo of combinations to smother a rival with leather and have him ready for powerful long-range deliveries that came with power and precision to land in the right places. It soon became clear, however, that Floyd had a somewhat fragile chin that caused him to go down whenever he was caught on the jaw as he came in with one of his kangaroo attacks. But he always bounced up, seemingly none the worse for the knockdown, and was back to a speedy attack to the consternation of his opponents.

Before he could challenge for the vacant heavyweight title, Patterson was put into an elimination contest with Tommy Jackson, a hurricane hitter, very durable and carrying a knockdown punch. It was Floyd's most severe test to date, but he scored well against a stronger rival and although the referee voted for Jackson, both the judges gave it to Patterson by a good margin. Floyd came out of the fight with a damaged right hand, otherwise he might have stopped Jackson, who was in a groggy state at the final bell that ended the 12 scheduled rounds.

Within five months Patterson was ready to face veteran Archie Moore for the championship. Moore was almost double Patterson's age and was boxing before Floyd was born. They made 'Ancient Archie' a favourite to win at 7 to 5, but he was never in the picture. Patterson took his best shots unflinchingly in the early rounds, then outspeeded the older man to have him weary by the fifth round when a dazzling left hook deposited Moore on the canvas. When Archie got to his feet he was met with a terrifying blast of punches that caused him to sink to the canvas for the full count. Patterson was the 20th heavyweight champion since the days of John L. Sullivan and the fifth coloured boxer to win the title.

Manager D'Amato was determined that his boxer should not become the monopolized property of the International Boxing Club that ruled the sport in New York. He refused all offers to defend the title there and took Patterson round the country. Floyd disposed of Pete Rademacher, former Olympic Games champion, in six rounds at Seattle; Roy Harris, a comparative unknown, in 12 rounds at Los Angeles, and Brian London, former British titleholder, in 11 rounds at Indianapolis. None of these challengers were of great class and by taking them Patterson lost considerable prestige. Both he and his mentor hoped to gain the popularity due to a world heavyweight champion, by finding an independent promoter to stage a fight in New York with Ingemar Johansson, a strong, hard-punching Swede, who had sprung into the limelight by virtue of a sensational one-round victory over Eddie Machen, one of Floyd's leading contenders.

Patterson entered the Yankee Stadium ring full of confidence, but found he could make little headway against Johansson, who checked his attacking spurts with a long left to the face for two rounds until Floyd lost patience, came out from behind his arm shield and leapt straight into a long right that came with the full force of the Swede's 14 stone and knocked the champion flat on his back. As usual, Floyd got up in time to beat the count, but although his spirit was as strong as ever, his nervous system had been paralysed by that tremendous blow and he was an easy target for everything that Johansson tossed at him – and it was plenty. Six more times Patterson was put down, and when the referee finally called a halt to the slaughter, Floyd was still on his feet.

Few men would have recovered mentally from such a beating, but Patterson was made of a rare quality of zeal and courage, plus an urgent desire to regain his lost laurels. He was still only 24 and when he had studied the film of his defeat by Johansson and analysed his own faults, he was ready, a year later, to meet his conqueror with the utmost confidence. This time he attacked from the start, coming off his stool to tear into the Swede and crowd him so close that Ingemar was never in range to fire his big gun. Patterson dominated the fight for round after round and in the fifth got through with a sizzling left hook to the chin that sent the big man sprawling. Johansson rose between 'eight' and 'nine', but he was done. Floyd timed another left to a nicety and cracked it home to put the champion on his back and out for the count.

So Patterson had broken tradition and regained the heavyweight title and nine months later when they met for the 'rubber', Patterson used the same tactics that had been so successful when he regained the championship, but received a rude shock when Johansson met his first rush with that mighty right that caught him smack on the chin and had him down. Up at 'seven', he was soon tumbled over again and although gamely on his feet at 'six', was given a mandatory count of two further seconds, precious moments that enabled him to last out this dramatic first round, even to drop the Swede momentarily from a neat left hook to the chin. It was all Patterson after that, and in the sixth he connected solidly with another left hook, struck Johansson with a whirling right as he was falling and it was all over.

There was a defence against Tom McNeeley in Toronto that lasted only four rounds, then Floyd was called upon to defend the title against Sonny Liston, a tremendous man with every physical advantage over Patterson, except courage. Unfortunately for Floyd that was not enough. He was mauled and bludgeoned into defeat inside a round and fared no better in a return meeting, except that he lasted four seconds longer this time, taking the full count in 2 min 10 sec of the first round.

Following two such crushing defeats, Patterson could have been excused if he had retired and lived comfortably on the large fortune he had amassed from his ring earnings. But the will to continue fighting would not be denied and it says something for this amazing man that twice more he tried his utmost to regain the championship, first against Muhammad Ali at Las Vegas in 1965, when he stayed 12 rounds against the 'Greatest' and then losing narrowly to Jimmy Ellis at Stockholm in 1968 in a contest recognized by the World Boxing Association as being for the world title. That was Patterson's 13th contest involving the heavyweight crown which in itself is quite an accomplishment.

Following his defeat by Ellis, Patterson stayed out of the ring for exactly two years, but at 36 he made a comeback. In the next two years he participated in ten bouts, winning the first nine and then meeting, for the second time, Muhammad Ali who was also engaged in a comeback. They met in New York, but again Patterson had to yield to the younger man, being stopped in the seventh round.

Sonny Liston

If ever a man was advantageously equipped to become the heavyweight champion of the world long before he did, it was Charles (Sonny) Liston (1932–1970), the ponderous, taciturn giant from St Francis County in Arkansas. At maturity he stood 6 ft 1 in and weighed 15 st 2 lb, but his greatest physical asset, from a fighting point of view, was his fantastic reach of 84 inches, and his 15-inch fist, bigger than any champion before him, larger even than Primo Carnera's by a quarter of an inch. Solidly built, Sonny was never stopped until he encountered Cassius Clay, and was such a deadly puncher, especially to the body, that 39 of his 50 victims, in a total of 54 contests, never heard the final bell.

Born in a Negro shanty town, he ran away from home at the age of 13 to run wild with the coloured rabble of St Louis until he was apprehended and committed to a reform school. There he picked up the rudiments of boxing and liked it, but he never recovered from that bad start and much of his career time as a professional fighter was lost through periods in prison. He was 21 before he was able to make a start, but made speedy headway, with six wins before he lost a points verdict to Marty Marshall. Liston's jaw was broken in the fourth round, but he stuck it out to the finish of their eight-rounder. The injury put Liston out of action for six months, then he resumed his career to twice defeat Marshall and win four other quick victories.

Liston seemed heading for the big time, but he lapsed by assaulting a policeman, for which he received a nine months' prison sentence. It took him a further year to get himself in the mood to resume his boxing life, but he got quickly into his stride and began to move up the championship ladder, making short work of such contenders as big Cleveland Williams (three rounds), giant Nino Valdes (three), Roy Harris (one), Zora Folley (three), Howard King (three), Williams again (two) and Albert Westphal (one). Only Eddie Machen stayed the distance in this whirlwind spell, taking Sonny to a 12-round decision at Seattle.

All was now set for a title fight with Floyd Patterson with the champion the

Liston knocks out Nino Valdes during his run of quick wins which led to a world title fight.

underdog in the betting at 7 to 10. Patterson was a small man by comparison, having to concede nearly two stone in weight and with nothing like the same power in his punching. Had it not been for the championship, it might have been regarded as a mis-match. As usual, Patterson was at the peak of physical fitness, a dedicated fighter keen to keep his title. The right way to beat Liston was to dance round him while gathering points at long range, but Floyd hadn't the strength to do that. His blows had not the slightest effect on the stolid challenger, who doubled him in half with rib-benders and worked havoc on his mid-section in the clinches, when he held the hapless champion with one hand and pounded him to destruction with the other. Floyd was floundering sadly when Liston switched to the head and had him down and out with thudding jaw punches to finish the fight in 2 min 6 sec.

A return fight in the Convention Centre at Las Vegas ten months later ended almost identically, but this time Sonny took four seconds longer to pulverize Patterson and it really looked as though Liston, at 31, would remain

champion of the world for a long time to come, especially as his foremost challenger was the 22-year-old Cassius Clay, with only 19 pro fights behind him, albeit all winning ones, but with no startling names among his victims.

Naturally Liston was favoured to win; in fact, those who did not appreciate Clay's brashness and buffoonery, both in and out of the ring, were looking forward to the trouncing they considered the 'Louisville Lip' had coming to him. The fight was staged at Miami Beach with a small crowd of 8,927 in the Convention Hall, but with the TV and radio receipts added, the gross amounted to 2,686,000 dollars, of which Liston took 40 per cent. In spite of Clay's cockiness, he did not show up as a likely winner in the early rounds in which he was chased round the ring by a determined-looking titleholder, who flung heavy punches at his flitting rival, connecting with quite a few and having the challenger looking far from comfortable by the end of round five. Then the tide turned and Clay became the aggressor with Liston allowing him all the latitude in the world. Then, to the utter astonishment of everyone, Liston refused to come out of his corner for the seventh round, complaining of a damaged shoulder, and in such circumstances, unbefitting a world champion, he resigned his title.

The return contest at Lewiston in Maine the following year had just as puzzling a result. Within a minute of the start Liston was down from a punch that even the slow-motion cameras could not specifically define and the last was seen of Sonny as a championship proposition. He stayed out of boxing for over a year then made a comeback that looked impressive on paper, but which ended when he was knocked out by Leotis Martin in nine rounds. Six months later, in June 1970, he disposed of Chuck Wepner in ten rounds at Jersey City, but by the end of the year he was dead, passing away at his home in Las Vegas from an illness no one knew he had. One is left to wonder just how far he would have gone but for those long spells of inactivity when he was engaged in sparring with the law.

Muhammad Ali
(Cassius Clay)

Surely no one can deny that the most colourful, and therefore the most entertaining, character to come into the boxing scene has been Cassius Clay, who adopted the Muslim faith just before becoming heavyweight champion of the world, and is now known as Muhammad Ali. The fight game is noted for its picturesque and controversial figures, but Clay surpassed them all with his antics both in and out of the ring. If one adds the undoubted fact that at his prime he was one of the finest exponents of the noble art of self-defence, he had every right to style himself the 'Greatest'.

Son of a signwriter, born at Louisville in Kentucky on 17 January 1942, Cassius Marcellus Clay bore the name of a man who employed his slave ancestors on a cotton plantation. He has resented this fact ever since and it has influenced his social outlook on life, but unlike many other coloured athletes, he has never allowed racial distinctions to come into his boxing career. From the time he stood on the rostrum at the Rome Olympics to receive his gold medal for winning the light-heavyweight class in the boxing events, he has done nothing but good for the boxing business. He may have irritated some by the boastful way he gained publicity and he provoked criticism for his refusal to go into the US Forces because of his non-war religious beliefs, but his worth as a magnetic ring personality has enabled him to attract capacity attendances wherever he has fought, while millions of people enjoy his television appearances, whether or not he is fighting.

Speed, perfect timing, sharp perception and correct punching have been the secret of Ali's success, plus a dedicated desire for physical perfection. He is a big man, standing 6 ft 3 in and weighing 15½ stone, yet he is so well proportioned that he does not have the appearance of a giant, while his fleet-footedness is an asset not usually attributed to one of his size. Of course, his boyish ebullience in the ring has provided problems for the majority of his opponents, and he knows it. Also his habit of prophesying the round in which he will win must have had an

adverse effect on many of his rivals. Adding his verbosity to his fistic talents has paid off, for when he was forced into temporary retirement because his licence was revoked and his title taken away by forfeiture, Ali had scored 29 wins in as many starts, 23 of them being inside-the-distance victories. Among these successes was the winning of the championship and nine defences against all comers with no one barred.

Before he competed in the 1960 Olympic Games, Ali knew there was a syndicate of boxing-minded business men who were prepared to back him in a professional career after seeing the way he won the National AAU and Golden Gloves tournaments as an amateur. He was three months short of his 19th birthday when he first took off his vest to fight in a ring. He announced that he intended to create a record by becoming the first man to win the heavyweight title by the age of 21, and he might have done so, had he not been held up for a year while Floyd Patterson and Sonny Liston fought a return contest. Even so, he was 39 days beyond his 22nd anniversary when he ultimately became king of the heavies.

He ran up ten wins in his first pro year in which he established himself as a pugilistic personality above the average. He used the outer perimeter of the ring to circle his opponents, holding his arms at his sides in the most unorthodox manner, bringing his left up as a jarring weapon to the face, whipping over a right, and dazing most of them into an early defeat, usually prolonging the contest so that it coincided with his prophecy. In his 11th bout Sonny Banks had the satisfaction of sending Ali to the canvas, but it was only a momentary triumph for Banks was a well-defeated fighter by round four. A four-round victory over Archie Moore put Ali into the contender ratings and he came to London to meet Henry Cooper in what promoter Jack Solomons advertised as a final eliminator for the world crown.

The fight took place at Wembley Stadium and beforehand Ali had told the Press that it would end in the fifth round. The British champion boxed determinedly in the first three sessions

without disturbing the somewhat lackadaisical American and it seemed that Ali was coasting through to the prophetic round. Then, just towards the close of the fourth, Cooper nailed his flighty opponent with his pet punch, a solid left hook to the chin that sent the coloured man flat on his back in a neutral corner. It seemed all over, that Cooper had brought off a sensational victory, but the bell saved Ali from being counted out and he was helped to his corner where skilful administration had him out for the

fifth looking as sprightly as ever. Now the fans saw the real Ali, who ripped into the Britisher and, opening a ghastly wound by the side of his left eye, had the referee calling a halt to save Cooper from serious injury.

Seven months later the burly, heavy-punching Sonny Liston got into the ring at Miami Beach to show the world the way to stop the youthful upstart, now known as the 'Louisville Lip'. The champion was favoured to win at the long odds of 5 to 1 and for the first five rounds he seemed likely to do it. He

chased the challenger, hustling him round the ring, ignoring his counter-punches and landing some very heavy blows to the ribs. Ali tied him up in the clinches, but Liston worked his way out of them to continue his attack and during the fifth round he looked like achieving an early victory when the challenger was seen to be rubbing his eyes and blinking as if he had been thumbed or something had got into them. Again his seconds worked miracles during the interval and he came out to assume suddenly the initiative and attack the champion with long-range punches that he could not avoid because of their speed and precision. In no time Liston was cut over the left eye, while his face puffed up under the hail of accurate shots from the challenger. Ali was going all out for a kayo win and had the crowd with him. But the bell sounded to end the round and Liston went wearily back to his corner. It was, however, a sensational surprise when he failed to come out for the seventh, complaining of a damaged left shoulder, and Ali went berserk when he realized that he had won the world title. He raced round the ring, leaning over the ropes to tell the pressmen that he had told them so and that he was, as he had always said, the 'Greatest'.

The first defence of his crown 15 months later was equally amazing, Liston going down and being counted out by the timekeeper from a punch that few saw, but which Ali claimed was his 'special' – a short right to the chin. There was a lot of confusion, referee Jersey Joe Walcott first allowing the fight to proceed when Liston got to his feet, then stopping the bout when he was informed that Sonny had failed to beat the count. The official time was 60 seconds.

Ali now demonstrated what a truly great champion he was. Inside a year he defeated six more challengers, only one of which stayed the full course with him, the tough Canadian

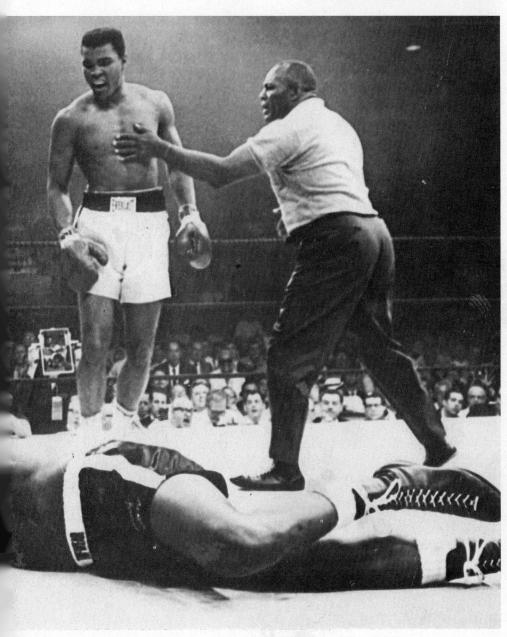

A snarling Ali stands over Liston after knocking him out in the first round of their return title bout. Referee is former champion Jersey Joe Walcott.

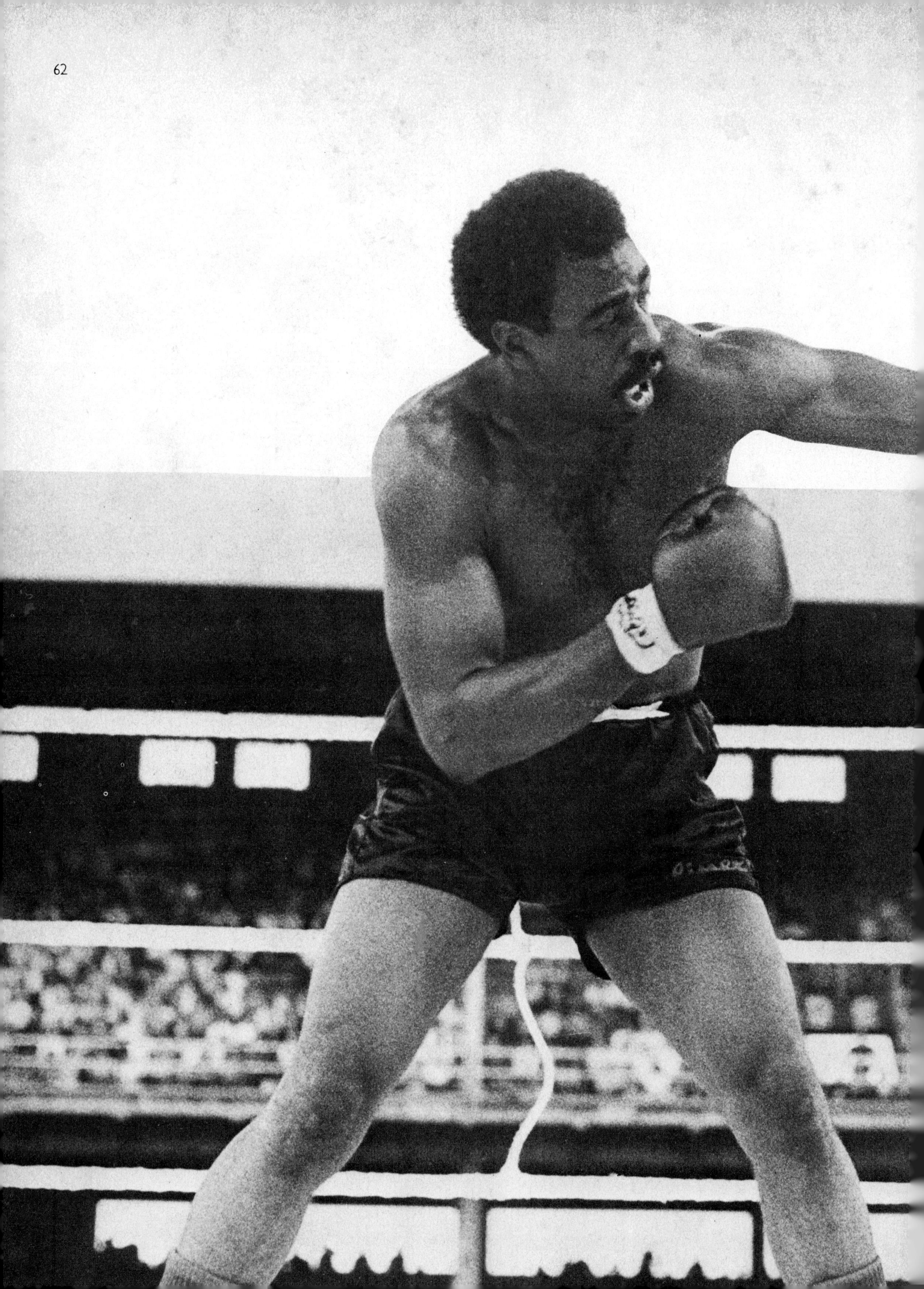

Ali easily evades a left lead from the unrated Al 'Blue' Lewis whom he met after his defeat by Frazier.
Inset: The end for Lewis, counted out with his feet in the air.

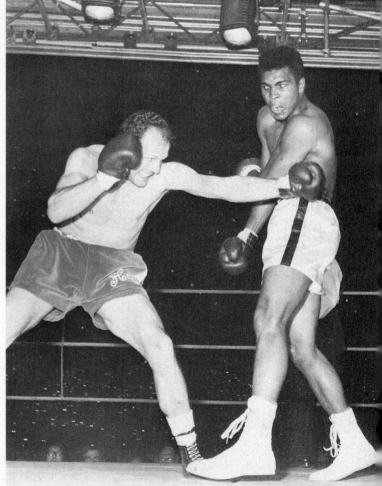

Muhammad Ali in action. *Opposite page:* **Ali beats Jurgen Blin** (*top*) **and Mac Foster** (*below*) **on his comeback campaign and evades a left from Henry Cooper in a title defence.** *Left:* **Ali takes a hard right from Frazier in his unsuccessful challenge for the title.** *Above:* **Frazier knocks Ali down in the last round.**

champion, George Chuvalo. Floyd Patterson was stopped in 12 rounds at Las Vegas; Henry Cooper in six rounds on the Arsenal FC Ground at Highbury in England; Brian London in three rounds at Earls Court, London; Karl Mildenberger, German holder of the European title, in 12 rounds and Cleveland Williams in three rounds at Houston, Texas. It was a triumphant cavalcade that fully demonstrated the world champion's skilful superiority and gained him unparalleled fame.

. Meanwhile, the World Boxing Association had not taken kindly to Ali's absence abroad and had installed Ernie Terrell as world champion, a move that made Ali insist on a meeting between them which took place at Houston's vast Astrodome, with 37,321 fans setting up a new indoor record attendance. Ali played with his opponent, taunting him as to who was the rightful champion, insisting that his name was Muhammad Ali, while at the same time giving his game 6 ft 6 in rival a thorough beating in each of the 15 rounds. There was a final title defence against Zora Folley that ended with a clean-cut knockout in round seven, then Ali's troubles with the US Army began and he was out of the ring for over three years, even announcing his retirement on 3 February 1970.

Fight fans clamoured for his return, however, and he came back to run up another series of wins that brought him face to face with Joe Frazier, the man whom the boxing world now recognized as his rightful successor, unbeaten in 26 contests, all but two of which had ended inside the scheduled course. Frazier had been installed as champion by the New York Boxing Commission and he enhanced his claim to the mundane crown by knocking out Jimmy Ellis, who had won a tournament sponsored by the World Boxing Association. Before he could be recognized as the undisputed champion, Frazier knew he must beat Ali.

Their meeting at Madison Square Garden, New York, created world-wide interest and was watched by millions of fight fans on television, while the 'live' attendance was 20,455. Both men received something like £1,000,000 or 2,500,000 dollars each, record pay in the new viewing era. Obviously carrying the extra weight that his 29 years demanded, Ali seemed no slower and boxed in his usual style, making full use of the ring and the ropes, perhaps overdoing it against a forward-plodding fighter, who came in like a coloured Marciano, hooking and jabbing, keeping his opponent on the run, taking the punches that came his

way with stolid indifference. Only once, in the ninth round was Frazier forced to take backward steps. Here Ali had his big chance to win decisively as he bounced his best punches on Joe's chin, to shake him to his heels, but not to put him down. By the 11th round Ali had begun to run out of gas, but he kept going, often trapped on the ropes, but always managing to keep on his feet under the persistent pressure from the champion. Midway through the final round, a little slow in slipping a punch, he was caught by a swinging left that collided with his chin and sent him sprawling. He beat the count and by skilful footwork denied Frazier the satisfaction of scoring a knockout. But he had been beaten for the first time in his career.

Since then Muhammad Ali has been engaged on a determined comeback effort with a run of victories over Jurgen Blin (seven), Mac Foster (15), George Chuvalo (12), Jerry Quarry (seven), Al Lewis (11), Floyd Patterson (seven), Bob Foster (eight) and Joe Bugner (12). He was all set for another big show-down, this time against the new world heavyweight champion, George Foreman, when he was narrowly beaten on points, and had his jaw broken, by Ken Norton, who was beaten in a return bout.

Henry Cooper

Henry Cooper's introduction to a boxing career was both short and sharp. On their fifth birthday Pa Cooper had given his twin sons a set of boxing gloves and they could not wait to put them on. Then George (who boxed professionally as Jim) swung a punch at Henry that landed full in his face and knocked him flat, the fall splitting his head open. The gloves were confiscated by Mrs Cooper, but were smuggled out at every opportunity, the boys being so keen on boxing that, as soon as they were old enough, they joined a local amateur club. The eldest – Henry was born 20 minutes before George – showed greater progress and in 1952 became the ABA light-heavyweight champion at the age of 18. He repeated his victory the following year and after boxing internationally on a number of occasions, he turned professional in September 1954 to start a fistic career that was to last nearly 17 years, with 19 championship fights, three titles and the winning outright of three Lord Lonsdale challenge belts.

A first-class, upstanding boxer, Cooper possessed an unerring straight left jab, a passable right cross, and a deadly left hook, known affectionately by the fans as "Enery's 'Ammer". With

its aid he won many famous victories and it enabled him to floor the great Cassius Clay in their memorable Wembley Stadium battle in 1963 when only the bell that ended the fourth round saved the coloured American from a knockout defeat.

All was far from plain sailing for Cooper. He had set-backs at the start of his career that would have discouraged most men, but he overcame defeat and disappointment, despite the handicap of eye injuries to which he was prone and which cost him a number of contests. Very often he had to give away weight, for at his best he scaled 13 st 6 lb, which made him lighter by almost a stone when he

challenged Clay for the world title in 1966. Three years later he was awarded the OBE for his services to sport and it is safe to say that no more popular man ever stepped into a British ring.

After a promising start, Cooper had a losing run that caused the critics to write him off as a serious heavyweight proposition. He lost in two rounds to an Italian, Uber Bacilieri; five rounds on a cut eye to Peter Bates; nine rounds to Joe Bygraves in a fight for the British Empire title; five rounds to Ingemar Johansson for the European crown, and was outpointed over 15 rounds by Joe Erskine for the British championship. All this in his first 20 bouts.

Three fights in Germany, only one of which he won, did not add to his prestige and he looked like being scrubbed out finally by Dick Richardson, only to get off the floor, land his 'ammer' and win by a knockout in five rounds. It was the turning-point. Brian London was outpointed for the British and Empire titles in 1959 and these honours were kept intact for ten years, with the European title won on three separate occasions.

There were further frustrations to be overcome: the losing fight with Clay that he was within a few seconds of winning, and disappointing defeats by Americans Zora Folley and Floyd Patterson. Any chance he had of

winning the world crown disappeared when his cut eye bogey prevailed in his second contest with Clay. He was at his greatest when defending his British laurels against such youngsters as Johnny Prescott (ten rounds), Billy Walker (six), and Jack Bodell (two), while he punched the fight out of Karl Mildenberger, of Germany (eight) and Piero Tomasoni, of Italy (five) in exciting battles involving the European crown.

In 1969, disgusted that the British Boxing Board of Control would not sanction a match between himself and Jimmy Ellis, of America, for the WBA version of the world heavyweight championship, Cooper handed in his

licence and relinquished his British, Empire and European titles. He stayed away from boxing for a year, then came back to astound everyone by outpointing Jack Bodell to become British and Empire champion once more, and to regain the European title by stopping Jose Urtain of Spain. It was an amazing return to the ring.

There was one more fight to come. Defending all his titles against young Joe Bugner at Wembley Arena in March 1971, Cooper was adjudged to have lost on points, a decision far from the liking of the majority of the onlookers, and a final disappointment that caused Henry to hang up his gloves for good.

Joe Frazier

Any man who can knock a 15½-stone opponent flat on his back after 14½ rounds of non-stop action, must be regarded as a fighter of considerable consequence. Joe Frazier did that midway through the final round of his bonanza bout with Muhammad Ali in the Madison Square Garden ring in March 1971, when not only did he clinch his claim to the undisputed heavyweight championship of the world, but also inflicted on the former titleholder his first defeat as a professional boxer.

Frazier hadn't the ideal build for a heavyweight champion. He was short at 5 ft 11½ in, and although weighing in the region of 15 stone, most of this was contained in his legs which, of course, was one of the reasons why he could keep going at a set pace almost *ad infinitum*. But Rocky Marciano was also on the short side. He was additionally handicapped by a limited reach of 68 inches, whereas Frazier boasted of 73½ inches. Well Rocky did quite well, retiring unbeaten after 49 bouts, while Frazier was undefeated in 29 starts before losing his title to George Foreman, only four of which went the full scheduled course. In his physical make-up, style of fighting, strength and durability, plus punching power, he was rightly named as the 'Black Marciano'.

Born at Beaumont, South Carolina, in 1944, the seventh son in a family of 13, Billy Joe Frazier was raised on a vegetable plantation that was worked by a shanty-dwelling coloured community who lived on the borderline of poverty. At nine he was working in the fields and it was then that he had the first dreams of becoming a national boxing hero like his idol, Joe Louis. He even filled a sack with moss and leaves and hung it on a tree to serve as a punch-bag for his small bare fists.

At 16 he married Florence, his schoolgirl sweetheart, and following the example set by his elder brothers, settled in Philadelphia where his bulk helped him to secure work at 75 dollars a week in a slaughter-house. Here he began to put on weight alarmingly, so went along to the Police Athletic Club where he was permitted to work out and incidentally attracted the attention

of Yancey 'Yank' Durham, the boxing instructor, who persuaded him to become an amateur scrapper, and was his manager when he decided to turn professional.

Durham encouraged Frazier by pointing out what winning an Olympic Games gold medal had done for Floyd Patterson and Cassius Clay. He made him see that it was a goal worth all the determination and hard work that dedicated training demanded; that his reward would be an end to money shortage. Joe responded so well that he won 38 of his 40 unpaid bouts, his two losses being to Buster Mathis. Frazier was twice lucky in his boxing career, the first occasion when he lost to Mathis in the trials for the 1964 Olympic Games team. The winner broke a thumb during the contest which automatically caused his elimination and Joe went to Tokyo to come home triumphant.

He did not turn professional until the following year and then set off at hurricane pace to score 19 wins in 28 months, only two of which went the full ten rounds. His second lucky break now manifested itself when Cassius Clay was deprived of his title by the various American boxing commissions, and the New York State body sanctioned a match between Frazier and his amateur conqueror, Mathis,

which was labelled as for the vacant world crown. Joe scored complete revenge over Buster, the referee stopping the contest in 2 min 33 sec of the 11th round, when Mathis had taken a long count after being sent sprawling from a dynamite-laden left hook to the chin.

Frazier enhanced his claim to the world title in his next four contests, all of which bore the championship label. Manuel Ramos, considered a distinct threat from Mexico, was put away in two rounds, but Oscar Bonavena, the brawny Argentinean, took him the full distance of 15 rounds before Frazier could gain a points verdict after what had been little more than a slugging match. It was their second meeting, Frazier having outpointed Bonavena over ten rounds in his 12th pro bout, but having to twice get off the canvas in the second round before he could secure a points win. He stayed on his feet during the second match to secure the unanimous vote of the three judges.

There was a ridiculous match with Dave Zyglewicz at Houston, which Frazier ended in 1 min 36 sec of the first round, which emphasized Joe as a wicked hooker, and he then defended his crown against Jerry Quarry, whom many thought would bring back the championship to the white race. Quarry took a terrible battering before the referee stopped the one-sided contest in round seven.

Meanwhile the World Boxing Association's eliminating tourney to find a successor to Clay had resulted in Jimmy Ellis, one-time sparring-partner to Cassius, emerging as the winner. He was at the ringside for the Frazier–Quarry fight and sprang on to the apron of the ring as Joe was leaving for the dressing-room, and they shouted abuse at one another, which was good publicity for a contest between them that would prove the undisputed championship. They met at Madison Square Garden on 16 February 1970 and it was no match.

Using the ring and boxing confidently, Ellis took the first round, but once Frazier was warmed up, his left hook began to play havoc with the WBA champion and in the fourth round it was all over. With a non-stop bombardment, Joe fired blow after blow to body and head until a savage left hook to the chin put Ellis down. He got up but was easy prey for another blasting left that sent him face forwards on the canvas. At 'four' he raised his head, a second later the bell sounded to end the round, but Jimmy remained down until the referee had continued to count until 'nine'. He got up and walked unsteadily to his corner. They could not get him fit for the next round and manager Angelo Dundee would not let him take any more. The fight went into the record books as a win for Joe Frazier in the fifth, although not a punch was struck in that round.

Next to be accommodated was Bob Foster, the light-heavyweight champion. No slouch himself, he had nothing to offer against the crowding assault that Frazier applied, and after being left-hooked to the floor for an 'eight' count, was put away for keeps in the second round, after 2 min 2 sec.

Now came the showdown between Frazier, now universally recognized as world champion, and Muhammad Ali, who had never been beaten for the title. It proved to be the 'Fight of the Century' from the financial angle, and

full of thrills with a terrific climax for the packed assembly in the Garden, with an estimated 300,000,000 watching on television. The former champion tried his old cat-and-mouse game, against Frazier, but it did not come off. He was forced to spend far too much time on the retreat and was frequently hard put to steer clear of disaster when pinned against the ropes.

Only in the ninth round did Ali appear to have Joe in trouble. Then, after being tagged by a hard jaw punch, Joe had to take several other fine shots to the chin that made his thick legs shake and go into reverse gear. But it was a mere flash and he recovered

quickly to resume his forward march until, midway through the 15th and last round he connected solidly with a great left to the jaw and Ali crashed on his back, his legs waving in the air, down for only the third time in his career. Somehow he managed to beat the count and then coast through the remaining time to the end of the round, when he went to his corner looking decidedly spent and with a huge swelling on the right side of his face, indicative of the force and weight behind Frazier's knockdown delivery.

Frazier beat Terry Daniels (four rounds) and Ron Stander (five), both set-ups, in 1972, but early the following year met a shock defeat at the hands of George Foreman, who floored him six times before the referee intervened in the second round. It was Frazier's first defeat, but one both unexpected and utterly devastating.

Frazier triumphant (*left*) after knocking out Foster (*below*). *Following page:* Frazier has Ali down in the last round of their championship fight (*above*), and (*below*) outpoints Joe Bugner in his first fight after losing his title.

George Foreman

The ninth coloured fighter to become the heavyweight champion of the world, George Foreman created the biggest upset among the big boys since Cassius Clay took the title from Sonny Liston. An underdog in the betting, Foreman disposed of Joe Frazier, the Black Marciano, in 1 min 35 sec of the second round at the National Stadium in Kingston, Jamaica, scoring six knockdowns – and what knockdowns – before the referee saved the champion the ignominy of a count-out defeat.

It was almost a one-sided victory as the young giant, with all the physical advantages, took Frazier apart with tremendous blows to the body, a long jarring left lead and a right uppercut of devastating power. Unbeaten in 38 professional contests, standing 6 ft 3½ in, weighing 15 st 10 lb, and with a reach of 78½ inches, Foreman represents a champion who is big enough, confident enough, and powerful enough as a puncher to reign for a long time. He is as tall as Muhammad Ali, and heavier, and only two previous champions Jess Willard and Primo Carnera were bigger.

Born at Marshall in Texas, on 10 January 1949, the fifth of seven children born to a railroad construction worker, Foreman was something of a delinquent as a youngster, spending two years hanging around street corners after he left school at 14. He then joined America's Job Corps and was sent to Fort Vannoy Conservation Centre at Oregon, where he learnt bricklaying and carpentry. In recreational sports he shone at boxing, taking tuition from Nick 'Doc' Broadus, the camp trainer. He encouraged Foreman to dedicate himself to boxing, pointing out that his size alone was a tremendous asset in physical combat. Foreman listened intelligently with the result that at the 1968 Olympic Games in Mexico City he stood on the rostrum as gold medallist in the heavyweight boxing, waving a tiny American flag in contrast to some of the other coloured athletes who had won awards.

His professional début was held back until June 1969 and he fought at regular intervals, winning most of his fights against nonentities in a few rounds, his most important victory being at the expense of George Chuvalo, the tough Canadian champion, who was finished off in three. Gregorio Peralta, from the Argentine, took him to a ten-round decision, but in a return bout the contest was stopped in the tenth with Peralta being saved by the referee. So far only three of Foreman's fights have gone the distance, a fact that makes him a terrifying prospect.

Frazier goes down for the last time in his fight with Foreman, who took the world title.

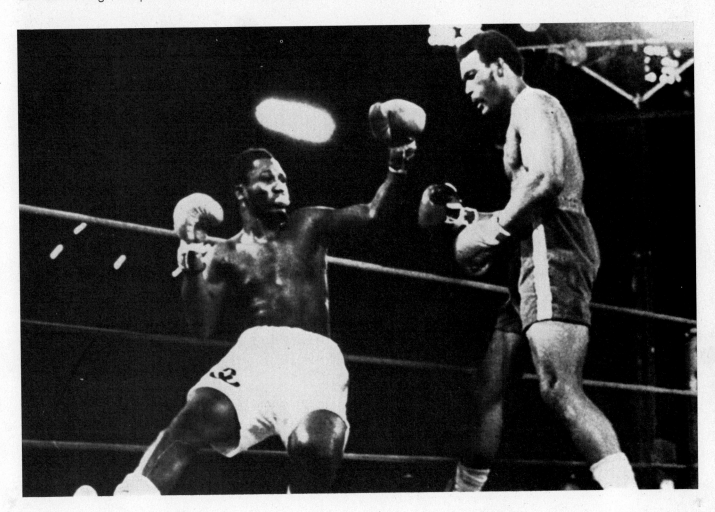

Not an impression of Jolson singing 'Sonny Boy', but Frazier losing his crown. *Inset:* Foreman applying the *coup de grâce*.

Georges Carpentier

Although he fought for the world's heavyweight championship, and he was heavyweight champion of Europe for nine years, Georges Carpentier, of France, was never any more than a light-heavyweight and it was in that class he became a world titleholder.

Born in the mining village of Lens in northern France in 1894, he was an active boy whose liveliness was spotted by François Descamps, a travelling one-man show, who entertained the country folk with acrobatics, hypnotism and political oration. He took a liking to Georges, which was reciprocated, and having made arrangements with the lad's parents, they set off together on a path that was to lead them both to fame and fortune. At that time boxing was unknown in France, where fighting for sport was conducted with the feet and not the hands and was known as *la savatte*. But Descamps had heard about *la boxe Anglais* and as soon as he and his protégé had seen a performance of it, they quickly added it to their repertoire of entertainment.

The young Carpentier proved so good at boxing that soon he was taking on anyone who cared to pull on the gloves with him. His fame as a boxer spread to Paris, where the sport had swiftly become very popular. The 13-year-old Georges won a four-round contest there to start an amazing professional career that was to make him the idol of France, not only for his amazing performances in the ring, but also because he grew into an athlete of beautifully proportioned physique, with handsome features that attracted women to boxing as never before. His lightning right-hand punching that won him so many victories also earned their admiration and hero worship.

At 17 Carpentier won his first title – the welterweight championship of France. Four months later he gained the European crown at this weight by stopping Young Joseph, the British champion, after ten rounds. Georges then garnered the European middle-weight title with a two-round victory over Jim Sullivan, the British titleholder, and made it a hat-trick of defeats for Englishmen when he beat Bandsman Rice in two rounds for the light-heavyweight crown. No one expected him to beat Bombardier Billy Wells when they met for the heavyweight championship at the Ghent Exhibition in 1913, but he got off the floor to knock out the British champion in the fourth round and at the end of the year, at the famous National Sporting Club, he repeated his victory over 'Beautiful Billy', winning sensationally in 73 seconds, including the count.

Victory earned the Frenchman a championship contest with 'Gunboat' Smith, of America, who claimed the 'white' world heavyweight title which had been instituted in the States in an effort to offset the fact that the boxing world was ruled by the hated coloured Jack Johnson. Smith and Carpentier met at Olympia, London, and Georges put up a tremendous battle with his heavier opponent until he slipped to the canvas in the sixth round, whereupon the Gunboat gave him a cuff while he was still down. Manager Descamps immediately demanded a 'foul', and the American was ruled out.

Nineteen days later the First World War broke out and Carpentier was denied the chance to cash in on his high status in the heavyweight ranks. Instead, he became an airman, was decorated for valour and did not resume his boxing career until 1919. Joe Beckett was champion of Great Britain by then and a match between he and Georges was the 'natural' of the day. Promoter C. B. Cochran was able to charge £25 for ringside seats at the Holborn Stadium and all they got for their money was 74 seconds, Beckett succumbing to a picture-book right to the chin that sent him down for the full count, rendering him a stepping-stone for Carpentier to a world title contest with Jack Dempsey.

To get the bout extra publicity and to give himself an insight into American ring conditions, Carpentier challenged Battling Levinsky for his light-heavyweight title and took it from him with a four-round knockout victory at Jersey City. Nine months later he stepped into a specially erected outdoor arena in the same city in what promoter Tex Rickard named the 'Battle of the Century'. This fight between a great war hero and the champion, who was accused of 'slacking', produced enormous interest and 80,183 fans paid 1,789,238 dollars to see it. Carpentier received a guarantee of 200,000 dollars (£40,000) and fought gamely against a stronger, more vigorous and heavier-punching opponent, breaking the thumb of his right hand in an attempt to knock the champion out in the second round and finally being battered to the canvas for the full count in the fourth.

The body battering he had received took a lot out of the Frenchman and when he defended his light-heavyweight title against coloured Battling Siki in Paris the following year, he suffered another set-back by being knocked out in the sixth round. He regained a lot of prestige when beating Beckett for the second time with another lightning one-round victory, but going to America in the hopes of securing a second world title chance, he was stopped by Gene Tunney in the 15th and final round and that was virtually the end of a scintillating career. Georges was 30 then and although he attempted a comeback two years later, it petered out and he returned to Paris to open a celebrity bar.

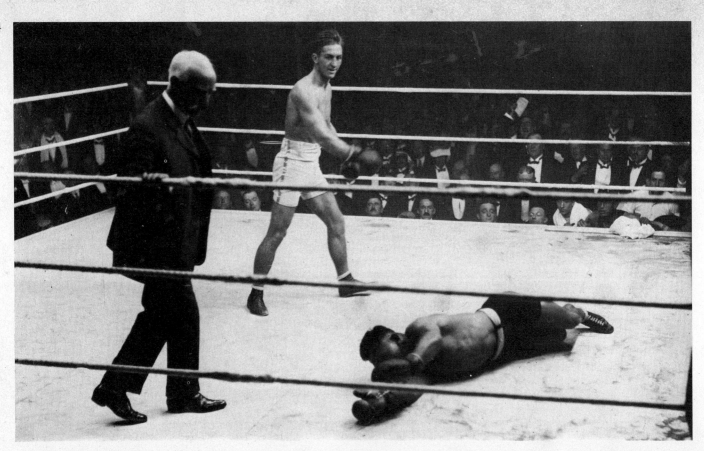

Battling Siki

Some earn greatness, others have it thrust upon them. Battling Siki (1897–1925), from St Louis in the French West African colony of Senegal, would never have been anything more than a rough-and-ready ring performer, had it not been that someone wanted to make a fight film featuring Georges Carpentier, with Siki in the chief supporting role. Up to that point he had been a willing, if wild, wielder of the gloves, a favourite with the fans because of his wild-man ring antics, but never regarded with any real seriousness as a candidate for championship honours.

As a boy, real name Louis Phal, he was brought to Paris by a French actress who had taken a fancy to him while she was engaged in playing a part at the local theatre. Siki stayed in her home quite happily until an engagement took her to Berlin, whereupon she found him a job in a restaurant, where he did dish-washing and odd chores and at the same time spent his leisure in a Montmartre boxing club. At 16 he took off his apron for the last time and embarked on a professional ring career, his unorthodox style of fighting gaining him more laughs than admiration.

During the war he was attached to an American unit, where his limited boxing ability was developed and between 1920 and 1922 he fought in Belgium, Holland, Germany, France and Spain, notching up 40 victories and only one points defeat. Even so, he was not considered to be in Carpentier's class, so when it was suggested that he should meet Georges for the world light-heavyweight title, everyone in Paris laughed, but at the same time made up their minds to be there to watch Siki being sacrificed on a boxing altar. Secretly, Siki had to agree to lose, being assured that Carpentier would not hurt him for six rounds when he would then go down and be counted out to make the appropriate ending to the movie. All went well until, in the third session, the champion shot a right to Siki's chin that carried a lot more power than was intended. Down went the coloured man and when he got up he was extremely annoyed. He fancied that Georges had taken a liberty, so he went after him, whirling both arms like a human windmill, one swinging right to the chin bowling over Carpentier to the amazement of the crowd. When he got up, Georges, too, was outraged, the film was forgotten and they went savagely at each other. It was Siki who got in the deciding swipe, another right to the chin that knocked the final stuffing out of the champion, who took the full count, leaving Siki a sensational winner.

Victory went to his woolly head and he behaved outrageously, even walking through the Paris streets with a lion on a lead. His tenure of the world title was short-lived. Six months later he made the psychological error of defending it against Mike McTigue, an Irishman, in Dublin, on St Patrick's Day and came off worst in a mauling fight that went the full 20 rounds, while the 'troubles' raged outside the arena, with rifle-fire and bursting bombs to add to the atmosphere.

Siki went to America where he had a number of contests, but lost the ones that mattered most, being stopped by Paul Berlenbach in ten rounds, after which his earning power diminished. He neglected his training and lived riotously, eventually being murdered in a Harlem brawl at the age of 28.

In a total of 74 recorded bouts, Siki won 54 (29 inside the distance), drew one, and there were six no-decision contests. He was stopped only once in his 12 years of fighting.

Opposite above: Carpentier knocks out Beckett, but (*below*) is on the receiving end himself to lose his title to Battling Siki in an astonishing upset.

John Henry Lewis

John Henry Lewis was the second man of colour to win the world's light-heavyweight title. The first was the notorious Battling Siki, the most fantastic figure ever to wear a boxing crown. And they differed as chalk from cheese. Whereas Siki had no pretensions to being a clever performer and was as wild out of the ring as he was in it, Lewis was a gentlemanly person who possessed boxing brains and fistic ability of high degree. He came into the title by outpointing Bob Olin at St Louis in Missouri, in 1935, and was never beaten for the championship, being forced to retire in 1939 with failing eyesight, after he had challenged Joe Louis for the heavyweight title and been knocked out in 2 min 29 sec of the opening round. He was half-blind at the time.

Born at Los Angeles in 1914, he showed great promise as an amateur and began boxing professionally at the age of 17. Victories over Jimmy Braddock, Maxie Rosenbloom and Tiger Flowers, gained him a beckoning finger from New York, where he fought Braddock in a return contest and was well outpointed. Lewis had shown such class, however, that he was provided with two further chances by the Madison Square Garden matchmaker within the next month, so returned home quite happily.

Ten months later he won the light-heavyweight title and his first challenger was the British middleweight champion, Jock McAvoy, who had electrified New York with a brand of punching that should have gained him a shot at the world 11 st 6 lb crown. Instead, they put him in with Lewis, whose perfect boxing proved too much for the visitor, who strained nerve and tendon to try and win with his big punch, but could not get past the champion's rapier-like left and short, accurate counters.

Next Lewis went to London where at Wembley Arena he defended his world title against Len Harvey, himself a highly skilled technician in the fistic industry. Lewis had to bring out his best to earn a narrow points victory,

but he returned home to make three more successful defences of his light-heavyweight title, beating Bob Olin (for the second time), Emilio Martinez and Al Gainer.

Having cleared the board of all logical contenders, Lewis made his abortive attempt to win the big title. He was only 25, the same age as the Brown Bomber, and it was thought that he

would give the champion a very good fight which would be a classic to watch. But the encounter was short-lived and Lewis opened negotiations to give Harvey a return title fight in London. He failed to pass the Board of Control's medical examination, it being disclosed that his eyesight was failing and he returned home to announce his retirement from the ring.

Len Harvey ducks but is caught by a Lewis left, Wembley 1936.

Billy Conn

As yet, no light-heavyweight champion of the world has won the heavyweight title. Many have tried, among them Billy Conn, the fighting kid from Pittsburgh, who came closer to doing it than anyone else. Born in 1917, his father came of Irish stock, his mother was raised in Ireland. They lived in a tenement district that was impoverished and wild. Young Billy was famed as a street scrapper during school-days, and his natural ability soon convinced the family that in the interests of everyone, especially from the financial aspect, the best thing he could do was to become a professional.

As he grew so his fistic skill developed. As a welter and then a middleweight he could mingle with the best and come out with the winning end of the decision. His record was not dotted with knockout victories, but the names of those he outpointed were of top quality, such as Fritzie Zivic, Babe Risko, Vince Dundee, Teddy Yarosc, Solly Krieger, Young Corbett and Fred Apostoli, all of whom he licked and each of whom claimed the title of world champion at one time or the other.

Conn won the light-heavyweight title from Melio Bettina in 1939 and defended it successfully on three occasions, twice against Gus Lesnevich. He then decided to take on the big boys, because making 12 st 7 lb had become something of a bore. He defeated Lee Savold, Gunnar Barlund and Buddy Knox, all aspiring contenders, and then was selected by promoter Mike Jacobs to go in with Joe Louis for the big title. They met at the Polo Grounds in New York on 18 June 1941, when Louis was at his peak at 27, with Conn three years younger and nearly two stone lighter; 54,487 fans came in the expectation of seeing the great Brown Bomber opposed to someone capable of giving him a real fight. They had got tired of the 'Bum of the Month' parade of so-called challengers and it would be interesting and exciting to see how Louis would cope with Conn's sweet science.

They were in for a pleasant surprise. Conn outspeeded the champion, walked round him, outboxed him, cockily confident as he stole the points and thwarted the champion's efforts to get in a decisive blow. At first they watched in disbelief, then they began to cheer, urging on the Pittsburgh Kid to take the title from Louis after a reign of seven years and 17 successful championship defences.

With only three rounds to go and being a mile in front, the challenger came out for the 13th as if he was intent on gaining undying fame. Conn's Irish blood had welled up and boiled over. Recklessly and foolishly he sailed into Louis as if going for the 'kill'. Fierce blows were exchanged, but those from Louis were dynamite. Hooks thudded against Billy's chin, he faltered, a snappy short right to the jaw saw Conn crumple to the canvas – out to the world.

There was a return fight five years later when both had done war service. But this time Army life had taken more out of Conn than it had out of Louis, and Joe won in eight rounds to cause Billy's departure from the ring.

Gus Lesnevich

Gus Lesnevich (1915–1964) enters the Hall of Fame not only because he was a fine boxer and superb puncher, but for the fact that he became light-heavyweight champion of the world after three attempts, defended the title six times, lost four years in war service with the US Coast Guard and then made a gallant attempt to win the heavyweight crown. Born at Cliffside, New Jersey, of Russian ancestry, he enjoyed an outstanding record as an amateur, which culminated in his winning a Golden Gloves Inter-City championship. He turned professional at 19 and went off to Australia.

In his absence Billy Conn had won the vacant world title and readily agreed to put it on the line against Lesnevich. Gus gave him a close contest, so close that they had a return six months later, when once again Billy's scientific stuff was a little too good for his challenger. When Conn elected to challenge for the heavyweight title, Lesnevich defeated Anton Christoforidis for the crown, defended it twice against Tami Mauriello, did his war stint, then, at 31 met Freddie Mills in London.

Lesnevich found 'Ferocious Fred' easy to hit, having him on the canvas several times in the opening round. But the Britisher made a good recovery, split open Gus's left eye and looked like winning on the referee's intervention when the champion tossed over a great right-hand punch that was a winner all the way, the bout being stopped in the tenth round.

Four months later Lesnevich was back in London, but failed to give weight and reach to Bruce Woodcock, the British heavyweight champion, who won by a knockout in the eighth round at Harringay Arena. Unperturbed Gus returned home to twice defend his world title against the much-fancied Billy Fox, knocking him out on both occasions, the last time in 1 min 58 sec.

A return fight with Mills in London saw Gus at last drop his crown on a close points decision, then he fought Joey Maxim for the American title, but again lost on points. In August 1949, at the age of 34, this courageous scrapper tried to win the world's heavyweight title, but was stopped in seven rounds by Ezzard Charles.

Freddie Mills

Pushing a milk float through the streets of Bournemouth, Freddie Mills (1919–1965) practised footwork and shadow-boxed, imagining himself to be his fistic hero, Jack Dempsey. On fight nights in the town, he would climb on to the roof of the local boxing hall and watch the fighting through the skylight. He took his holidays by attaching himself to a West Country travelling boxing booth and learnt the sport the hard way. Born at Parkstone in Dorset, he was wrapped up heart and soul in fisticuffs and before his 17th birthday had won a novices' competition, a start in a professional career that was to make him one of the most popular boxers of all time.

Freddie could not fight often enough, averaging a contest a month in his first four years. There wasn't a lot of science about his work, but there was plenty of energy and most of his victims caved in under such a fierce and sustained assault that he soon picked up the name of 'Ferocious Fred'. He could, however, use a perfect straight left when he felt in the mood. Outside the ring, he was a happy, light-hearted person, generous to a fault and with good will towards all men. In the ring, although he strove determindedly from the opening bell to annihilate opponents as quickly as possible, he never struck an illegal blow or acted unfairly, and his record of 96 contests is without a blemish in this respect.

When he was 22 Mills had developed into a 12-stoner, but this did not prevent him from taking on heavyweights and beating them. His path to fame, however, began when he stopped Jock McAvoy, the British middleweight champion, in the opening round of a catchweights contest, and then knocked out Len Harvey in two rounds to win the BBBC version of the world's light-heavyweight championship. This incredible victory also made Freddie the British and Empire champion, but before he could capitalize on these possessions, he was called up for national service and joined the Royal Air Force as a sergeant-instructor.

Mills (right) and Lesnevich had two great title fights.

He was permitted to engage in the occasional pro contest and in one of these he took on Jack London, from West Hartlepool, for the heavyweight championship left vacant by Harvey's retirement. Freddie was outweighed by three stone, yet he hustled the bigger man around and lost only on points. It was the first time in his life that he had ever travelled 15 rounds.

He was sent to India and stayed there a year. Then one day he poked his shaggy head into Jack Solomons's London office and asked cheekily if he had a fight to offer him. 'You are a blessing in disguise,' answered the promoter. 'I had planned to put Woodcock in with Gus Lesnevich, but Bruce can't make it. Will you fight Gus for his world title?' Would he? Mills could not get to a gymnasium quickly enough. His own claim to the world crown had always been disputed in America. Here was the opportunity to prove who was the real champion. Unfortunately, it turned out to be Lesnevich. Short of practice, Mills was caught by some fine rights to the jaw in the opening round and took several counts. It seemed that he would not last long, but he staged an amazing recovery and by the end of the ninth round had made up a lot of leeway and had the American bleeding badly from a cut over his left eye. They sent Gus up for one more round and he came out to toss a right that was to win the fight. It caught Freddie by surprise and dropped him in a heap. Even so he got to his feet, but was subjected to such an all-out bombardment from the desperate Lesnevich that the referee rightly called a halt. Many thought the official's action had been premature – but not Freddie.

He remained to fight another day and so he did, taking the world title from Lesnevich in a return match two years later with a fine points victory. He also won the European title by stopping Paul Goffaux of Belgium in four rounds. But against class heavyweights Freddie found he could not give away the poundage. He fought bravely against giant Joe Baksi, but was beaten in six rounds; he went 14 gruelling sessions with Bruce Woodcock in an effort to capture the British heavyweight title, to drop more from exhaustion than a punch and to be counted out.

These defeats, plus his long and strenuous campaigning, took a lot out of the seemingly imperishable Mills and when he came to defend his world title against the scientific Joey Maxim, he suffered his worst defeat, taking the full count in the tenth round and losing a few teeth in the process. He retired immediately to become a radio and television personality of some account and a boxing promoter for several years. It therefore came as a shock to his many admirers when he was found dead from a gunshot wound at the age of 46.

Mills attacking Joey Maxim, who knocked him out to take the light-heavyweight crown.

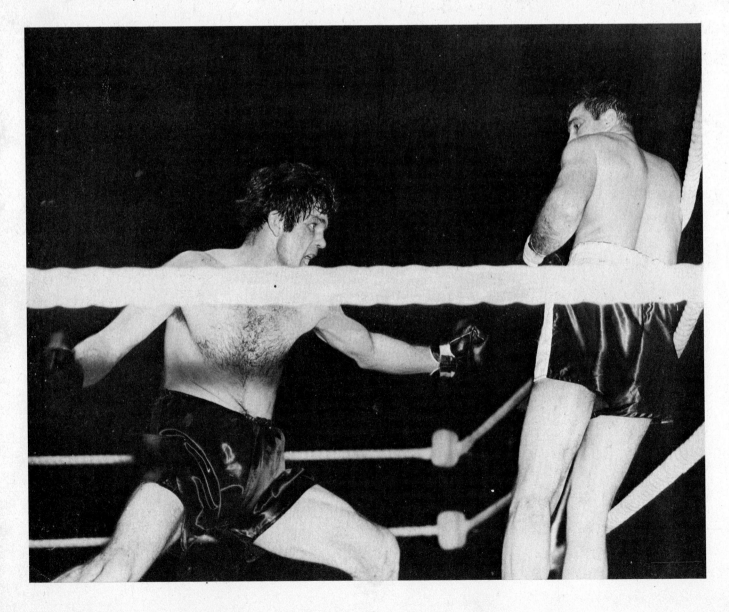

Archie Moore

When Archie Moore retired from the ring at the age of 50, no one believed it. He had been around so long, had fought so many contests and had taken part in so many championship matches, that he seemed a permanent fixture in the fight game. A well-muscled, nicely proportioned figure, he put defence before aggression, developing into an expert all-round boxer of such degree that he was able to enjoy a fighting life that lasted 30 years – and you have to be good to stay that length of time. The record book shows him as having 228 contests, of which he won 193 (140 inside the distance) with nine drawn. Several dozen more can be added during the days he was learning his trade as an amateur.

He won the light-heavyweight championship of the world when he was four days past his 36th birthday and he defended the title nine times and never lost it in the ring. Twice he fought for the world's heavyweight crown, against rugged Rocky Marciano, who knocked him out in nine rounds, but not before he had put the champion down for a count; and against young Floyd Patterson, who stopped him in five. In both these attempts he was an old man in comparison with his opponents, and it is a credit to his wide knowledge of the sweet science that he stayed four rounds with Cassius Clay when that loquacious gentleman was 20 and Moore was close up to his 46th birthday.

Real name Archibald Lee Wright, he was born at Benoit, Missouri on 13 December 1916, although his mother maintains that he was born three years earlier than that. Like many other coloured boys of that time who came of impoverished homes, he ran wild and was sent to a reform school, where he learnt to box more from a sense of self-preservation than with any eye to the future. When he turned pro, boxers were a dime a dozen and coloured fighters even cheaper. Archie had no trouble in getting cheaply paid bouts with boys of his own race, but to secure a contest with a white boxer often meant being prepared to be the loser if it went to a points verdict. A succession of managers took him for very long rides, promoters welshed, controlling bodies

turned deaf ears to his pleas for recognition.

Moore bought an old jalopy and drove himself from fight town to fight town, arriving in time for his contest, battle it out, then drive off to the next job. It took him 17 years to get a title fight with Joey Maxim and he had to defeat him three times before he was in the clear to make money out of his championship holding. Having been a logical contender through the reigns of three world titleholders, he now invited any challenger to come and get it. Six months after beating Maxim the third time, he stopped Harold Johnson in 14 rounds, whipped the giant Cuban heavyweight, Nino Valdes, in 15 rounds, then successfully defended his laurels against Carl (Bobo) Olson, who

was put away for keeps in round three.

The victory over Valdes earned Archie a title fight with Marciano. Moore had campaigned for such an opportunity for a long time, writing to the sports editors of every important newspaper, challenging him from the ring and gradually getting public sympathy on his side. He really thought he could halt the pulverizing progress of The Rock and it looked that way, too, when he dropped the champion in the second round. Moore always reckoned that he fought two men that night in New York's Yankee Stadium. 'I was unlucky to lose to Rocky. When I put him down I went in for the "kill", but the referee got there first. He gave Marciano a mandatory count, which wasn't applicable in a title fight anyway, then wasted time in wiping his gloves before telling us to box on. Those valuable seconds gave the champ time to recover and ruined my chance of winning there and then. By the ninth the gas had run out for me against Marciano's persistent attacking and I lost.'

In London, Moore defended his world title against Yolande Pompey from Trinidad, and after being reprimanded by the referee for 'not trying', promptly shook the challenger to his heels with a left hook to the chin and then set about him with such intent that the contest was stopped.

Moore again showed his championship calibre in his first title defence against Yvon Durelle, the Canadian champion. Put down three times in the first session from roundhouse rights to the chin, dropped again in round five, this amazing man used all his boxing artifice to make a full recovery and floored his challenger four times to put him down and out in round 11. It was voted the Fight of the Year. Archie went to Rome and dropped a ten-round non-title decision to Giulio Rinaldi. The Italian demanded a championship chance and got it, but found himself bamboozled out of the verdict by the crafty veteran. It was the last time Moore defended the title and in 1962 most of the boxing commissions withdrew their recognition of him as champion – but he had run out of challengers anyway and after the Clay disaster Archie retired to his ranch in San Diego, California.

Left: **Moore on his way to his 127th knockout victory, a record, against Yvon Durelle.** *Top:* **A left to Durelle's nose in their return contest.**

Centre: **A right to the jaw in the same fight.** *Bottom:* **Moore blocks a right from Yolande Pompey, Harringay, 1956.**

Dick Tiger

When Dick Tiger (1929–1971, real name, Richard Ihetu) left his native Nigeria to try and make a name for himself in England, he was long past 26 and the middleweight champion of his country. He based himself in Liverpool, and could not have made a worse start, losing his first four contests. Following a number of impressive wins, he was picked as a stepping-stone for new star, Terry Downes. A five-round win gained him a match with Pat McAteer for the Empire middleweight crown which he won conclusively in nine rounds. Five fights later, one a victory over Yolande Pompey, and Tiger took off for America and that was the last British fans saw of him.

America suited Tiger, and once he had settled down he soon proved to be of world class, his tough frame and his resolute fighting enabling him to run up a remarkable record. He lost his Empire title to Wilf Greaves of Canada on a points decision, but he got it back, together with his revenge, by stopping Greaves in nine rounds, then waited patiently for two years before getting his first crack at the world crown, taking a points decision off equally tough Gene Fullmer. They met twice more before Fullmer was convinced that he had met his master, a seventh-round loss before Tiger's own people at Ibadan, bringing an end to their series.

Joey Giardello snatched a verdict off Tiger to assume the championship and kept the Nigerian waiting for nearly two years before giving him a chance to win it back. This Tiger did, only to drop it to Emile Griffith six months later. So Tiger, now 37, turned his attention to the light-heavies and caused an upset when outpointing for the title the Puerto Rican Jose Torres, who had built up a big reputation and was seven years younger. To show it was no fluke, Tiger did it again, but when he made his next defence, against Bob Foster, he was meeting a formidable challenger, 13

Dick Tiger (*left*) beating Yolande Pompey at Wembley in 1958 before going to America to win the world middleweight crown.

years his junior, and suffered the one and only knockout defeat of his career, taking the full count from a solid left hook to the jaw in the fourth round. If Tiger hoped for a return bout he was unlucky, but at the age of 40 he confounded everyone by beating Nino Benvenuti, but lost a ten-round points verdict to Emile Griffith. This was his last contest and in July 1971 he announced his retirement and went home to live in the conquered Biafra, the place of his birth, where he had sent considerable funds during its fight for independence from Nigeria. Five months later the boxing fraternity was shocked to hear that this likeable, popular warrior had died from cancer. Tiger was honoured with an OBE for his services to sport.

Bob Foster

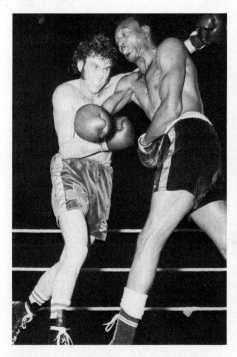

When a man quits the fight game without getting anywhere, it is very seldom that he comes back to it and makes the grade. Bob Foster, born at Albuquerque, New Mexico, in 1942, built up such a good amateur record that it seemed certain he would make similar progress as a professional when he joined the paid ranks just a month before his 19th birthday. He made a good start, but some bad matchmaking against such heavyweights as Doug Jones, Ernie Terrell and Zora Folley, when he was only a light-heavy, caused him to bid adieu to boxing and find work in a munitions factory.

Foster moved his wife and four children to Washington, DC and there met a fight enthusiast named Morris Salow, who convinced Bob that with his height of 6 ft 3½ in and corresponding long reach of 79 inches, he should, with five years of ring experience behind him, return to action with every prospect of making good. The new partnership proved productive. In a year Foster had won his eight bouts, all but one inside the distance, and now they resolved on a bold stroke – a challenge to Dick Tiger for the light-heavyweight championship

The Biafran champion was willing enough provided he was guaranteed 100,000 dollars (£41,667). This meant that even if he won Foster would be out of pocket to the tune of 25,000 dollars. Therefore, he could not afford to lose. Tiger was as tough a fighter that it was possible to meet. He had twice been middleweight champion before becoming light-heavyweight king. It would take a very good man to beat him, but lanky Bob, after ramming a long left into the champion's face for three rounds, produced a stunning left hook to the chin in the fourth to send Tiger flat on his back, knocked out for the first time in his long career.

There were three successful title defences in the following year, then Foster followed the example of so many previous light-heavyweight champions,

Two views of Foster beating British champion Chris Finnegan in a title defence at Wembley in 1972.

and challenged for the heavyweight crown. It was a courageous gesture, because Joe Frazier happened to be occupying the throne at the time and he had a knockout record that was awesome to behold. Foster found that his long reach and his maximum hitting power was not enough to stem the aggressive titleholder and it was not long before Frazier got through with a left hook that floored his challenger for 'nine', while another put him away for the full count.

A devastating defeat like that made Foster's challengers think he was ready for the cleaners, but in the next 18 months he made six successful title defences and the following year was brought to London to face Chris Finnegan, the British champion, whose backers thought would be too fast and too young for the 30-year-old titleholder. Finnegan put up a great fight, but Bob's punching was too much for him and when put down in the 14th, he could not summon up the strength to get to his feet and was counted out. Foster went home to try once more to break into the heavyweight picture, but Muhammad Ali put him in his place by winning in eight rounds.

Stanley Ketchel

The middleweight division has supplied some of the greatest fighters the world has ever seen and one of them was Stanley Ketchel (1886–1910), real name Stanislaus Kiecal, but known among the fight fraternity as the 'Michigan Assassin'. Born at Grand Rapids, of Polish ancestry, he got tired of being a farm-hand and set out to see the world. He was 17 then, strong, vigorous, full of life and wanting to get as much out of it as possible. At a fair he came across a boxing booth and decided to try his luck when the 'barker' tossed a pair of gloves at him with the invitation to come up and stay three rounds for a dollar. Young Ketchel knocked the star of the show out with a swiping right, pocketed the silver coin and made up his mind that fighting was the easiest way to earn a living.

No one taught him to box and Ketchel did not bother to learn. Few could stand up to his big punches and after he had stopped 35 opponents out of 41 bouts, he boxed a 20-round draw with Joe Thomas, who fancied himself as champion. They were then matched by a San Francisco promoter with the middleweight title at stake, and Stanley won by a knockout in the 32nd round. He beat Thomas again, knocked out Mike (Twin) Sullivan in a single round, and defeated Billy Papke, a dangerous contender. In a return match with Papke he lost his title. When they came up for the first round Ketchel extended his glove for the usual handshake, but Billy belted him between the eyes with a blinding right-hander and for the first time in his life Ketchel took a count. He never recovered from that unsporting blow and the fight was stopped in the 11th round after he had taken an unmerciful beating. He gained full revenge two months later when he battered Papke into helplessness in 11 rounds and then took on Philadelphia Jack O'Brien, the light-heavyweight king. When the bell sounded to end the tenth and final round, O'Brien was out to the world from a tremendous right swing and could never have beaten the count.

This feat caused Ketchel to think that he could tackle Jack Johnson, the magnificent coloured heavyweight champion. There were plenty of people who hated Johnson and urged Ketchel to knock him out – and if ever a man tried to bring this off, it was the Michigan Assassin. They met at Colma in California and for the first 11 rounds the far shorter and lighter man swung his big punches at the smiling Negro who picked them off in the air or contemptuously moved out of line to make his rival miss. But midway through the 12th Stanley got one home to sit the heavyweight champion on the canvas while the crowd roared excitedly. Johnson got up and as the confident Ketchel charged in for the 'kill', he was caught with an uppercut to the chin that sprayed his front teeth and knocked him unconscious before he fell. Stanley went back to the middleweights, but never again defended his title. Eight months after the Johnson disaster he was murdered by a jealous cowhand on a ranch where he was resting between fights.

Middleweight champion Ketchel floors heavyweight champion Jack Johnson, who got up to knock out Ketchel in the same round.

EAST-SIDE

EL. — JOHNSON.

Les Darcy

When a fighter reaches 21 and is already regarded as a world-beater by his fellow-countrymen, there is every reason to suppose that he is destined for the highest honours in the ring. Tragically, not so for Les Darcy (1895–1917) who died before he could fulfil his great promise. One of the hardest punchers the middleweight division has known, he had time only to participate in 39 contests, of which he lost three by decision and one on a disqualification. The remainder he won, 21 of them inside the distance. In Australia he was regarded as champion of the world at his weight.

Born at Woodville in New South Wales, James Leslie Darcy had to become the family bread-winner while a youngster because of his father's semi-invalidism. At 15 he had the build, the courage and the yen to go into the professional ring and was undefeated in his first 17 contests. At 18 he boxed 20 rounds for the Australian welterweight title, but lost on points to Bob Whitelaw. In a return fight, he stopped Whitelaw in five rounds to win the title and become a national idol. He built up such a reputation that he ran out of Australian opposition and the promoters had to import top-ranking Americans.

The first of these was Jeff Smith, who had a strong claim to the world title. He struck Darcy so low in the fifth round that the Australian boy was unable to continue and the fight was awarded to the American. The same thing occurred in a return match, but this time Smith was disqualified in the second round for foul hitting and Darcy's friends claimed the title on his behalf. In a 20-round contest advertised as for the world middleweight crown, Darcy delighted the fans by belting out Eddie McGoorty, also from America, in the 15th round, and he beat McGoorty again, this time in eight rounds, to prove that his winning of the title had not been a fluke.

After that there was no holding Darcy. Twice he outpointed celebrated Jimmy Clabby over 20 rounds, but his final and most brilliant victory was over George Chip, yet another American claimant to the middleweight championship, who was disposed of in nine rounds. At this point in his career he had taken part in 39 paid bouts, of which he had won 35 (21 inside the distance); had lost three points decisions and been ruled out once for an alleged foul in the 18th round of his contest with Fritz Holland. He had never been stopped or knocked out.

Tex Rickard, the great American promoter, invited Darcy to come to New York for some very lucrative matches, but his country was now at war with Germany and the young fighter could not get permission to leave. He foolishly jumped ship for the United States, only to find when he got to New York that the Governor would not issue him with a licence and he was branded as a 'slacker'. Away from home, ashamed at the bad publicity he was getting, he went down with fever and without putting up a fight for his life, died in a Memphis, Tennessee hospital. His body was shipped home and laid in state while thousands of Australians paid silent homage to their dead hero.

Harry Greb

If ever a man could be defined as a truly professional fighter, it was Harry Greb (1894–1926), who stepped into the ring no less than 290 times in 13 years of torrid scrapping in which he used unbounded energy and non-stop aggression. If it is added that he was the one and only man ever to beat talented Gene Tunney, and give him such a going-over that he had to spend a week in bed afterwards, then some idea of Greb's special brand of belligerency will be appreciated. Not a great puncher – he did not give himself time to place his blows or put precise power behind them – he just swarmed over his rivals from first gong to last and the majority of them must have felt that they had been put through a wringer at the end of the contest.

In all those fights he was outpointed only five times and stopped once – in his very early days. Strangely enough, for all his rough-and-ready tactics, he was disqualified but once. He won 111 contests (46 inside the distance) and the remaining 168 bouts were of the no-decision variety, for Greb fought mainly in the days when it was illegal to render verdicts in most of the United States. It was not for nothing that they called him the 'Human Windmill'.

Born at Pittsburgh, Edward Henry Greb was a fighter from birth, it being reported that at a day old he gave his mother a black eye. At 16 he was badgering promoters to give him fights and in two years was an established pro. Averaging 22 bouts a year, he never had time to train – it wasn't necessary anyway – and he spent his purses as fast as he earned them. He was booed every time he stepped into the ring and all the way to the dressing-room on the way back. He loved it.

A look through Greb's record shows that he travelled the length and breadth of the United States and there wasn't a fight town in which he did not appear. Only once did he box outside his own country, this being when as a seaman in the American Navy he fought in the Inter-Allied Tournament after the First World War at the Albert Hall, London, where his rough tactics met with the displeasure of the fans.

Greb (*right*) and Walker before Greb's successful world middleweight title defence in 1925.

Greb became middleweight champion of the world from southpaw Johnny Wilson after he had won and lost the American light-heavyweight crown in hectic battles with Tunney to whom he conceded a stone in weight. The middleweight title he defended successfully on six occasions, having his toughest fight with Mickey Walker in which they tossed leather at each other for the full 15 rounds without pausing to take breath. Several hours later they met by chance in a New York restaurant and began a battle of words that ended with a punch-up on the pavement outside that had to be stopped by the police. At the age of 32 he was still champion and was challenged by coloured Tiger Flowers, whose arms whirled a little faster than Greb's and enabled him to sneak the title on a points verdict. A return fight six months later ended the same way, then Greb, who had fought for many years with the sight of only one eye, went into hospital for an operation on the other and died under the anaesthetic.

Mickey Walker

Only two fighters have ever won three world titles, Bob Fitzsimmons and Henry Armstrong. Mickey Walker did his best to win four and although he did not succeed, no one could accuse him of not trying, and he might have done it had nature been a little more bountiful with his physique. Sturdily built, he stood only 5 ft 7 in and was very short in the arms.

To assess Walker's true capabilities as a fighting machine one must examine his professional record. It began when he was 17 and occupied 17 energetic years during which he participated in 148 bouts, winning 93 (58 inside the distance). He fought 32 no-decision contests, having the best of the majority of them and there was one bout that was declared 'no contest'. Four times he fought to a drawn decision. On the losing side he was outpointed only 11 times, disqualified twice and stopped five times, once at the very beginning of his career and the others when he was giving away too much weight or towards the end of his long career.

Born at Elizabeth, in New Jersey, in 1901, Edward Patrick Walker was the champion scrapper in Keighry Head, the rough Irish section of the town. Liked for his good nature, there was nothing amiable about his boxing and when he turned professional at the age of 18, he quickly established a reputation as a knockout specialist. Then, when he was walking in to demolish Phil Delmont, he was caught by a right-hander that knocked him cold. 'It was the best lesson I ever had,' Walker said afterwards.

In his 19th bout, when he was five days past his 20th birthday, Mickey's manager thought fit to put him in with veteran champion, Jack Britton, who dropped Walker with a clip to the chin in the opening minute, just to let him see who was boss, but was surprised when the youngster got up and contested every inch of the way to the end of their 12-round bout. Eighteen months later Walker won the welterweight title by outpointing Britton over 15 rounds, the first time Mickey had travelled that far. He successfully defended his crown against southpaw Lew Tendler, who was a high-class performer, and also against

Dave Shade, another near champion. But weight-making difficulties caused Walker to drop the title to Pete Latzo after he had held it for four years.

Outfought by the redoubtable Harry Greb in a rugged battle in which no quarter was asked or given, Mickey's first attempt to win the middleweight crown was unsuccessful, even though he had the better of their famous Broadway brawl several hours after they had left Madison Square Garden. But within seven months, Greb had lost the title to Tiger Flowers, who passed it on to Walker on a very narrow points decision. Walker, who now had Jack Kearns as his manager, then took a £30,000 offer from C. B. Cochran to put his championship at stake against Tommy Milligan, the British titleholder, and on getting to London found that the challenger was such a favourite to win that they bet the whole purse at generous odds. Mickey then proceeded to beat Milligan in ten rounds and the pair went off to Paris with their loot.

When Mickey got home he faced a dangerous challenger in Ace Hudkins, known as the 'Nebraska Wildcat', but was still champion at the end of ten give-and-take rounds. He then startled the boxing fraternity by challenging Tommy Loughran for the world's light-heavyweight title. Mickey had been well outboxed by the end of their ten-round championship bout, but laughed off his defeat. To avoid the chore of weight-making, after one more middleweight defence, in which he again had a blistering set-to with Hudkins, he resigned the championship and started work among the heavies.

This meant giving away all from a physical standpoint, but that did not bother Mickey. He worked his way through the contenders without loss and then startled everyone by holding Jack Sharkey, leading challenger for the heavyweight championship, to a draw after 15 rough rounds. Six wins at the expense of the Beef Trust came next, then the intrepid Walker stepped into the ring with Max Schmeling, who three months previously had lost the heavyweight title on a split decision to Sharkey and was now desperately anxious to qualify for a chance to win back the championship.

It was a case of David and Goliath all over again. The German was six inches taller, had a reach of 76 inches, and outweighed Mickey by two stone. Moreover, he had a bomb in his right hand and he exploded this on Walker's chin midway through the first round causing him to make a complete somersault, before rolling in the resin. The game Toy Bulldog, groped around, stuffed his gumshield back into his bleeding mouth and got up at 'eight' for more. He got it and took so much punishment that his manager refused to let him come out for the ninth.

Walker made one more attempt to win the light-heavyweight title, but was outpointed by Maxie Rosenbloom, who kept out of his way for 15 rounds while he clouted Mickey open-gloved at long range. When he found himself being beaten by boys he would not have condescended to meet a few years earlier, Walker decided to call it a day. He was 34 then and took up painting as a hobby, finding it less painful to put paint than opponents on the canvas.

King Levinsky takes a wild swing at Mickey Walker and misses by a mile. Walker won this fight in Chicago, 1932.

Len Harvey

Len Harvey was the complete boxer. They named him 'Master of the Fistic Art'. He studied glove-fighting from childhood, being paid five shillings for his first professional fight at Plymouth at the age of 12½. He continued to box for a living for the next 19 years, during which time he made a habit of collecting titles, becoming the only British boxer to win the middle, light-heavy and heavyweight championships, and to make a Lonsdale Belt his own property in the process. In all he took part in 21 championship bouts, two of which involved a world title.

When it is remembered that Harvey fought in each of the eight weight divisions, passing from less than flyweight to heavyweight, it stands as a remarkable achievement. In his early growing years he did not remain in one division long enough to reach championship class, but from welterweight onwards he was a top-of-the-bill boxer and stayed in championship class to the end of his career. He was a clever boxer who developed an amazing talent for defence.

Born in the tiny Cornish village of Stoke Climbsland, Leonard Austin Harvey had elder brothers who boxed and thus became early acquainted with the sport. Watching others slug each other at the Cosmopolitan Club in Plymouth, he decided that one could win contests and come to the least possible harm by using brain as much as brawn, so he planned, firstly to build himself a superb physique and secondly, to learn the scientific side of boxing.

It paid off in all directions, for he came out of hundreds of contests mentally unimpaired and without a mark to show that he had ever fought the best in the world for so many years. He had his first title fight at the age of 18, earning a draw after 20 fast rounds with Harry Mason for the British welterweight title. Three years later he became British middleweight champion by knocking out Alex Ireland in seven rounds, then made six successful title defences, being denied the winning of two Lonsdale Belts, because one of these championship bouts was declared a 'draw'. Subsequently, when it had become a strain to make the middleweight limit, he was narrowly outpointed by Jock McAvoy to lose his crown, but within two months had become British light-heavyweight champion by outpointing Eddie Phillips.

Against Marcel Thil, of France, for the world middleweight title, and against John Henry Lewis, for the world light-heavyweight crown, Harvey lost by extremely narrow points verdicts, but he achieved his best-ever performance when he outpointed Jack Petersen, to whom he conceded almost two stone, to become heavyweight champion and thus complete a hat-trick of British titles. He won the Empire crown when giving weight and a beating to Larry Gains, of Canada, but he lost both titles in a return match with Petersen, after courageous 12 rounds.

In July 1939 he and his old enemy McAvoy, had a hard-fought struggle at London's White City in a match billed as for the world's light-heavyweight crown. Harvey won on points and although receiving recognition from the British Boxing Board of Control was never acknowledged as world champion in America. He retired after losing to Freddie Mills in 1942, when he had been out of the ring for three years and was serving in the Royal Air Force.

The fourth fight between Len Harvey and Jock McAvoy was recognized in Britain as for the world's light-heavyweight championship. *Right:* **McAvoy covers up.** *Far right:* **Harvey connects with a left lead.**

Jock McAvoy

Without any doubt the toughest and most destructive of all the British middleweight champions was Jock McAvoy (1908–1971). In a long career he was never stopped, except by Freddie Mills in 1942, when he took a punch that injured his spine and was no doubt responsible for him becoming a polio victim in the last 23 years of his life.

Born at Burnley in Lancashire, Joseph Patrick Bamford chose the fighting name of Jock McAvoy in order to prevent his mother from finding out that he spent his Sunday afternoons in boxing six rounds for a few shillings at a small arena at Royton. When she discovered that her son was a professional fighter she made him promise to give it up until he was 21. He did, then bounced back into activity leaving a trail of victims in his wake. The family had moved to Rochdale and McAvoy became known as the 'Rochdale Thunderbolt'.

At the second attempt he took the British middleweight title from talented Len Harvey. This he defended against all comers on four occasions, and was never beaten for this championship. He won and lost the British light-heavyweight title, and tried hard to take the heavyweight crown from Jack Petersen, to whom he conceded over a stone and was at every physical disadvantage. Twice more he fought Len Harvey in close contests for the light-heavyweight crown, and put up a great fight to try and win the European light-heavyweight championship from that tough Frenchman, Marcel Thil.

It was in America, however, that McAvoy reached real glory, although he did not profit greatly thereby. He went to New York in 1935 and after giving a good beating to Al McCoy, the Canadian light-heavyweight champion, he astounded the fight fraternity by blasting out Ed (Babe) Risko, the world middleweight champion, in 2 min 48 sec of the first round. Such a conclusive victory should have gained Jock a shot at the title, but he had been too good. Instead, they put him in with John Henry Lewis for the light-heavyweight world title, against whom the Britisher was outreached and skilfully outboxed, to lose narrowly on points after 15 close rounds. In spite of this good showing, he was never allowed to challenge for the middleweight crown and had to come home empty-handed.

Tony Zale

If for nothing else, Tony Zale is famous for his three great bruising battles with Rocky Graziano, considered the hardest-hitting, free-punching slugfeasts ever seen in the middleweight division. These three fierce battles took place within a period of 21 months. In each they fought until one or the other had been flattened, and the punishment they absorbed and what it took out of them in dealing it out, finished both off as fighters. In Zale's case he fought only once more after their third meeting.

Born at Gary in Indiana in 1913, Anthony Florian Zeski came of Polish forebears and was as tough as the steel city in which he grew up. As a youth he took to boxing as a duck to water, joining the local amateur club and spending all his time in the gymnasium when he wasn't working in the mills. His strong physique had steel-like qualities that enabled him to hit hard and take a punch in return unflinchingly, and he won 50 of his 95 unpaid bouts

inside the distance and was beaten only eight times.

A fortnight after his 21st birthday he turned pro, but his ambitious manager overworked him with 28 contests in his first year and he lost interest as well as a few bouts, and retired for two years, by which time he had grown into a sizeable middleweight. Sam Pian and Art Winch, who managed a team of fighters with considerable success, persuaded Zale to return to the ring and under their experienced guidance he had two and a half years of steady grooming until they thought it time to put him in with Al Hostak, a tough Czech from Minneapolis, whom the National Boxing Association recognized as world middleweight champion. They boxed ten rounds at Chicago and Tony took the decision.

Victory earned Zale a title shot which came six months later, this time at Seattle. Hostak, who had a tremendous knockout record found himself

outpunched in a fight that was far more furious than their first affair. His best punches just bounced off the challenger, who slugged back with such effect that the champion took the full count in round 13. Twice Zale defended his NBA title, knocking out Steve Mamakos in 14 rounds and Hostak, in a return match, in two rounds. Then he went to New York to meet Georgie Abrams, who was challenging his claim to the championship, and Zale won on points over 15 rounds to establish himself as undisputed titleholder.

Three months afterwards he failed to give weight away to light-heavyweight Billy Conn and lost on points, then he went into the US Navy and was out of the fight game for four years, during which time his title was 'frozen'. On his return Tony found that a young fellow named Rocky Graziano, nine years his junior, had been making the headlines with a display of vicious punching that had won him a number of sensational

knockout wins. Everyone wanted to see if the 'Man of Steel' could stand up to the bombs that Rocky could toss with both fists.

Zale had six warming-up bouts in five months that ended in an aggregate of 22 rounds, then he was ready for Graziano. They met in New York's Yankee Stadium in a fight that had the 40,000 fans roaring with excitement as they punched it out with all the force and fury they could muster. It was a sheer battle of survival and it was the challenger who hit the floor first, going down from a sizzling left hook to the chin midway through the opening round. He got up to charge into the champion and they stood toe-to-toe swapping punches. All through the second round they fought like cavemen, then in the third, two belting rights under the heart and a swinging right to the chin sent Zale skating under the bottom rope with no hope of getting up in time to beat the count. The bell came to his rescue at

'three', but he was so dazed he walked into Rocky's corner by mistake.

Making an amazing recovery in the minute's rest, Zale came out full of fight and again they hammered each other with no attention paid to defence. Graziano could see but one target – his opponent's chin, but Zale used all of Rocky as a punching-bag and gradually had him weakening, a left hook after 1 min 43 sec of the sixth round putting the challenger down for the full count.

Of course, there had to be a return by public demand, this time in Chicago. It was the same kind of battle all over again, but this time with Zale doing the greater damage, in fact, at the end of the fifth round, with Graziano bleeding badly from cuts it seemed as though it might be stopped. But Rocky staged such a furious assault in the sixth that Tony took a fearful battering and was on the point of collapsing when the referee called a halt and the title had

changed hands. It came back into Zale's possession 11 months later when they had the 'rubber' match. Again it was total war, but Zale got through with the finisher in the third round when Graziano had punched himself out.

Marcel Cerdan came from France to challenge for the championship and Zale made the mistake of taking on the tough Frenchman just three months after the final fight with Graziano. Obviously the 35-year-old champion had not given himself time to recover, but he punched it out with the fierce-hitting Cerdan, finally being beaten into the ropes and bombarded with blows until he pitched forward out on his feet. The bell sounded, his seconds conveyed him to his corner, but Tony was done and they daren't send him up for any more. He never fought again.

Zale versus Graziano. A left from Zale puts Graziano down in one of their three great fights.

Rocky Graziano

It was boxing that prevented Rocky Graziano from becoming a confirmed criminal. Born in a Brooklyn tenement cold-water flat, the fifth son of a third-rate Italian fighter, Rocco Barbella had the roughest and toughest of upbringings and at school age was running wild with a gang of youngsters who regarded stealing as an exciting adventure. Before long his busy fists had made him leader, but he was caught breaking open slot machines and sent to a reform school. Eventually he found himself in prison, where he was given solitary confinement for assaulting a warder. Drafted into Army service he was in serious trouble through striking an officer, and ran away.

It was wartime, all his former pals were in uniform or in prison. Passing a boxing arena he saw a chance to earn five dollars by taking part in a novices'

competition. He won, and had eight fights in 55 days, winning five of them by knockouts, before the military police caught up with him and he was back in the Army. Within a year, however, it was decided that the war could be won without his services, so he went back to boxing, where he could use his big fists as savagely as he liked – and get paid for it.

In the next year and a half he had 38 contests, winning 20 of them by the kayo route, although being outpointed by one or two too clever to be caught by his swiping punches. The matchmaker at Madison Square Garden in New York put him in with Billy Arnold, a coloured middleweight of great promise, but Graziano punched him stupid in three rounds, then defeated the reigning welterweight champion, Freddie Cochrane, twice in ten rounds apiece and butchered Harold Green in three

savage sessions. Marty Servo had become welterweight king, but he was no match for Rocky who battered him into subjection in two rounds and ruined his career. Now the way was clear for a battle with Tony Zale for the world title. It promised to be the punch-up of all punch-ups – and it was.

Down in the first round, Rocky bounced up to put the champion through the ropes in the third, the bell preventing the title from changing hands. Then the nine-years-younger challenger punched himself out in an effort to score a knockout and was finally floored by a Zale special left hook that had him sitting bewildered on the canvas unable to continue. His great showing earned him a return fight that had the fans clamouring to see it. The Chicago Stadium was packed to the rafters, the receipts being 422,009 dollars paid by 18,547 spectators.

This time Graziano found the champion in far better fighting trim and although he threw his big right with great frequency, Zale's punches were more accurately delivered and he gave the resolute Rocky such a hiding that at the end of the third round and after each succeeding session, the referee visited the challenger's corner to make sure that he was fit enough to continue. At the end of the fifth it was decided that Rocky, now with cuts over both eyes and one almost closed, could come up for one final round. He left his corner with the fixed intention of selling his life dearly and fought in a mist of his own blood. Suddenly he felt a slap across his face and found he was fighting his trainer. It was all over. Zale was being picked off the ropes, a battered unconscious hulk and Graziano was champion of the world.

Rocky returned to Brooklyn as a hero, but not for long. The newspapers revealed that he had served a prison sentence and had been an Army deserter in wartime. They wanted to know why the Boxing Commission had given a licence to such a character. So he was suspended for nine months, forfeiting the right to earn big money in a third meeting with Zale. All that time he was unable to earn and had to resist pressure from his old companions to go back to crime. Finally the 'rubber' match was made for Newark in New Jersey, where they drew 21,497 fans and 335,646 dollars. But the long lay-off had affected Rocky more than it had Zale and he was sent sprawling for the full count in the third round after another punch-swapping spree.

He stayed out of the ring for a year, then started a comeback that lasted for 21 contests with 18 impressive wins inside the distance and no defeats. It looked as though Graziano was back at the top again and when he challenged Sugar Ray Robinson, who was now reigning as middleweight champion, it seemed that Rocky, although now 30, might stand a chance of regaining the title with one of his roundhouse swipes. But he was up against a perfectionist this time, who allowed him to weary himself in misses that were wide of the mark and then put him down and out with a right-hand precision punch to the chin. There was one more bout five months later when Rocky was outpointed by up-and-coming Chuck Davey, after which he retired to become a television personality.

Opposite: Graziano has Zale down in the second round of his first title fight, but Zale got up to win. Below: A Graziano right explodes on the jaw of Tony Janiro in a drawn fight.

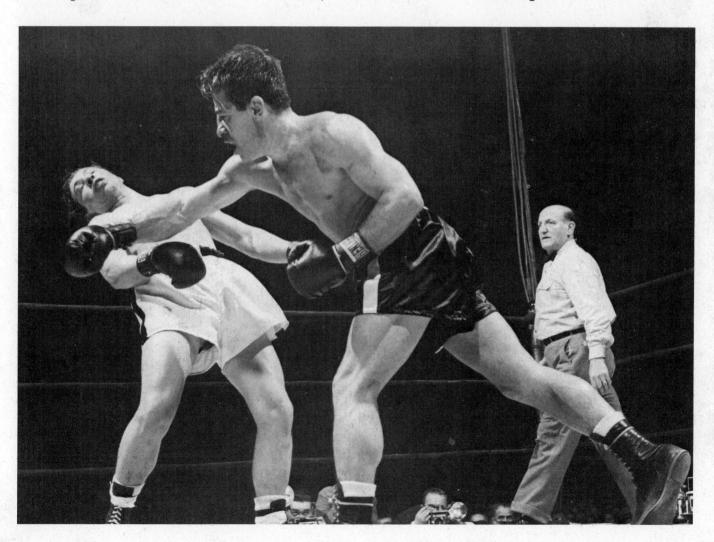

Jake LaMotta

Born in this slum district of New York in 1921 of an Italian father and a Jewish mother, Jake LaMotta had to fight for self-preservation from the time he was old enough to set foot in the street. After a scuffle with the police over a pavement battle, a friendly cop lured him into the local boys' club and turned him over to the boxing coach.

A Diamond Gloves winner when he was 19, LaMotta went into the paid ranks to help swell the family budget and also to save. When he found it hard to get opponents, he converted a cinema into a fight arena and promoted matches with himself a star performer. He was as good a business man as he was a fighter. He became the first person to defeat Sugar Ray Robinson.

By the time he was 28 Jake had accounted for all the other contenders to the middleweight title and secured a title fight with Marcel Cerdan at Detroit. It was one of the toughest fights on record and ended when the Frenchman was tossed to the canvas, injured his shoulder and was forced to retire. Now LaMotta set out to make the most of his good fortune.

First he outpointed Tiberio Mitri, of Italy, in New York, then faced Laurent Dauthuille, of France, at Detroit. Here he came close to being beaten. For 14 rounds the Frenchman outsmarted him all the way and it looked 100 to 1 on LaMotta dropping his title when midway through the 15th and final round, he slung over a mighty punch that caught his tiring opponent solidly on the jaw. He sagged into the ropes and LaMotta hammered him down for the full count.

Ray Robinson was the next challenger and Jake met him just five months after the fight with Dauthuille. But his rugged, bull-dozing methods were of no avail against a sharp-shooter of Sugar Ray's class and by the 13th round, LaMotta had been punched to a standstill and had to be rescued by the referee. A knockout defeat by Bob Murphy when he turned to the light-heavies convinced LaMotta that at 30 he was past his peak.

Jake LaMotta (*right*) knocks out Georgie Kochan.

Sugar Ray Robinson

If any man has been the complete boxer it is Sugar Ray Robinson, a superb artist and brilliant perfectionist, throughout his fabulous career that lasted 25 years, during most of which he was a fistic star of the highest order. His list of achievements rates him very high in the Hall of Fame and his skill was such that after 202 contests he was able to leave the ring at the age of 45, physically sound and as mentally alert as ever. His study of his chosen profession, his personal discipline and intense dedication to his vocation, is an object-lesson to all those who aspire to fame in the boxing game.

Born at Detroit in 1920, Walker Smith changed his name when he substituted for a boy who had failed to pass the doctor. Not having a licence to box, teenage Smith borrowed the disappointed lad's card and was announced as Ray Robinson, a name he was to make famous. He won his first contest and a great many amateur bouts afterwards, including the Golden Gloves featherweight title in New York in 1940, and when he decided to become a professional he continued to use his adopted name. When he had run up a long sequence of quick wins, someone told his manager, George Gainford, that he had a sweet fighter. 'Yes, as sweet as sugar,' came the reply, and Sugar Ray Robinson it was thereafter.

Only one points defeat marred his first 132 contests. In Detroit, before his own people, he was adjudged to have lost to Jake LaMotta, a toughie from the Bronx area of New York, and a man he had already defeated. Subsequently he defeated LaMotta four times, the last giving him the greatest satisfaction as he stopped Jake in 13 rounds to win the world's middleweight crown.

There were other successes before that, however. During the war Robinson had grown into a welterweight, but although good enough to fight for the title, he had to wait until peacetime as the championship was frozen while champion Freddie Cochrane was in the US Navy. Then Cochrane lost his crown to Marty Servo and although Sugar Ray was nominated as leading contender, the match never came off as Servo rashly took on Rocky Graziano and was so badly battered that he was forced to

From a camera mounted in the lights: Robinson (*left*) and Basilio about to swap punches.

retire from the ring. Robinson then outpointed Tommy Bell to win the vacant welterweight championship, a title which he successfully defended on five occasions in the next four years, and which he gave up when becoming middleweight titleholder.

A smooth mover, precise puncher, with a thought-reading brain and a knowledge of anatomy that enabled him to place his blows where they did most damage, Robinson was at his best when he challenged LaMotta for his second world title. He outboxed the rugged 'Bronx Bull' so completely that by the 13th round Jake was in a stupefied state and had to be rescued by the referee. That was in February 1951, which meant that Sugar Ray was long past 30, but as it happens, just reaching his prime. He took off on a European business-cum-holiday tour, winning in France, Belgium, Italy and Germany, then accepted an offer from promoter Jack Solomons to visit London and defend his championship against the British titleholder, Randolph Turpin.

Robinson did the thing in champion style when he travelled. His large entourage consisted of his manager, trainer, sparring-partners, golf companion, secretary and a few others, including a court jester. Perhaps there was a little too much of the holiday

spirit in his camp, for when the bell ended the contest after the 15th round, Sugar Ray found he had been outpointed and an excited throng were cheering a new champion. Just 64 days later, before a record crowd at the New York Polo Grounds, he came from behind, with the handicap of a severely damaged left eye, to produce a pay-off punch in the tenth round that floored the Britisher for a long count. An expert finisher, Robinson showed no mercy and was punching Turpin at will when the referee rightfully called a halt.

Sugar Ray successfully defended his regained title against Carl (Bobo) Olson, outpointed over 15 rounds, and the former middleweight champion, Rocky Graziano, who was put away in three. Then he startled the fight fraternity by challenging Joey Maxim for his light-heavyweight crown. It meant giving away a full stone, two inches in height and a couple of years in age, but Robinson wanted to put his name among the immortals who have won three separate world titles, and for the first 12 rounds he looked like doing it. Only Maxim's long experience and expert defence kept him going, but doing all the forcing in a heat-wave temperature of 104 degrees, took so much out of the challenger that he collapsed in his corner at the end of the 13th round and could not come up for the next. Even so, he did better than the referee who staggered out of the ring at the end of the tenth and had to be replaced.

Robinson had come so close to achieving his ambition and the manner of his defeat, plus his age, made him decide to retire from active boxing while still middleweight champion and go into cabaret work. For two and a half years he stayed away from boxing, during which time Olson beat Turpin for the vacant title. Then Sugar Ray announced his return to the ring at the age of 35, which most of his friends thought unwise, especially when he was beaten by a second-rater in a warm-up bout. But this amazing man was merely getting his second wind and by the end of the year he had caused a sensation by

Following pages: **Robinson throws a left but misses in his losing title fight with Turpin.**

but in his very next title defence he was outpointed by Carmen Basilio, who had relinquished the welterweight crown to compete as a middle. It looked like an upset from which Robinson would be unable to recover, yet once more he was to show that he was a superman among ring warriors. Basilio kept the title for the usual six months' respite, but had the surprise of his life when the now 38-year-old Sugar Ray walked away with a points victory rendered by both judges, even if the referee did not agree.

Robinson had set up a record by becoming middleweight champion of the world five times, something that is hardly likely to be equalled, certainly not surpassed. He remained champion for nearly two years, then was outpointed by little-known Paul Pender, a sound boxer but scarcely reckoned to be in Sugar Ray's class. However, when the inevitable return match took place, Pender did it again, and Robinson was back among the challengers. The National Boxing Association refused to recognize Pender as champion and Gene Fullmer was promoted into the championship seat as the result of a victory over Basilio. At once he was challenged by Robinson, now in his 41st year, who had the fans cheering when he held the champion to a close drawn decision. Three months later they fought again, but Father Time appeared in Fullmer's corner and he gained a points verdict that finally saw the end of Sugar Ray as a championship contender. He remained active, however, until December 1965 when he retired finally at a resplendent farewell party.

stopping Olson in two rounds to regain the championship.

So he was king of the middleweights for the third time, but there was a lot more to come. He beat Olson in four rounds in a return title encounter, then dropped a decision to Gene Fullmer and once again was an ex-champion. He had taken the precaution of having a return-fight clause included in the contracts and precisely four months later he stepped into the ring to flabbergast the fans and bewilder Fullmer with a characteristic display of phenomenal fighting power that saw him the winner by a perfect knockout in round five.

So Sugar Ray was back on top again,

Left: The referee pushes Robinson away from Turpin and awards him the fight in their second encounter.

Below: Joey Maxim avoids a right from Robinson when retaining his light-heavyweight title.

Randolph Turpin

No one captured the imagination of the British sporting public more than Randolph Turpin (1928–1966), whose vigorous fighting and dynamic punching brought him to world fame at the early age of 23. He was a box-office draw from his first professional fight to his last, 16 years later, because he had gained a tremendous reputation as an amateur. At 17 he was the ABA welterweight champion, becoming middleweight titleholder the following year. But his greatest moment while wearing a vest came in a match between Great Britain and the USA when he scored a sensational victory over Harold Anspach by knocking him out in 90 seconds.

Born at Leamington Spa, of a coloured father and white mother, Randolph Adolphus Turpin was the third son in a fighting family, his eldest brother Dick, being the first coloured boxer ever to win a British title, while Jackie gained considerable success as a feather. Randy, the youngest, picked up a lot from the others, but his ability to punch with devastating power was a natural gift. All he did was to develop it into a match-winning weapon. After service in the Royal Navy as a cook, he became a professional three months after his 18th birthday and with success after success his name soon became a household word.

His mother insisted that he let brother Dick have first crack at the middleweight crown and when he lost the title to Albert Finch, Randy redeemed the family honour by stopping his brother's conqueror in five rounds. It was a title he never lost. The European crown was added with a dynamic 48-second victory over Luc van Dam of Holland, four months later, and the world title garnered in five months after that. To achieve this high honour he was faced by none other than the fabulous Sugar Ray Robinson, but Randy did not turn a hair about meeting such a celebrity. At the Exhibition Hall at Earls Court, London, Turpin proved himself the best man of the night by scoring an undisputed points victory that had the 18,000 capacity crowd standing up and singing 'For He's A Jolly Good Fellow', followed by a sustained ovation that lasted all the long way to the dressing-rooms.

Alas, in New York 64 days later, before a record crowd for middleweights of 61,370 excited fans paying 767,626 dollars, he fought a little under par against a man determined to regain his lost laurels, and did not look like a winner until Robinson sustained a badly cut eye and had to do something

Above: **Turpin's fine physique.**
Right: **Turpin gets a left to the face of Don Cockell when winning the British and Empire light-heavyweight title.** *Far right:* **Turpin ducks very low when winning the world middleweight title from Robinson.**
Far right, above: **A Turpin left flattens Charles Humez's nose.**

desperate to keep in the fight. He did just that with a desperation right-hander that caught Turpin by surprise and had him down and dazed for a long count. Randy got up and gamely took a merciless going-over with his back to the ropes until the referee decided that he was too far gone to take any more and Turpin came home as ex-champion.

Disappointed but undismayed, Turpin next turned his attention to the light-heavies and took the British and Empire titles from Don Cockell, who was stopped after 11 thrilling rounds; then Randy gained the Empire middleweight championship by beating George Angelo, from South Africa. Meanwhile Robinson had temporarily retired leaving the world throne vacant, so Turpin outpointed a strong contender in Charles Humez of France, to qualify to fight Carl (Bobo) Olson for the world middleweight crown. In New York, worried by domestic troubles, he was far from his best and lost a fight he should have won, and worse was to follow. Defending his European crown against Tiberio Mitri in Rome he suffered the humiliation of being counted out in the first round.

With sadness his army of admirers thought that this was perhaps the end, but Randy came back with a bang by regaining his British light-heavyweight crown with a startling two-round victory over Alex Buxton. He gave this up for the second time, but in November 1956, when he was 28, he became British light-heavyweight champion for the third time, thus winning a Lonsdale Belt outright. There was one more title fight, in which he defended his crown successfully against Arthur Howard, but following six more wins over a variety of opponents, a knockout defeat at the hands of Yolande Pompey decided Turpin to call it a day. His well-earned retirement lasted a bare eight years, when tragically he ended his life by his own hand.

Dave Sands

Gene Fullmer

It is doubtful if the fistic world ever saw the best of Dave Sands (1926–1952) for at 26 he was killed in a motor accident near his home at Newcastle in Australia. At that time he had been boxing professionally for ten years, had participated in 104 contests, of which he won 93 (62 inside the distance), had been beaten seven times on points, mostly in his early days, and had been stopped just once and that when he was suffering from a badly cut eye. He was champion of his own country at three weights, middle, light-heavy and heavy, and he was also Empire middleweight titleholder, an honour he never lost.

Real name David Ritchie, he was born at Burnt Ridge, 312 miles south of Sydney, New South Wales, of an

Aborigine mother and a Puerto Rican father. His four brothers became top-of-the-bill scrappers, but Dave outshone them all, his sound boxing and solid punching quickly taking him to the top. A quiet, unassuming chap out of the ring, so shy that it was impossible to interview him, he became a destructive fighting machine when he came from his corner.

Going to London he made himself popular when scoring a fine victory over tough Robert Villemain, of France, in a toe-to-toe battle that had the fans on their feet. He followed this with a 2 min 35 sec win over Dick Turpin to gain the Empire middleweight crown, and now everyone wanted to see him in action against Randy Turpin, a 'natural' if ever there was one. This keenly anticipated match was never made as Turpin engaged himself to fight Sugar Ray Robinson, so Sands went home where he gained an important win over Carl (Bobo) Olson, a leading contender for the world crown, then won the Australian heavyweight title to become a triple champion.

Returning to England he notched up two more wins, then went to Chicago where he again beat Olson. Back in London to try and force a match with Turpin, he accepted an offer to fight Yolande Pompey, a high-ranking light-heavyweight from Trinidad. At the end of six rounds he had the West Indian on the verge of defeat, but in the next, when it seemed likely that the referee might intervene, Sands sustained such a bad cut over his left eye that the fight was stopped, leaving Pompey a most fortunate winner.

To give his wound time to heal Dave returned to Australia and three months later he was back in action, having three title bouts in four months in which he successfully defended his Australian and Empire middleweight crowns, and twice beat off challengers for his light-heavyweight championship. His last contest was on 9 July 1952 and 33 days later, when driving a truck back to his training camp, it slipped off the road and rolled down an embankment. Even Dave's tough physique could not survive an accident like that. He was severely injured and died soon after being taken to hospital.

It was generally agreed by the critics that Gene Fullmer, the Mormon fighter, had little idea of boxing science, was painfully awkward to watch, had a pitiful left jab, could be hit by anyone and had no fan appeal. Yet he twice became middleweight champion of the world, twice defeated the renowned Sugar Ray Robinson, and in the last five years of his boxing career took part in no less than 11 title bouts which netted him a fortune, ten per cent of which he donated to the Mormon Church.

In a career that covered 12 years, 18 months of which was lost due to service in the American Army, Fullmer notched up 62 bouts, the majority of which were exceedingly hard fought. He won 54 contests (24 inside the distance), was three times held to a drawn decision, and never won a fight on a foul or lost one through being disqualified. While he was fighting he had a code system of switching his punches as they were called out in prearranged numbers by his manager, Marv Jenson. Whether this achieved its purpose is doubtful, but it had the effect of disturbing Gene's opponents, especially Carmen Basilio, who was twice stopped in title bouts with Fullmer.

Thickset at 5 ft 8 in, he possessed a strong, well-muscled physique that had been developed while working as a welder in the local mining industry. His immense strength and general toughness made up for his lack of polish and enabled his rugged style of battling to see him through contests against the best in the world. Only three opponents outpointed him, but he was stopped on two occasions, once by Robinson, who knocked him out cleanly with a left hook to the chin, and Dick Tiger, who stopped him in seven rounds to conclude Fullmer's career.

Born at West Jordan in Utah, in 1931, his mother named him Gene because her sports hero had been Gene Tunney. He thus received every home encouragement when he started to box at the age of 11, and more so when he embarked on a pro career at 20. There were five years of making the grade, then a succession of victories over well-placed contenders saw him secure a title fight with Sugar Ray in New York. Robinson was a hot favourite to keep his crown, but found himself uncomfortably hustled by his uncouth rival, who had him on the canvas in the seventh round for seven seconds from a left to the jaw and a right smash to the body. It was the first time Robbie had ever been put down and it upset him so much that Fullmer was able to go on from there and pile up enough points to win the decision and the world's middleweight championship.

That he remained titleholder for only 119 days was sadly disappointing, but two years later he fought Carmen Basilio for the NBA version of the middleweight crown and won in the 14th round when the battered Basilio could take no more. Now came a succession of successful title defences,

Spider Webb, Joey Giardello, Basilio, Robinson (twice), Florentino Fernandez and Benny Paret, all failing to remove the laurels from his broad brow. Then defeat met him in the person of Dick Tiger, who won the championship on a points verdict after a gruelling, bitter bout in San Francisco. In a return at Las Vegas, Fullmer almost recovered his crown, but had to be satisfied with a 'draw', and in their third meeting at Ibadan in Nigeria, with Tiger fighting before his own people, Fullmer was stopped in seven rounds and never fought again.

Fullmer (*right*) sinks a right to Robinson's ribs when taking from him the world's middleweight crown.

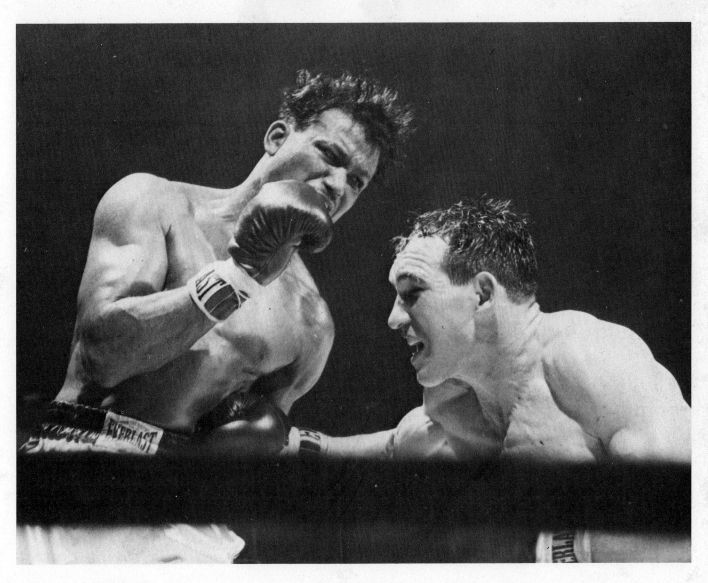

Carmen Basilio

One of the bravest men ever to come out fighting was Carmen Basilio, who came from Syracuse in New York State, measured up to only 5 ft 6½ in, never got beyond welterweight, but who drank a gallon of water each time he wanted to go in with the middles so that there should not be too much disparity when the time came to go on the scales. Born at Canastota in 1927, one of a community of onion-growers, he was a lean, craggy individual who looked as if his physique had been carved out of rock. No one stopped him until very late in his career and then it was tough Gene Fullmer, who had a stone advantage in natural weight. He lost a few decisions to better boxers.

After four years of grim schooling Basilio was ready to go into championship class. He defeated Billy Graham to be recognized as welterweight champion in New York State, but when he fought Kid Gavilan, the tough 'Cuban Hawk', in a bout that carried the world crown, he lost on points. He had to wait 18 months before getting another title shot and then he made the most of it by fighting Tony DeMarco to a standstill in 12 rounds to once more become welterweight king. He beat DeMarco again, but was surprisingly outpointed by Johnny Saxton six months later.

Basilio did not think he had lost his title and in a return bout he proved his point by disposing of the champion in nine rounds to become welterweight champion for the third time, and when Saxton made the plea that he had been unlucky to have lost on the referee's intervention, Basilio proved him wrong by knocking him cold in two rounds when they met on the third occasion. Basilio then created a stir by challenging Sugar Ray Robinson for his middleweight title, and caused an even bigger one by walking off with a points decision.

The first Basilio versus Robinson fight in September 1957 was one of the bitterest and most savage battles the ring has ever seen, even taking the renowned Zale versus Graziano brawls into account. Both fought with eager intensity, with Basilio producing that little bit extra that turned the scales in his favour. When they met again six months later there was even more emnity between the pair and another grimly fought duel resulted with Robinson just getting the edge. When Sugar Ray lost his crown to Paul Pender, whom the NBA refused to recognize as the new champion, Basilio was selected to box Gene Fullmer and was holding his own until the 14th round when the task of giving away a stone to the rugged warrior from Utah proved too much and the fight was stopped. Gamely Basilio tried again but was halted in 12 rounds after putting up a brave resistance. There was one final fling at the middleweight crown, this time against Paul Pender, who was too clever for the 34-year-old Carmen, who was outpointed and promptly called it a day.

Basilio crosses a right to Tony DeMarco's chin, just before the fight was stopped.

Carl (Bobo) Olson

Hawaii has produced a number of top-class boxers, but none more amazing than Carl (Bobo) Olson, if only because of his toughness and durability, plus a passion for fighting that enabled him to compete for 20 years and to notch up his 90th victory on his 38th birthday. Born in Honolulu in 1928, his father was a narcotics inspector who taught his son to box when he returned home from school with two black eyes.

Like many other boys in his locality, Olson attached himself to Sid Flaherty, who ran a large stable of Hawaiian boys. Carl made such progress that he was boxing in San Francisco at the age of 17, won seven bouts in a row, then returned home to perform before his own people and become a popular star. After four years he was thought good enough to be matched with Sugar Ray Robinson at Philadelphia, in a contest that the Pennsylvania Boxing Commission recognized as for the middleweight title.

Stopped in 12 rounds on the first occasion, he took Robinson the full distance when they fought for the middleweight crown proper 18 months later. Then Sugar Ray decided to retire and Olson came to his peak, well beating Randolph Turpin in New York when they fought for the vacant crown. Unfortunately for Carl his nemesis did not stay put, but elected to return to the ring and did so with such determination that he regained the championship with a two-round knockout. It should be stressed, however, that Olson had defended his title on three occasions, whipping Kid Gavilan, Rocky Castellani and Pierre Langlois before taking on Robinson for the third time; also barely six months earlier he had had the audacity to challenge the redoubtable Archie Moore for the world's light-heavyweight title and had been put in his place by the veteran who had knocked him out in round three.

His quick dismissal by Robinson, this being his third defeat by the same man, should have convinced Olson that in Sugar Ray he had met his master. But Olson, entitled to a return contest, was as optimistic as he was fearless, so in due course he faced Robbie for the fourth time, but was again stopped, a clear-cut knockout coming in the fourth round.

Terry Downes

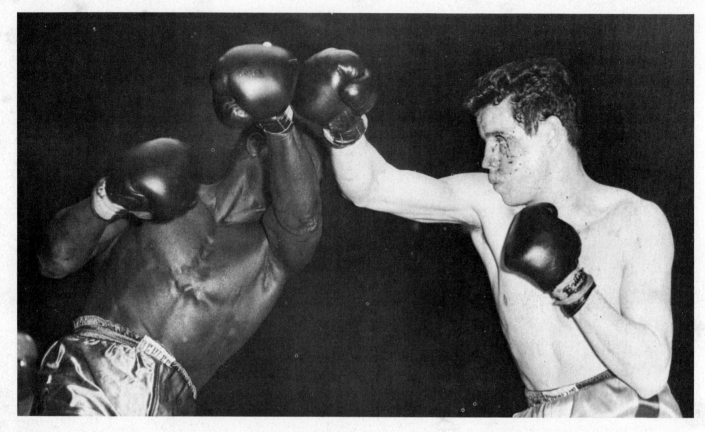

No one loved a fight more than Terry Downes, the London Cockney kid who learnt to fight the American way in America after picking up the rudiments of the noble art from a North London amateur club. He went to the United States with his parents when his sister was in hospital from a road accident, and in due course he joined the US Marines, and performed so effectively that they chose him for the Olympic Games team in 1956. But Downes never got to Melbourne because it was discovered he had been born in England and therefore could not compete for the United States.

Downes all-action style and tendency to 'lead with his face' caused him to suffer cuts as he battered his way to the top, and his earthy complaints about the way his 'bleedin' hooter' bled made him a popular figure whenever he appeared on TV.

When the family moved back to Paddington, where Terry was born in 1938, he resumed his amateur career, but gave it up very quickly to become a professional, when his whirlwind, non-stop, fierce-punching style made him a box-office draw whenever and wherever he appeared. Damage round his eyes and nose caused him to lose bouts he should have won, but he put middleweight champion Pat McAteer out of business and then defeated Phil Edwards most conclusively for the vacant British title by stopping him in 13 rounds.

A title defence against John McCormack a year later saw Downes flooring his challenger several times before being ruled out for an alleged low blow in round eight. To say Terry was annoyed would be a gross understatement and when he got the Scottish champion back in the ring again, he stopped him in eight rounds. He defeated Edwards once more, this time in 12 rounds, and having won a Lonsdale Belt outright, he never again defended his British title. Following a worthy win over Joey Giardello, later to become middleweight champion, Downes went to Boston to challenge Paul Pender for the world crown, but had to return empty-handed when an injury to his nose caused the referee to intervene. A return match at Wembley Arena saw the reverse,

A cut eye lost this fight for Downes(right) against Michel Diouf.

Pender retiring in his corner with a nasty eye wound at the end of the seventh round. Back to Boston went Terry for the 'rubber' match and although he fought furiously for 15 rounds, he found Pender's precise left-hand leading beyond his scope and had to leave the title behind in America when he came home.

Downes turned in a fine performance when outpointing Sugar Ray Robinson at Wembley, then he begged his manager to get him a shot at the world light-heavyweight title, then in the possession of talented Willie Pastrano. They fought at Manchester's Belle Vue and Downes looked a winner all the way, his fast non-stop attack having the American wilting until Willie pulled one out of the blue, a beautifully timed right to the chin that floored the Britisher and had him so groggy that the referee stopped the contest midway through round 11. Terry tore off his gloves in disgust and never fought again.

Emile Griffith

When Benny (Kid) Paret lost his life as well as his world welterweight title when defending it against Emile Griffith in 1962, no one could blame his conqueror for the tragedy. Griffith was out to regain the championship he had lost to Paret six months earlier and having got his rival cornered and in trouble in the 12th round, he proceeded to finish him off. That Paret took unnecessary punishment was the fault of the referee, if anyone at all was to blame. Fortunately the unhappy event did not adversely affect Griffith's boxing career, who went on to fight many more championship contests and to win a second world title.

Born in the Virgin Islands in 1938, Emile Alphonse Griffith made his way to New York at the age of 19 and settled in Brooklyn, where he became an apprentice hat-designer and took up amateur boxing as a hobby. He did better with his hands when they were enclosed in gloves, becoming a Golden Gloves champion at welterweight and joining the paid ranks at the age of 20.

A fast, penetrative puncher, who used both fists briskly and intelligently, he disposed of all competition in his first 24 contests, then took the world title from Paret, who was knocked out in round 13. After he had lost, then regained, the championship from Paret, he remained champion for another seven years, apart from a period of 79 days when he 'loaned' the crown to Luis Rodriguez in

1963. Griffith beat off all other challengers, including Brian Curvis, the British champion, who fought gamely, but could not cope with Griffith's powerful punching.

Heavily muscled for a welter, it was no surprise when, in 1966, he challenged the renowned Dick Tiger for the world middleweight title and came out the winner on points after a fierce battle in which he put the champion down, the first time the tough Nigerian had ever been decked. Then, as well as defending his welter crown, Griffith took on any middleweight challenger there happened to be around, proving to be one of the few champions who have operated successfully in two weight divisions at the same time. He lost the middleweight title to classy Nino Benvenuti, of Italy, regained it five months later, but was beaten in the 'rubber' match in March 1968.

Dick Tiger down for the first time in his career at the feet of Emile Griffith, who stepped up a weight and took Tiger's crown.

Griffith was 30 then, a time when some think about retiring, especially after ten years of hard and sustained warfare, but Emile was far from through, even when he lost his welter crown to Jose Napoles. In 1971 he made a big effort to regain his middleweight laurels by challenging formidable Carlos Monzon, who had twice stopped Benvenuti. For nearly 14 rounds he put up a terrific battle, but the tough Argentinean finally caused the referee to intervene with only 14 seconds of the penultimate round remaining. In June 1973 he again challenged Monzon, holding him to a close points verdict, a remarkable achievement for a man aged 35.

Nino Benvenuti

An idol of the Italian people since he came home from the Rome 1960 Olympic Games with the welterweight gold medal, Nino Benvenuti set up an astonishing record as a professional in a busy career that started at the beginning of 1961 and came to an abrupt halt ten years later. Born in the fishing village of Istria near Trieste, in 1938, his father a fisherman, he was one of a family of four brothers and a sister. All the boys took up amateur boxing, but Nino surpassed the others, having all the physical and mental equipment required by a perfect boxer.

He had style, a varied repertoire of punches that was full of surprises, a knockdown left hook and a straight right of damaging quality. He was Italian champion in two years, European titleholder in four, and picked up the world light-middleweight crown in between. It was when defending this 'half-way' title against Kim Ki-Soo at Seoul in Korea that Benvenuti suffered

his first defeat, losing on points, but it was of no consequence, except to his pride, and in 1967, having successfully defended his European middleweight crown in Berlin and Rome, both with inside-the-distance wins, he went to America to try conclusions with the redoubtable Emile Griffith.

They met in New York, in the new Madison Square Garden, and Nino delighted the 18,096 paying customers by outboxing and outsmarting the coloured champion, bringing matters to a crescendo when he nailed Emile with a left hook, then dropped him with a combination right-left, that brought cries of 'Nino, Nino', from his Italian supporters. Griffith took a mandatory count and tried desperately to turn the tables, but Benvenuti was on top and stayed there to win on points. Griffith regained the crown five months later, but Nino made it third time pays for all when he won the 'rubber' match. He defended his championship against Don

Fullmer, Frazer Scott, Luis Rodriguez and Tom Bethea in quick succession, beating the latter in eight rounds after being sensationally stopped by the same man in eight rounds in Australia two months earlier. A remarkable recovery.

When Carlos Monzon, from the Argentine, came to Rome at the end of 1970 to challenge for the world middleweight title, the Italians were shocked to see Benvenuti go down and out in the 12th round from the vicious-punching South American. They were stupefied when six months later at Monte Carlo, Nino was demolished in three rounds. It was the end for Benvenuti who went back to the insurance agency business he had had the sense to set up during his long and lucrative career.

Benvenuti (*right*) winning the middleweight title from Griffith. Both men were down during the fight.

Carlos Monzon

Many famous fighters have been scrappers from boyhood, energetic youngsters who find they have a natural aptitude for boxing. Not so with Carlos Monzon, who drifted into a gymnasium as a refuge from the harsh, impoverished existence that he shared with his parents and ten brothers and sisters. The idea of getting out of the lowly ruck and becoming someone inspired him through a successful amateur career during which he developed into a strongly built middleweight, technically correct in his boxing moves and punching, with an astonishing coolness when under fire and an uncanny ability for getting out of trouble. A thoughtful calculator, he set traps for his opponents with the foresight of a chess master.

Born at San Jairer in Sante Fé, a province in the Argentine, he waited until he was turned 20 before becoming a professional and began building up an amazing career, not venturing out of South America for over seven years and thus being left out of the ratings, in spite of the fact that in 81 contests, he had been beaten only three times, all points losses, and that 45 of his wins had been gained inside the scheduled course.

The first fight he had outside his own country was the most important of his career, no less than an opportunity to fight for the world's middleweight title. But it meant going to Rome and boxing under conditions completely foreign to him. He was also facing Nino Benvenuti, a god in the estimation of the Italian fans, and he must have known that he had been brought there to provide a typical Roman holiday. This was emphasized most clearly by the fact that whereas the champion was being paid 100,000 dollars, Monzon was receiving less than a sixth of this amount.

It mattered little, for the champion realized from the start that he was up against a fighter of class whose punches hurt wherever they landed. He found himself outpointed in the early rounds and although he turned on a fierce attack in the fifth and sixth rounds which went to his credit, his fury had no effect whatsoever on the calm and collected Argentinean, who gradually wore down his resistance and then knocked him out with a straight right to the chin in the

12th round. Nino will surely win the title back when they have a return battle, thought the Italian fans, but they were wrong. Monzon had summed up Benvenuti's weaknesses and stopped him unceremoniously in three rounds to keep his crown. Four months later he turned back veteran Emile Griffith whose effort to regain his old title ended with the referee's intervention in the 14th round. Monzon, 30 years old in 1972, made three title defences that year, beating American Denny Moyer in five rounds, Jean-Claude Bouttier, of France in 13 rounds and Tom Bogs, of Denmark, in five rounds. In June 1973 he was given an extremely hard fight by Emile Griffith before keeping his title by a narrow points margin.

Monzon (*right*) makes Bouttier's hair stand on end with a hard right during a successful title fight in 1972.

Ted (Kid) Lewis

When Ted (Kid) Lewis (1894–1970) had his first professional fight at the age of 14, he received sixpence and a cup of tea. Later he won a competition and came home with a 'silver' cup, but this prized trophy melted on the mantelpiece overnight. From such sparse encouragement he became a multiple British titleholder and twice welterweight champion of the world. His forceful style had the fans calling him the 'Crashing, Dashing Kid', and he remained noted as a colourful performer throughout a 20-year career that involved 253 contests, of which he won 155, with nine drawn and 65 of the no-decision variety.

Born in London's teeming East End, real name Gershon Mendeloff, he became a boxer for two good reasons – he liked it and it seemed a sure means of adding to the family income. Near his home was the Judaens Club which offered its members cheap entertainment on a Sunday afternoon. There were always plenty of youngsters eager to battle one another for next to

nothing and from such competition Lewis emerged as a boxer of exceptional zeal and no small amount of natural talent.

At 17 he became British featherweight champion, adding the European title before campaigning in Australia, at one stage participating in five 20-round contests in 63 days, losing only one of these by a close points decision. Putting on weight, he moved off to the United States where he stayed for five years and met the cream of the welterweights and middles that that productive country could provide. At 20 he became champion of the world with two wins over Jack Britton, a man he was to meet on 18 more occasions in rings all over America. Between them they monopolized the welterweight championship for six years, their series ending with Britton the final winner.

Lewis returned to London and immediately proved a menace to the leading British middles and welters, winning championships at both weights, with Empire and European honours

thrown in for good measure. His swarming style overwhelmed Johnny Basham, a skilful boxer, who was stopped on three occasions after some brilliant exchanges. Then Lewis beat Jack Bloomfield for the middleweight Lonsdale Belt and won the Empire title by knocking out Frankie Burns of Australia in 11 rounds.

In 1922 he challenged Georges Carpentier for the light-heavyweight championship of the world and the pair met at London's Olympia. There were many who thought Lewis capable of beating the famous Frenchman, but in the opening round he turned his head to look at the referee who had spoken to him, exposed his chin and was promptly knocked out. As he got older he lost his titles to more youthful men, but he kept ring-active up to the age of 35.

Lewis (*left*) throws a left to the head of Boy McCormick, British light-heavyweight champion, whom he stopped in 1921.

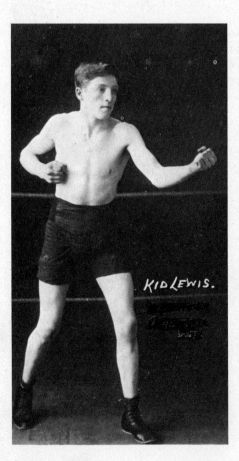

Jimmy McLarnin

They called Jimmy McLarnin 'Babyface' because he was only 16 when he started boxing professionally and had a cherubic countenance. There was nothing angelic about his fighting, his record being liberally strewn with quick knockout victories. He came to championship status in the fabulous 1930s and his trio of title bouts with Barney Ross were epics.

Born in Belfast in 1907, his family emigrated to Vancouver in Canada when he was a mere child and he was brought up there together with a large brood of brothers and sisters. 'Pop' Foster, an ex-boxer, who was running a small gymnasium in the city, saw McLarnin fighting in a street battle and took a fancy to him. He coached the boy, found he had a natural aptitude for boxing, and relieved his parents of the responsibility of feeding him by taking Jimmy under his wing.

Thus began a partnership unique in the fight game. Soon McLarnin was making a name for himself in the arenas of San Francisco and Los Angeles. Jimmy was just turned 20 when Foster finally responded to an offer to box in Madison Square Garden in New York. McLarnin's opponent was Sid Terris, a lightweight of near championship class. It was all over in 1 min 47 sec of the opening round and McLarnin had arrived in the big time.

His sensational victory gained him a shot at Sammy Mandell for the championship, but Jimmy was outpointed by the cagey champion, mainly because it had been something of a strain to make the weight, and from then onwards his manager built him up to the welterweight limit. Fans flocked in to see a run of electrifying victories. Phil McGraw went in one round, so did Sammy Baker, while the highly rated Ruby Goldstein, the idol of New York was demolished in two. Al Singer, the reigning lightweight champion was put away in three rounds.

McLarnin became world's welterweight champion in 1933 by knocking out titleholder, Young Corbett III, in 2 min 37 sec, a record

quickie for the class at that time, and then came the three thrilling matches with Ross, all taking part within a year and each one in the open air, a tribute to their drawing-power. Ross won the first on points, McLarnin recovered his title in the second, but lost again in the third on a verdict that did not meet the approval of either the critics or the fans. A year later McLarnin retired, having won 63 of his 77 bouts, and with a fortune in the bank. And when 'Pop' Foster died 20 years afterwards, he left his entire estate, amounting to 200,000 dollars, to his fighting partner.

McLarnin (*right*) on his way to outpointing Lou Ambers.

Barney Ross

Speedy punching, without a lot of knockdown power, plus a courageous fighting heart enabled Barney Ross (1909–1967) to travel through 82 pro bouts without ever being stopped inside the distance and to acquire two world championships in the process. The majority of his contests went the contracted course, including seven title bouts over 15 rounds, which gives an indication of his supreme physical fitness and the quality of his boxing ability. He fought twice for the lightweight title, which he relinquished to save weight-making; seven times for the junior-welterweight championship, for which he was never beaten, and six times for the welter crown, which he won, lost and regained. He was 29 when he was fought to a standstill by the phenomenal Henry Armstrong to whom he ultimately conceded the crown.

Born Barnet Rosofsky at New York, the family moved to Chicago where his father opened a grocery store. One day two gunmen demanded the contents of the till, Barney's father reached for the bacon knife and was shot dead. The eldest in the family, Ross became the principal bread-winner. Having been a keen amateur boxer since the age of 16 and just recently the winner of a Golden Gloves title, he persuaded his mother to let him try professional fighting, at which he could earn far more than at an ordinary job. In his first 50 bouts he dropped only two decisions and then secured a match with Tony Canzoneri for the lightweight championship, with the pseudo junior-welter title thrown in for good measure. He twice beat Canzoneri, a great dual champion himself, and then turned his attention to the welters, sandwiching six defences of his 'junior' laurels in between.

No one thought he would beat Jimmy McLarnin for the welterweight championship when they had the first of their three historic battles, but Ross dodged the champion's lethal punches and outboxed him to gain the decision. He could not cope with McLarnin's determined efforts to regain his crown and was, in the opinion of many, somewhat lucky to win the 'rubber' match.

Ross proved himself a worthy champion, however, beating off hot challenges from Izzy Janazzo and Ceferino Garcia, his contest with this tough Philippino saving promoter Mike Jacobs's famous Carnival of Champions at the New York Polo Grounds in 1937. For the full 15 rounds they fought at a fast clip with the challenger striving desperately to win by a knockout, while Ross defied his efforts and outboxed him to win a popular verdict. Eight months later Barney put his title on the line against the most dangerous fighter of the year, the all-conquering Henry Armstrong, a man with an astonishing kayo record and a hustling style that few could fathom. Ross was given a rough going-over that few boxers would have survived, but bruised and battered he fought back to the bitter end, to leave the ring as an ex-champion and never to fight again. He served with the US Marines at Guadalcanal and was wounded and decorated for bravery. He died from cancer at the age of 58.

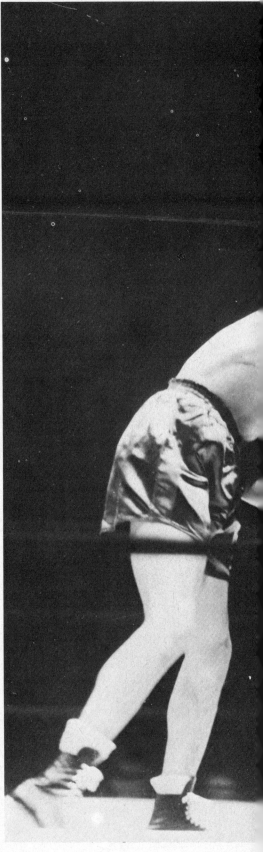

Henry Armstrong

The furious, all-action, non-stop style of fighting as demonstrated by Henry Armstrong had to be seen to be believed. It is not likely that his counterpart will ever be produced or that his record of being a world champion at three weights at the same time will ever be duplicated. Armstrong was a fistic phenomenon. He had an abnormally slow heartbeat and had to warm up in the dressing-room with ten rounds of fast shadow-boxing before going into the ring to fight a torrid 15-round battle. He tossed punches incessantly and they came from all angles. He fought so furiously that it was impossible to count the blows he struck and it must be recorded that in his haste and fury he was guilty at times of using wrists, forearms, elbows and even his head in addition to his busy fists.

Apart from being a triple world titleholder, Armstrong set up a record with 20 defences of his welterweight crown. He also made a gallant attempt to win a fourth world title, challenging the tough Philippino, Ceferino Garcia, for the middleweight championship, but being held to a drawn verdict. He won 58 of 62 bouts as a *paid* 'amateur' and a number of early pro fights that never got into the record books. On paper he is credited with 175 contests in 14 years of furious fighting, of which he won 144 (97 inside the distance) drew eight and lost 23. Only twice in this long career was he stopped, once very early when he was a novice pro, and once by the notorious Fritzie Zivic, when he was attempting to win back the welter title.

Real name Henry Jackson, he was born at Columbus in Missouri in 1912 and took to boxing to escape the downtrodden life meted out to Negroes in those parts. Coloured fighters were grossly ill-used and poorly paid, but the training routines appealed to the youngster and he was fascinated by the glare of the arc-lights and the general showmanship of the boxing arena. He adopted his non-stop attacking methods more as a means of defence than anything else, because he was often

Ross (*right*) trying to get through Armstrong's defence when losing his title in 1938.

called upon to give away considerable poundage to boys bigger than himself, especially if they happened to be white.

Finally, he and another coloured boy, rode the rails to San Francisco where they were mishandled by a manager who preyed on young fighters, until he attracted the attention of Al Jolson, the jazz singer, who was a keen boxing follower. He bought Armstrong's contract and handed him over to Eddie Mead, a manager of sound repute, who saw the potential in the boy from Missouri and steered him skilfully through the ranks of the contenders until he was ready to challenge for the championship. No manager could have had a more willing fighter, and from August 1936, when Armstrong was 23, until October 1937, a matter of 14 months, Mead put his man in the ring on 31 occasions, which must have made training unnecessary. That 'Homicide Hank', as the newspaper boys were now calling him, lost only once and that on a disputed foul, while all but three of this long sequence of bouts ended inside the distance, is proof of his destructiveness at this stage of his career.

Petey Sarron, stumpy featherweight champion, stood up gamely to the irrepressible Armstrong for six rounds and then had to acknowledge defeat.

Then with 14 more wins under his belt, only one of which went the full course, Armstrong went into the Long Island outdoor arena in New York to challenge Barney Ross for the welterweight crown he had held for three years. Henry was probably giving away well over a stone to an accomplished performer of long experience. He never gave the champion a moment in which to draw an extra breath, putting up an all-out, never-ending assault, that carried him to his second world crown over a courageous, but badly battered champion, who suffered such physical torture that he never ventured into a ring again.

Now holding two world titles, Armstrong went after the hat-trick, and a mere 78 days after the defeat of Ross he was climbing into the Madison Square Garden ring to challenge Lou Ambers for the lightweight crown. Ambers himself was a busy-fisted champion, but not quite busy enough to contain Armstrong on that particular night and Henry left the ring the holder of three championships to create a world boxing record. It was a unique status, but one that could not be expected to last for long. He gave up the featherweight crown at the end of 1938 to concentrate on the more lucrative welter title, but after packing in seven successful defences, including one against Ernie Roderick, the British champion, in London, he ventured back into the lightweight class to give Ambers a chance to regain his laurels. The sudden reduction in weight had an adverse effect on Armstrong, who tired, and at the end of 15 toe-to-toe rounds, Henry was declared a points loser.

He took a month off and then began another long series of welterweight championship defences, defeating 12 challengers in the space of 11 months, sandwiching in between an attempt to win the middleweight title from Ceferino Garcia and a non-title bout with Lew Jenkins, a former lightweight champion, who was beaten in six rounds. If ever a pitcher went too often to the well it was Armstrong. Just 11 days after successfully defending his championship against Phil Furr in Washington, DC, he agreed to meet his No. 1 challenger, Fritzie Zivic, the roughest of a family of fighting brothers, who had a rule book of his own that wasn't very pleasant for his opponents.

He and Armstrong put up one of the most gruelling fights the welter division has ever known, and at the finish of their 15-rounder it was Armstrong who was the more used up. Zivic took his remaining title and when, three months later, they had a return fight for the championship, it became obvious that the once smooth-running fighting machine had started to slow down. Zivic again lasted better, and at the end of the tenth round Armstrong had been so badly battered that the referee went to his corner and advised him to retire. Henry requested one more round and came out fighting as if the bout was just beginning. He set up such a furious assault that the stronger Zivic was beaten back step by step while the frenzied record crowd of 23,190 that filled the famous Garden to the rafters, were standing up and cheering. Armstrong tried hard to beat down his rival, and it looked as though Zivic would cave in under the furious bombardment. But he was there at the bell and the referee permitted Armstrong yet one more round. It was the last. Armstrong had taken so much out of himself in that death-or-glory effort that Zivic could punch him at will and midway through the 12th the contest was stopped.

Everyone thought that Homicide Hank would now live peacefully in retirement, and he did stay away from the ring for 18 months, but the old urge to do battle was still very strong in this amazing man and in June 1942, at the age of 29½, he made a comeback, fighting just as fiercely and just as frequently as ever, notching up 40 wins in 49 bouts that took him to February 1945 when, after dropping a ten-round points decision to little-known Chester Slider, who had already held him to a draw, Armstrong finally decided to call it a day.

It was difficult for a man who had spent so much time in ring warfare to find another vocation suitable to his temperament, but when Henry did it was at the reverse end of occupations. In 1951 he became an ordained minister of the Baptist Church, and now devotes his time to persuading others to love their neighbours.

Armstrong handed out two tremendous batterings to two world champions in winning his first two titles. *Opposite above:* Ross pokes a left into Armstrong's face in his welterweight defence, and lasted the distance, but never fought again after taking severe punishment. *Below:* Armstrong delivering a terrific right to Petey Sarron who lost his featherweight title when knocked out in the sixth.

Ernie Roderick

Ernie Roderick, born in Liverpool in 1914, crept in every Thursday as a boy, often without paying, to watch the boxing at the local stadium. He joined a local boxing club, and won a junior championship of Lancashire and Cheshire. When he started to box for money he was managed by Billy Metcalfe who subsequently passed him on to Ted Broadribb, who had another great Liverpool boxer in his stable – Nel Tarleton. So Ernie got to know 'Nella' and also his pretty sister, whom Roderick married a little later. Subsequently, when Tarleton retired he took over the management of his brother-in-law and it proved a most profitable partnership.

After a trip to Australia, he began an assault on the many welterweights that abounded in those days, beating the majority of them with his solid left-hand leading, accurate right cross and busy fists at close range. In 141 bouts, he scored 112 wins, 45 inside the distance, and there were four drawn contests. Only twice was he stopped.

The competition was so strong in the 10 st 7 lb division that Ernie was turned 25 before he climbed into the ring to challenge the hard-hitting Scot, Jake Kilrain, for his title. It was quite a punch-up for the seven rounds it lasted and it was Roderick who struck the last blow, a magnificent right-hander that dropped the champion as if he had been shot, to remain unmoving until he had been counted out. Roderick then outpointed the resolute Norman Snow and the talented Arthur Danahar to make the Lonsdale Belt his own property. It had taken him two and a half years to capture this prized possession.

As soon as he had become British champion, the Liverpool Stadium promoter, Johnny Best, gave Ernie the biggest chance of his life – or was it? At Harringay Arena, where he had assumed the matchmaking, Best brought over the phenomenal Henry Armstrong to defend his world title against Roderick, who jumped at the opportunity, although he knew full well that 'Homicide Hank' had not earned that name for nothing. Against this non-stop fighting machine Ernie was swamped in leather, barged and

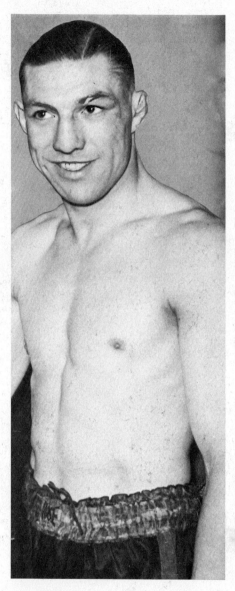

buffeted about the ring like a human punch-bag. Yet, he defended himself well, hit back whenever he got the chance, got himself out of difficult situations and was still on his feet at the finish of what must have seemed a fistic nightmare. He lost the decision but the crowd rose to him for his courageous stand against an almost superhuman battler.

With things in the doldrums in the welter division, Roderick challenged Vince Hawkins, a model boxer, for the middleweight title and caused an upset by winning on points. Then he went back to the welter class and added to his laurels by outpointing Omar Kouidri for the European championship. Dodging

between two weights did not appear to be in his best interests when he lost the middleweight title back to Hawkins four months later, and in his next fight he had to retire to vigorous Robert Villemain, of France, at the end of the tenth round because of a damaged eye after a below-par performance.

So it was back to his own division and the quest for a second Lonsdale trophy. First challenger to be served up was that crafty Welshman Gwyn Williams, who was cleverly outpointed, then came a 'natural' with Eric Boon, former British lightweight king of great kayo reputation, who had just returned from a successful tour of South Africa. Seven years earlier they had fought out a thriller that went the distance with Roderick a close points winner at the finish.

Their welterweight championship battle was equally dramatic with the powerful Boon striving relentlessly to win the title by knocking out the champion, and Roderick producing his very best boxing artistry to keep his determined rival at bay. It seemed all up for the 33-year-old champion when he was floored by a tremendous right-hander in the 12th round, and although he got up to fight back, a lot of his strength had been sapped by that mighty blow and he was hard pressed to keep on his feet as his challenger swung over his big punches in an effort to score a knockout. The last round saw Roderick entirely on the defensive and the fans roared as he made Boon miss and slipped and slithered out of trouble to receive a well-earned points victory after a tense battle.

One more Belt match to win and Roderick would have a second trophy, one he hoped for each of his children. Challenger was Henry Hall, eight years his junior. Roderick dropped his challenger for a count in round 12 and plastered him with punches, but at the finish the referee gave Hall the verdict, a decision that was most unpopular and caused a ringside disturbance. So Roderick had to be content with one Belt and made a record by being the first-ever boxer to qualify for the Board of Control pension of a pound a week at the age of 50, having retired soon after his 36th birthday.

Kid Gavilan

Like many of the great boxing champions, Kid Gavilan, real name Gerardo Gonzalez, came from the humblest of beginnings. Born on a sugar plantation at Camaguey in Cuba, he was out in the fields working at the age of nine, wielding a bolo knife, weighing between six and seven pounds. Using it developed fine muscular shoulders, ideal for swinging punches, especially the whipping 'bolo' uppercut that Gavilan made famous. When the family moved to Havana he found his way to a boxing club and soon became a star member. The many boys in the club were exploited and a few months after his 17th birthday he was boxing four rounds as Kid Gavilan – his pay, five cents.

Quickly he developed into a main-event fighter and at the age of 20 was given a trial in New York. Winning this in five rounds, he stayed on for two further victories, went back home to notch up five quick wins then returned to America where his remarkable durability and wholehearted swings made him a popular attraction. Soon they began to bill him as 'The Hawk' and he swarmed into his opponents, slugging with wide-open arms to batter his way to a decision. No one in their right mind would have termed him a boxer, nor was he a precision puncher, for his tally of 144 contests contains only a small proportion that ended inside the distance. He was never stopped and although beaten 30 times, most of these were at the tail end of his 15-year career.

Staying ten rounds with Sugar Ray Robinson earned him a title fight with the welterweight champion which he lost on points after a strenuous effort

Kid Gavilan (*right*) welterweight champion of the world, on his way to a knock-out victory over middleweight Walter Cartier.

that was foiled only by Robinson's superior boxing ability. Two years later Gavilan became champion by outpointing Johnny Bratton and he remained titleholder for three years, fighting off such notable challengers as Billy Graham (twice), Bobby Dykes, Chuck Davey, Carmen Basilio and Johnny Bratton. Stepping out of his class to challenge Carl (Bobo) Olson for the middleweight title, Gavilan lost on points. What's more, he took a great deal out of himself, and next time out he dropped his welter title to Johnny Saxton on a close decision and that was his end as a champion.

There were four more years of ring

activity, during which he twice visited London to fight Peter Waterman, the British welterweight champion. Gavilan was adjudged to have lost and he and his manager, Yamil Chade, gave a passionate demonstration in the ring, the like of which had never before been seen in British boxing. In a return bout he well trounced Waterman, but a subsequent run of losses caused him to announce his retirement in 1958, by which time he was 32.

Jose Napoles

One of the last professional fighters to come out of Cuba, when Fidel Castro put his ban on all pro sports, Jose Napoles settled in Mexico City to resume a boxing career that began in Havana when he was 18. He was fighting from boyhood as a means of self-preservation among his six brothers and showed such prowess with his fists that his entry into the local amateur club was a matter of course. Here he showed class above the average which encouraged him to become a professional, but the pay was pitifully poor, even when he was given a ten-rounder in his eighth bout, which he lost on points. Napoles thought he had been robbed of the verdict and secretly decided that in future he would not allow his efforts to be left to the tender mercies of a referee.

There was not a lot of style about his work. He came in behind a crouch that made him difficult to hit and did his punching at close range, his adopted stance enabling him to put plenty of weight behind his jabs and hooks. He carried terrific power in his short-arm blows, and of his first 72 contests, 48 saw his opponents stopped, many of them in the early rounds, with only five defeats on the debit side.

Born at Santiago in 1940, Napoles found contentment among the Mexicans, marrying one of them and settling down as a pro battler whose winning style soon made him a popular favourite among the local fans. He had no urge to box in American rings, despite many tempting invitations. He lost a contest during this period to L. C. Morgan, who gave Jose a bad eye wound with his head. But there were no other set-backs, and eventually he was given a title fight with Curtis Cokes, a coloured Texan who was thought to be too strong and experienced for the ex-Cuban.

Napoles proved them wrong by outpunching Cokes to win in 13 rounds. Two months later he beat Cokes again, this time in ten rounds, then brought off another fine performance by outpointing the great Emile Griffith over 15 rounds. One more contender, Ernie Lopez, was beaten in the last of another 15-rounder, then Napoles made his first trip to New York where he treated the fans to a sample of his powers by stopping Pete Toro in nine rounds and then defended his welterweight title for the third time, against unranked Billy Backus from Syracuse. It went only as far as the fourth round when a gushing wound over the champion's left eye forced the referee to stop the fight and the title had changed hands. But not for long. In a return match six months later, Napoles stopped Backus in eight rounds, scoring two knockdowns, and regained the championship. There have been several successful defences since – against Ralph Charles, the British champion, who could stay only seven rounds in London, and Adolph Pruitt, who was no match for Napoles in Mexico City and was belted out in two rounds. 1973 saw Napoles into his fifth year as world champion, with thirteen successful title defences to his credit.

Jose Napoles (*right*) on his way to a knockout win over Ralph Charles.

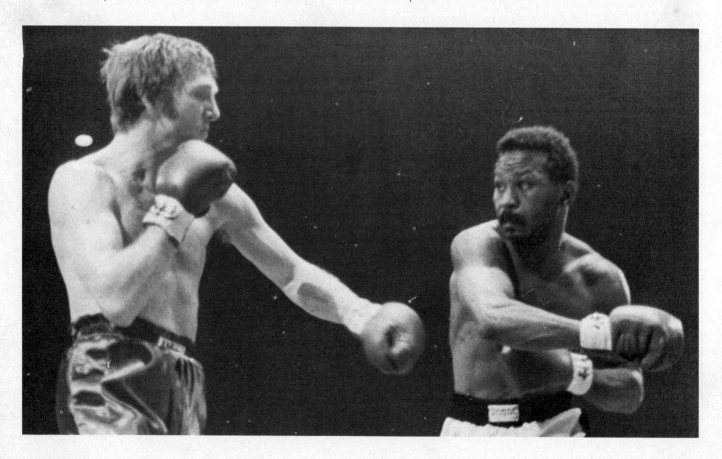

Joe Gans

An ultra-skilful boxer, Joe Gans (1874–1910) was also a simple soul, with the result that he was exploited and tricked and did not get the full fruits of his ability out of his long boxing career. An upstanding boxer, with a crisp punch in either hand, he was the first coloured man to win the world's lightweight title, and in his day, when Negro boxers had to fight racial prejudice as well as their opponents, this was a considerable achievement. In later years, when he defended his championship seven times successfully, they called him the 'Old Master'.

Real name Joseph Gaines, he was born at Baltimore in Maryland. He came of a poor family, enjoyed the minimum of schooling and was out on the oyster wharves picking up a few cents in competition with other boys of his age. He learnt to defend himself with his fists and by the age of 17 was eager to box in the clubs to earn a dollar or two to take home to his mother. His earnings enabled the family to eat such luxuries as bacon now and again and when he was an established pro and boxing away from home, Joe would let his mother know he had won a contest by sending her a telegram that read: 'I am bringing home the bacon.'

By the time he was 26 he had risen out of the ruck and was fighting contests of 20 and even 25 rounds' duration. When he got a title chance, however, he was stopped by Frank Erne in 12 rounds because of an eye injury, and had to wait over two years before being given a second opportunity. This time he made no mistake, knocking out the champion in 1 min 40 sec, feinting with a left and banging over a right where he guessed Erne would move his head. He remained champion for six years, meeting the best lightweights available, even boxing a 20-round draw with Joe Walcott, the welterweight titleholder.

His most dangerous challenger was Battling Nelson, a rough character, who was contemptuous of Gans, and would not agree to meet him unless he received two-thirds of the purse-money, 20,000 dollars to champion Joe's 10,000. The challenger also insisted that the lightweight limit should be reduced by two pounds, to 9 st 7 lb, which forced Gans to weaken himself. The title fight, promoted by Tex Rickard at Goldfield in Nevada on 3 September 1906, drew a record 700,000 dollars for lightweights. It was scheduled for 45 rounds, but Nelson, who had repeatedly fouled Gans with kidney and liver punches, was ruled out in the 42nd round for low hitting. The bout took a great deal out of the 32-year-old coloured man, who contracted consumption from which he died in 1910, but not before he had gone in with Nelson twice more, each time being knocked out by the younger and stronger man.

Battling Nelson

A hard-hitting lightweight and cruel with it, was Oscar (Battling) Nelson (1882–1954) who reigned as world champion for two years, but was the scourge of his division for more than 25 years. He was a close-range hooker and an artist at infighting, where he would slash away, more often than not holding with one hand while he battered his rival's kidneys and liver with the other. In a total of 132 bouts he was twice disqualified and was lucky that it was not a lot more.

Born at Copenhagen, real name Oscar Matthew Nielson, he was taken to the United States when a child and brought up at Hegewisch in the lake district of Illinois. Here, in the winter months, he found boyhood employment cutting and packing ice for the Chicago meat markets. It was rigorous work that was interrupted from time to time by fist fights. When he made a career of boxing at the age of 17, he had already established a reputation as a hard and durable scrapper.

His big opportunity came in 1906 when the mining town of Goldfield was anxious to put itself on the map by staging an important prize-fight. Tex Rickard, who ran a gambling saloon in the main street, offered the then unheard-of sum of 30,000 dollars for a match between Nelson, who claimed the white lightweight title and coloured Joe Gans, the rightful champion.

For most of the fight Gans outboxed his rival, but having been forced to reduce his weight by two pounds below the normal lightweight limit of 9 st 9 lb, he suffered severe punishment during the infighting, where Nelson used his famous 'scissors' punch, a left hook to the liver that he nipped with thumb and forefinger at the moment of impact, the thin gloves used in those times allowing him to inflict this added discomfort. Even so, he found himself being steadily outpointed and in the 42nd round struck a low blow that the referee could not ignore. It dropped Gans in agony and Nelson was ruled out.

There was a return bout in San Francisco two years later, by which time Gans was ravaged by consumption and Nelson was far too strong for him, winning by a knockout in the 17th round. Two months later they met for the third time, but after a courageous stand, Gans was knocked out again, this time in 21 rounds. Nelson's reign came to an end when he accepted a challenge from Ad Wolgast, a younger man by six years, who was known as the 'Michigan Wildcat', a description that sums up his style of combat. He and Nelson put up the most savage battle ever known in the lightweight class. It was a fight to a finish and it was Nelson who weakened first, being knocked out in the 40th round. There was no return battle and although Nelson continued to fight for a number of years, he could never regain his former high standing.

Nelson (*right*) in his first fight with Gans, in which he was disqualified.

DANA Photo.

Nelson-Gans Contest. Goldfield. Nevada. Won By Gans. 42 Rou

Freddie Welsh

Strange to relate, Pontypridd-born Freddie Welsh (1886–1927) started his celebrated boxing career in America where he went at the age of 16 to seek fame and fortune. The ring was the last place in which he expected to achieve this, but becoming employed in a sports shop, he took a great interest in physical culture. This led him to join an athletic club, where he was attracted to boxing. Not being particularly robust, he applied himself to the defensive side, becoming an artist at punch evasion at long range and a tricky, but destructive, infighter. Although his tally of 167 bouts shows only 24 won inside the distance, he was stopped only once, right at the end of his 17-year career.

Real name Frederick Hall Thomas, he adopted the name of Welsh because of his origin and principally to avoid his mother finding out that he was a professional boxer. When he came home after an uninterrupted run of 28 bouts without defeat, he was so sure of himself that he did not mind her knowing. His first contests in England took place at the National Sporting Club in London's Covent Garden and the members were agreeably impressed by the quality of his boxing and the businesslike way he went about it. He stayed home for nine months, then returned to the United States where he was now recognized as a main-event fighter, participating in bouts ranging from ten to 25 rounds against the leading lightweights of the day.

Recalled to fight Johnny Summers at the NSC for the first of the Lonsdale Belts to be put into circulation, he won on points to become British lightweight champion. He was then induced by newspaper publicity to meet his fellow-countryman and friend, Jim Driscoll, the featherweight titleholder, in a match that neither of them were keen about. Those behind it thought it would prove a classic contest, but the 'needle' element that had been implanted by others, caused both men to box below par and ended in Driscoll being disqualified in the tenth round for 'butting'.

Surprisingly Welsh lost his British title to ex-amateur champion, Matt Wells, but regained it the following year and did not lose another contest

either in Great Britain or America for the next six years. In that time he fought the very best in the world. He became British Empire champion when defeating Hughie Mehegan, of Australia, and won his Lonsdale Belt outright with only two notches on it instead of three, simply because no one good enough to meet him could be found.

His points defeat by Matt Wells, the only occasion he ever lost in Great Britain, took place at the National Sporting Club. It was his first title defence and he made the 'mistake of treating his challenger too lightly. Freddie appeared to box rings round his opponent, jabbing him freely with his left, causing Wells to bleed profusely. The verdict went to Matt because of his sustained attacking. When he went through the kitchen on his way to the dressing-room, the cook threw her apron over her face as she could not bear to look at his bloody countenance. 'If that is the winner, whatever must the loser look like?' she gasped. But Welsh was unmarked.

Although there was nothing colourful about his boxing, nor were sensations to be expected when he fought, the purists

among the fans flocked to see him. He had to wait a long, long time for a chance at the world championship and had to see Battling Nelson and Ad Wolgast come and go before getting a title bout with Willie Ritchie. Even then he had to persuade London theatre impresario, Charles Cochran, to pay the champion an enormous fee that left nothing for Welsh beyond his bare training expenses. They fought at Olympia and the Welshman had to produce all the art and craft at his command to win by the narrow margin of a quarter of a point.

At once he returned to America to cash in on his crown, engaging principally in no-decision contests that were essential in those days because of stringent laws against boxing and which, of course, enabled Welsh to protect his title on an adverse points verdict. He did, however, defend his crown against former champion Ad Wolgast, who was disqualified in round 11 for low hitting, and against Liverpool-born Charlie White, who was outpointed over 20 rounds.

Welsh was 30 by now and looked like remaining as champion for several more years to come, his immaculate boxing and ring guile enabling him to outbox the roughest of opponents. In fact, the crude fighters were as clay in his hands. Then in May 1917 he engaged to fight Benny Leonard, a New York lightweight, in a ten-round no-decision bout at the Manhattan Sporting Club. Leonard was ten years younger and had boxed ten rounds previously with the champion. This time he set a faster pace that had the Welshman tiring and in the ninth round Benny got through with a nasty left hook to the chin that put Welsh down for one of the few times in his long career. Dazed, he got up almost immediately, to be punched freely round the ring and finally left draped over the ropes, whereupon the referee stopped the contest. As both men had scaled under the lightweight limit, Leonard was acclaimed champion. It was almost the end for Freddie. He stayed away from the ring for three and a half years, made a brief comeback and then retired to run a health farm. This failed and when he died at the age of 41 he was penniless.

Benny Leonard

A long-reigning world lightweight champion, Benny Leonard (1896–1947) modelled himself on the great Joe Gans, his boyhood hero. He applied to his own boxing the same scientific approach, learnt to punch correctly and with knockdown power, and was never defeated for the championship which he defended successfully on nine occasions. In 209 professional bouts he was beaten only four times, was held to a draw on one occasion and lost one fight on an inexplicable foul. A clean-living, likeable character, Leonard was coolness itself in the ring, finishing off a beaten opponent with cold fury, recovering quickly when hurt, and talking his way out of trouble to demoralize his opponents.

Born in New York, his real name was Benjamin Leiner, and he was encouraged by his Jewish mother to box when she realized that he was a top-quality performer. Mostly in his early days he fought around New York, but the first time he boxed in another city, he rushed to the telegraph office as soon as he was in his street clothes and sent his mother a telegram in imitation of Joe Gans, telling her that he had won by saying that he was 'bringing home the bacon'. She replied instantly: 'Never mind the bacon, bring home the gelt', which Benny proceeded to do in increasing amounts throughout his long career.

He was a bare 15 when he started earning with his fists and it is not surprising that he was stopped twice in the early days by boys more experienced than himself. But he learnt his lessons thoroughly and did not lose a contest for the next nine years, in which he engaged in 120 bouts, frequently boxing as often as five times in a month. Because he punched correctly, he never suffered a hand injury; because he knew how to defend himself, he usually left the ring unmarked; because he kept himself in the pink of condition he could travel ten fast rounds and look as fresh as when he started, his sleek black hair, that he parted down the middle, being quite unruffled.

Leonard was just past his 21st birthday when he was matched in a ten-round no-decision contest with champion Freddie Welsh in Brooklyn.

He was determined to knock him out, the only way he could win the championship. No one had ever achieved that feat so far, but Leonard set a fast pace until the ninth round when the tiring champion made a lapse in his defence and Benny got through with a pay-off punch that brought him victory.

In the next six years Leonard defended his title at every opportunity, never refusing a challenger and picking up good pay every time, because those he faced were worthy contenders. He beat such great ring warriors as Johnny Kilbane, the reigning featherweight champion, who wanted a second world crown; dangerous left-hook artist Charlie White; slugging Joe Welling; and tough Rocky Kansas, who had three tries. All with the exception of a 15-rounder with Kansas, ended inside the distance.

Against White, he came closest to defeat, being caught by a left hook that sent him through the ropes. In the excitement the timekeeper forgot to record how long the champion had been out of the ring. White's supporters said it had been longer than ten seconds. Leonard knocked White out in the ninth round, to keep his crown.

Leonard's greatest challenger was Lew Tendler, a southpaw of great talent. They fought a 12-round no-decision bout at Jersey City that was so close that there had to be a return match with the championship at stake by public demand. They fought in New York's Yankee Stadium before 58,519 excited fans who paid 452,648 dollars for the privilege of seeing this well-matched pair, with opposing styles, fight it out for supremacy. At one point in their closely fought contest Tendler hurt his rival and Leonard was glad to drop into a clinch. 'Is that your best punch?' he asked his opponent. 'You'll have to do better than that if you want to win.' Tendler's confidence was shaken and at the finish Leonard had taken the decision and kept his crown.

In 1922 he challenged Jack Britton for the welterweight championship. It was a match that caught public imagination, for Britton was a classic boxer himself, although the older man by 11 years. The 23,000 fans who crowded into the Metropolitan Velodrome in New York saw a battle of wits until the 13th round, when Leonard dropped the veteran with a neat left clip to the chin and then, while Britton rested on one knee, gave him a cuff to the head that caused his instant disqualification. It was the one and only time in his career that Leonard lost his head.

He retired unbeaten as lightweight champion in 1924, but made a comeback seven years later at the age of 35. It lasted a year and ended when he was stopped by the much younger Jimmy McLarnin. Leonard then became a referee for the New York State Athletic Commission and proved an efficient 'third man', serving in that capacity for four years until, in 1947, he dropped dead in the middle of a round. For a man who had spent almost his whole life in the ring, there could not have been a more fitting ending.

Tony Canzoneri

Tony Canzoneri (*left*) outpointing Jimmy McLarnin in New York in 1936.

They called Tony Canzoneri (1908–1959) 'Little Pisan' and it was an apt description. Small, compact, with strong shoulders and well muscled, he was a worrying fighter, difficult to hold at bay because of his determination and zest for punch-swapping, plus a seemingly inexhaustible stock of stamina. In 181 contests, 138 of which he won, he was stopped only once and that in the final fight of his long career. Canzoneri enters the pugilistic Hall of Fame on several counts. He was featherweight champion of the world, twice lightweight champion of the world, and the holder of the synthetic junior-welterweight title. He also boxed a draw for the bantam crown when he was 18.

Born at Slidell in Louisiana of Italian parents, he was taken to New York where he had his schooling, both academically and pugilistically, it being a rough neighbourhood where all arguments were settled with the fists. He was the most enthusiastic member of the local boys' club and at 16 won the New York State amateur bantam title, although he weighed only a bare 7 stone at the time. Within two years he was considered to be in the championship class.

Making two abortive attempts to win the bantamweight title in torrid battles with Bud Taylor in Chicago, he took the featherweight crown from Benny Bass in New York on a points decision, but lost it seven months later to André Routis, of France, whose extra experience enabled him to gain a points victory. It was a big disappointment to Tony, but within a year he was challenging for the lightweight championship only to be outpointed over the short distance of ten rounds by Sammy Mandell.

Next came the first of his three furious contests with Jack (Kid) Berg of London, himself a whirlwind scrapper with boundless and sustained energy. Canzoneri was outpointed, but by the end of the year he fought again for the lightweight title and astounded the fight fraternity by knocking out champion Al Singer in the short time of 66 seconds which still stands as a lightweight record first-round win. Naturally he was challenged by Berg, who happened to be the holder of the junior-welterweight crown at the time. So two championships were at stake for the second meeting and Canzoneri proved that his new-found knockout punch was

no fluke by stopping the brilliant Londoner in three rounds. The 'rubber' match between them, as fiercely fought as the others, saw Canzoneri edge out a narrow winner on points.

Now came a period in Tony's career when he was in and out of titles like a jack-in-the-box. He fought a magnificent battle with the renowned Kid Chocolate, from Cuba, to defend his lightweight title and held out against hard-punching Billy Petrolle for 15 slashing rounds to keep his crown. But against Barney Ross he met his master in two title fights and lost his junior championship to Johnny Jadick, twice being outpointed. He regained this 16 months later by beating Battling Shaw.

Canzoneri kept among the top-notchers and in his 27th year created a surprise by winning the lightweight title for the second time, outpointing Lou Ambers, himself a hurricane type of warrior. It was the first of a trio of meetings between this pair, each one being non-stop for the full 15 rounds

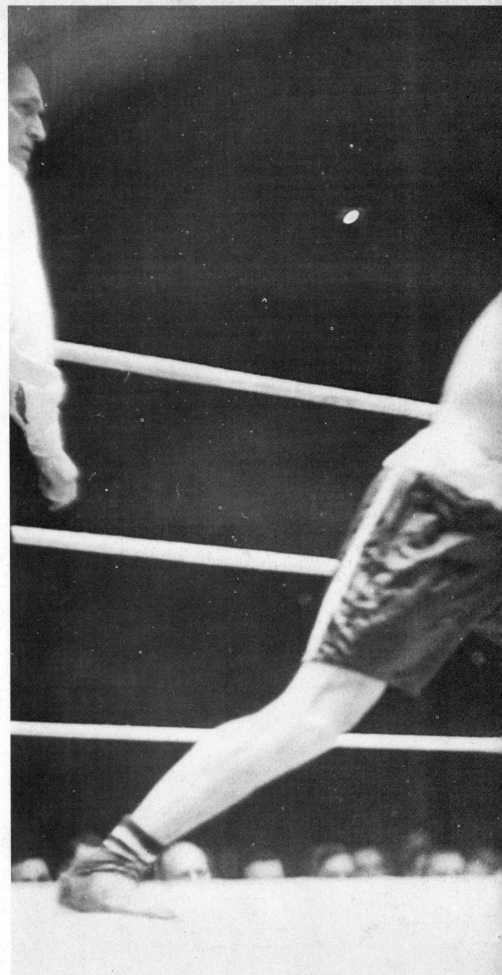

Canzoneri (*right*) avoids an attack by Leo Rodak when getting a ten-round points decision in Chicago, 1935.

and having the fans on the edges of their seats from start to finish. Ambers took the title from Canzoneri in their second match and retained it when they fought out the 'rubber'. Tony was in his 29th year then and could have called it a day, but the lure of the arc-lights was too strong and he continued to box for another year until he came up against Al Davis, a savage left-hook specialist who broke through Canzoneri's guard in the third round and twice floored him. The game ex-champion tried hard to get to his feet following the second knockdown, but his legs would not support him and the referee intervened. Canzoneri kept a restaurant after that and also did some cabaret work with success. He died of a heart attack in New York.

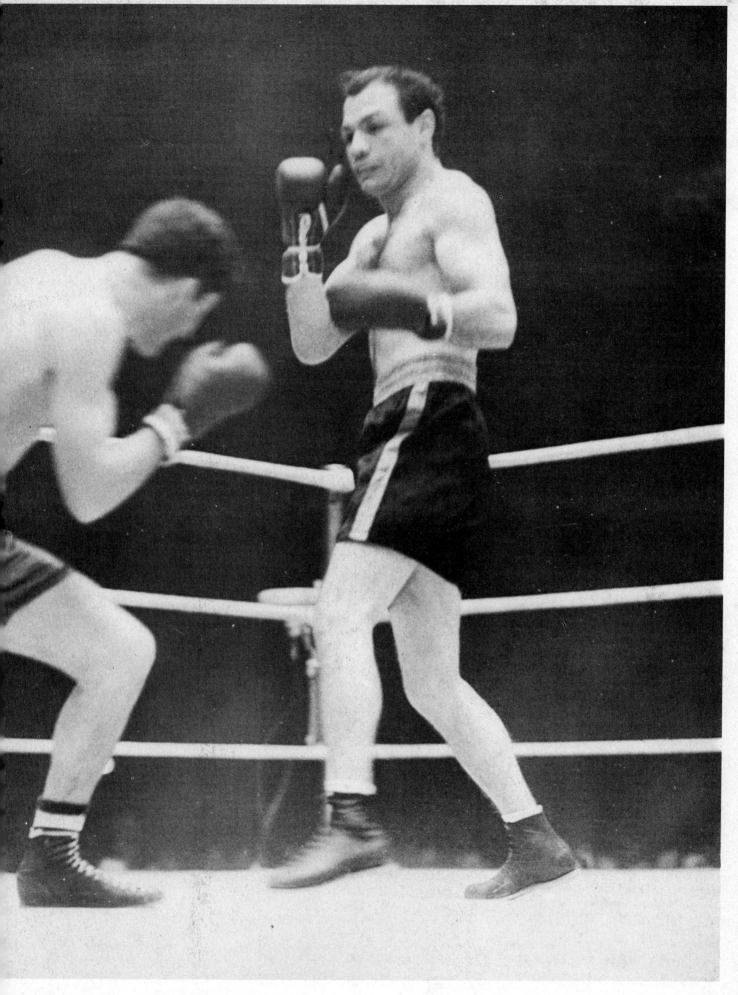

Jack (Kid) Berg

The greatest disappointment in Jack (Kid) Berg's fighting life was his inability to win the world's lightweight title. And how hard he tried. Holder of the junior-welterweight championship of the world which he had gained at London's Royal Albert Hall by stopping Mushy Callaghan, of America, in ten dynamic rounds, he beat the current holder of the lightweight championship, Tony Canzoneri, on points. Sixteen months later he was confident that he could do so again when they met for the title in Chicago. But rushing into the attack in characteristic fashion, he ran into trouble and to his great grief the referee stopped the contest in the third round. Berg was only 21. In a second attempt, five months later, he fought his heart out in an effort to win the title, only to find himself on the losing end of a close points decision.

Born at Whitechapel in London's East End in 1909, real name Judah Bergman, the nearby 'Premierland' where boxing shows were staged every week, became his boyhood focal point. Eventually he worried the promoters into giving him a bout, even though he was three weeks short of his 15th birthday. He was so successful and so colourful in his fighting style that in next to no time he was a great favourite, particularly on a Sunday afternoon, being elevated into the 15-round class in his eighth paid bout.

For the next four years he fought with great frequency, 21 contests in 1925, with only two points defeats, both by Johnny Cuthbert, a future dual British champion. Then Berg whisked himself off to America where he was a great success, his crowding, all-action attack earning him the name of the 'Whitechapel Whirlwind'. He stayed in the United States for eight bouts with one defeat, returned home for Christmas and three winning contests, then went back to New York for 16 bouts, at the rate of two a month without defeat, culminating in a victory over the formidable Canzoneri. Berg came home to win his 'junior' crown, then went to and from the United States on several

occasions until in 1934, at the age of 25 he challenged Harry Mizler for the British lightweight title and won on the referee's intervention in the tenth round.

In London Berg had furious battles with 'Tiger' Gustave Humery, of France, a man after his own heart when it came to exuberant hitting; went to South Africa, where he was upset by the altitude and lost to Laurie Stevens for the Empire title, and returning home was surprisingly beaten for his British crown by Jimmy Walsh, who stopped him in nine rounds. It was the end of Berg's championship contests, but he went on scrapping until 1945, by which time he had engaged in 197 contests, of which he won 162, 59 of them inside the distance. A great record.

Berg (left) under attack from Harry Mizler when winning the British lightweight championship.

Eric Boon

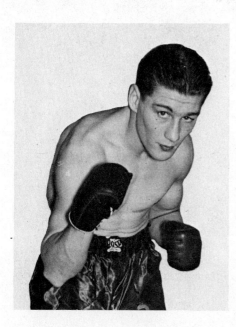

thriller from start to finish, with Boon looking like a loser until he managed to connect with his big punches and so turn the tide of battle. This bout was historic in the fact that it was the first-ever boxing contest to be televised 'live'. Knocking out Crowley in seven rounds, Boon made the Lonsdale Belt his own property in the second record fastest time of 11 months and 24 days. He had only 12 contests in the next five years because of war service, then lost his title to Ronnie James by a knockout in ten rounds.

That seemed to be the end for Boon, but at 26 he returned to action as a welterweight with much of his old vigour, and after beating Danahar in an eliminator and winning five out of six bouts in South Africa, he challenged

Ernie Roderick for the British welterweight championship to lose by a close points margin. He fought himself to a standstill against tough Frenchman, Robert Villemain, dropping from sheer exhaustion in the tenth round. There were not many fights after that epic and at 30 Boon decided to hang up his gloves for good. Of his 116 contests, he won 91, 62 of these inside the distance, a great tribute to his punching power that had been developed at the anvil in his father's blacksmith shop in Chatteris.

Boon's great fight with Arthur Danahar in February 1939 is still remembered as a boxing classic. The referee restrains Boon as Danahar begins to rise from a knockdown.

There is a legend that Eric Boon, at the age of 15, cycled from his home in Chatteris, Cambridgeshire, to the Devonshire Club in Hackney, London, to fight a six-round contest for promoter Jack Solomons one Sunday afternoon. He leaned his bike against the wall of the hall, went in and fought his six-rounds bout to a draw, then bruised and happy, he pedalled the 72 miles back home. It was the first of many fights he was to have in Hackney where he rarely suffered defeat. It was the springboard for his sensational leap into fame, the start of a highly successful career that might have resulted in his winning a world title, but for the intervention of the Second World War.

A natural free-punching fighter, Boon had courage in abundance and supreme confidence that was backed by the power he could put into his punches, especially with a left hook. His progress was fast, his long list of knockout wins impressive. When he challenged Dave Crowley for the British lightweight championship at Harringay Arena in North London, and won by a knockout in round 13, he was 13 days short of his 20th birthday, one of the youngest boxers ever to win a native title.

Two months later he stopped Arthur Danahar in 14 rounds after one of the greatest fights ever seen between lightweights, the contrasting styles of boxer versus fighter producing a

Joe Brown

If ever a fighter won a championship on borrowed time it was Joe ('Old Bones') Brown. He gave himself the nickname because he was turned 30 before he got his first chance to win the world's lightweight title. Before that there were ten long years of struggling to the top, so there was every incentive to want to hang on to his laurels for as long as possible. This he did with 12 defences in the next six years, fighting anywhere a worthy challenger could be found. When he finally lost his crown he was close up to his 36th birthday, yet he went on fighting for another eight years, having his last contest at 44. Of his 149 bouts he lost only two decisions, and although stopped nine times these were either at the very beginning or the tail end of his long campaign.

Son of a carpenter, Brown was born at New Orleans in 1926, but the family moved to Baton Rouge in Texas when he was quite young. He never gave boxing a thought until at 18 the war swept him up and he joined the US Navy, taking up boxing in order to be excused other duties.

He took a sound licking in his first bout, but he stuck at it despite set-backs at the hands of such class men as Sandy Saddler and Johnny Bratton, subsequently feather- and welterweight world champions. At 5 ft 7½ in Brown was a nice height for a lightweight. He was lean and strong in the legs, hard in the upper body and quick, with delicately long hands. He fought with a slick economy of moves, was a blistering counter-puncher who could throw well-measured combinations when pressing an attack. His right hand brought him 47 inside-the-distance wins out of 104.

When he finally caught up with Wallace (Bud) Smith, he won the championship on points, but once he was king of the lightweights he let most of his challengers know who was boss by stopping short their title ambitions. Smith in a return bout lasted 11 rounds, then came Orlando Zulueta, halted in the 15th, Joe Lopes (11), Ralph Dupas (eight), Paolo Rossi (nine), Dave Charnley (six by cut eye); the others stayed the full course. He seemed lucky to get the verdict when meeting Charnley for the second time, in London, but Carlos Ortiz relieved him of his crown on a points verdict and never gave him the courtesy of a return.

Brown (*left*) avoids a right from Joe Lopes and won in the 11th round.

Dave Charnley

One of the best southpaws ever produced in Great Britain, Dave Charnley was also one of the hardest hitters in the lightweight class. He was capable of putting his punches together in effective style and there was no mercy for an opponent who showed the least sign that he had been hurt.

Born at Dartford in 1931, his sturdy physique and zest for fighting made him a highly successful amateur and at 19 he won the ABA title at featherweight. Towards the end of the year he turned professional and quickly fought his way to the front as a lightweight, taking the title from Joe Lucy on a points verdict in a battle of southpaws.

His attempt to add the Empire championship failed when he was skilfully outpointed by Willie Toweel of South Africa, but Charnley gained full revenge a year later when he knocked out Toweel in ten rounds. As a dual titleholder Charnley now set off in pursuit of the world crown, going to Houston in Texas to tackle Joe ('Old Bones') Brown, a man five years older and of far greater experience. The

champion succeeded in keeping his title when Charnley was forced to retire in round six, but there was some consolation for this unfortunate defeat when he stopped Mario Vecchiatto, of Italy, to win the European crown.

He defended the EBU title against Fernand Nollet of France and then had his heart's desire, a return championship match with Joe Brown this time in London. Charnley chased the world champion from start to finish of a scintillating 15-rounder which went the full distance. The majority of the spectators thought that the Englishman had won by a clear margin of points and were dismayed when the referee elected to give the verdict to Brown. Two years later, when the coloured American was no longer champion, Dave knocked him out in six rounds.

Charnley successfully defended his European title in Rome, then knocked out David (Darkie) Hughes, of Wales, in 40 seconds to keep his trio of titles. He went to Kingston, Jamaica, but came away without his Empire crown as the result of a dropped decision to Bunny

Grant. Then he outpointed Maurice Cullen to make the Lonsdale Belt his own property and thereafter confined his attention to the welterweights.

In this new field, however, he met with disaster. A terrific battle with Brian Curvis, the welterweight king, saw Charnley put his southpaw opponent down for a count of 'eight' in the eighth round and seemingly to have won by a clear margin of points. But the referee decided otherwise to the annoyance of the fans. Dave beat rated American, Kenny Lane, and then took on Emile Griffith, at that time champion of the world and one of the best welters ever to hold the title. Charnley put up a game fight against overwhelming odds, being saved by the referee in round nine. Soon afterwards he retired, having won 48 of his 61 bouts with one draw, and being undefeated as British and European lightweight champion.

Charnley's second fight with Brown. Charnley receiving (left) and handing out (right).

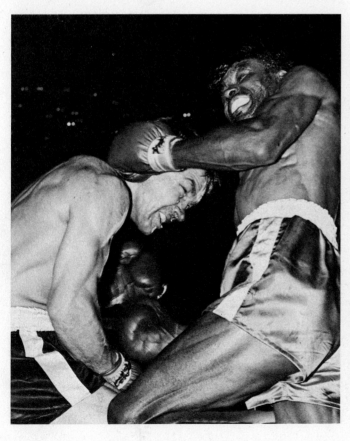

Ken Buchanan

In the summer of 1969, Ken Buchanan, lightweight champion of Great Britain announced his retirement from the ring after 32 professional contests all of which he had won. He was then 24 and had been titleholder for six months. He gave as his reason the feeling that he had been mismanaged, that by boxing almost exclusively in clubs he had not earned as much as he might otherwise have done. The Board of Control did not uphold his request for a severance of his contract with manager Eddie Thomas and it looked as though the British fight scene had lost one of its most promising performers. A month later they resumed their partnership.

Panama Negro had won, lost and regained the championship and was thought to have too much experience for the Scot, but Buchanan brought off the upset of the year by winning on a split decision. He thus became the first Britisher to win the lightweight world title for 56 years.

Born in Edinburgh in 1945, Buchanan began boxing at the age of eight when an aunt gave him a set of gloves for Christmas. He pestered his father to be

Buchanan forces Al Ford to cover up (*left*) and misses with a right against Carlos Hernandez (*right*), stopped in eight rounds.

possible for him to go in against the best in America with the greatest of confidence. He beat Donato Paduano over ten rounds in New York, defended his title successfully against Ruben Navarro at Los Angeles, stopped Carlos Hernandez in eight rounds in London, then retained his title in a return match with Laguna in New York.

It was a remarkable run for a man who at one time was prepared to quit the ring, but it was to end very disappointingly when Buchanan was savagely mauled by Roberto Duran, of Panama, in another title defence in Madison Square Garden, New York. The challenger's street-fighting tactics

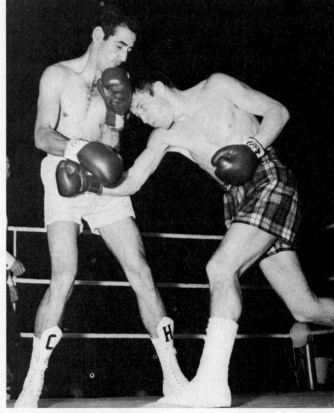

It did not get off to a very successful start, because Buchanan had the decision given against him when he fought Miguel Velazquez in Madrid for the European title, but he gained a second notch on his lightweight belt by knocking out challenger Brian Hudson in five rounds, and then slipped off to San Juan in Puerto Rico to face Ismael Laguna for the world crown. The

allowed to join a local boxing club and won a medal in his first year, although he was below the entry age of ten. After that there was no stopping him. He won the ABA featherweight title in 1965 and later in the year became a professional, using a nice left jab with good footwork and an effective right cross to win.

As a lightweight he could put more power into his right and this made it

upset the Scot who went down claiming that he had been fouled by an obviously low blow after the bell had sounded to end the 13th round. A return fight seemed required, but instead Buchanan elected to try and regain the British lightweight crown which he had relinquished, challenging champion Jim Watt in Glasgow and winning on points after a particularly hard bout.

Terry McGovern

There have been many strong punchers among the little men, but none fought fiercer or hit harder than Terry McGovern (1880–1918) who won two world championships with his dynamic fighting ability. None of his nine title bouts went the scheduled distance and he was so ruthless in the ring that they called him 'Terrible Terry'. McGovern did not bother about the finer points of boxing; he just waded in, determined to batter the opposition into pulp as quickly as possible.

Born at Johnstown in Pennsylvania, his family moved to Brooklyn where he set up as a newsboy outside the railway station. It was a good site and he had to fight hard and often to keep it. A month after his 17th birthday, he was boxing ten-rounders at Brooklyn's rough fight arena and he soon became highly popular with the rough-and-ready fans, especially those of Irish blood.

In 1899, when the world bantam title was vacant, Tom (Pedlar) Palmer, the British champion, who because of his extreme cleverness, was known as the 'Box o' Tricks', went to America to fight McGovern for the championship. He was supported by a strong British contingent who backed him up to the hilt. When they came from their corners, Palmer stuck out a left 'feeler' but was promptly crossed by a right to the chin that put him down and out in the short time of 75 seconds. He was one of the youngest ever to win a world crown.

Four months later he won the featherweight championship by knocking out the celebrated George Dixon, in eight rounds, and the same year kept his title against such formidable opponents as Eddie Santry, Oscar Gardner, Tommy White and Joe Bernstein, all of whom were put away in a combined total of 18 rounds. It was phenomenal fighting, and when the following year he beat Gardner again, this time in four rounds, and knocked out the highly rated Aurelio Herrera in five rounds, it seemed that Terry would remain champion for many years. Six months after beating Herrera he went to Hartford in Connecticut, to defend his crown against Young Corbett, a rugged battler who was expected to provide a good punch-up but nothing more. As he passed McGovern's dressing-room on his way to the ring Corbett yelled: 'Come out you Irish rat and take the licking of your life,' an insult that seemed likely to cause the challenger a lot of pain and suffering before long. McGovern was infuriated and could not get into the ring quickly enough. When the bell started he dashed across the square to annihilate his cheeky opponent, but ran into a belting right to the jaw that bowled him over like a shot rabbit. He suffered more knockdowns and took the full count in round two.

Corbett did it again in a non-title fight 16 months later, this time in 11 rounds, and after that McGovern's fighting powers deserted him and he retired at 28. He died ten years later.

Jim Driscoll

They called Jim Driscoll (1881–1925) 'Peerless Jim' and not without good reason. At his peak there was no one to touch him for sheer ring artistry and perfection in punching. Although 27 of his 70 recorded bouts ended within the scheduled course, he often declared that he had no need to cultivate a big punch. 'They knock themselves out trying to get pass my defence,' he often declared. That he never lost a decision is a tribute to his great boxing skill. But he lost on a foul after being provoked into doing so by Freddie Welsh, a disaster that no one thought could possibly happen to such a clean operator, and he was stopped once, in his last contest when he foolishly allowed himself to be matched with Charles Ledoux, 12 years his junior, when he (Driscoll) was a sick man.

Born at Cardiff in South Wales, his father died when he was a boy, so Jim had to do odd jobs while he was at school and was then employed on the local paper as a printer's devil. He and the other apprentices used to spar together in their lunch break, wrapping old newspapers round their fists in lieu of gloves. Soon Driscoll was earning extra money in the local boxing booth, where the men admired his clever boxing, the women his good looks. His genial personality made him very popular, and when he turned professional while still in his teens he enjoyed a big following.

He was 23 before he caught the attention of the matchmaker at the famous National Sporting Club in London, but once the members had seen him, his services were always in demand. He won the British featherweight championship by knocking out Joe Bowker in 17 rounds; took ownership of the first Lonsdale Belt to be assigned to the nine-stone class, by stopping Arthur Hayes in six rounds, and won it outright by knocking out Spike Robson in 15 rounds, then stopping him in seven. He became the undisputed, if unrecognized, champion of the world when he gave a boxing lesson to titleholder Abe Attell in New York in 1909. Only the fact that it was a no-decision bout deprived Driscoll of the full reward for his brilliant victory, his immaculate left lead being rarely out of the champion's face.

Driscoll then defeated Jean Posey, of France, by a knockout in 12 rounds to win the European title. In 1913 he defended all his honours against experienced Owen Moran, but did not box again until 1919, when he was in no condition to return to the ring. In the intervening time he had served as a sergeant instructor in the British Army. When he retired a testimonial fund organized by the NSC produced £25,000 as a mark of esteem, but he did not enjoy it long, dying from pneumonia at 43.

Driscoll's last fight. *Below:* **Ledoux sinks a left to his body.** *Right:* **Driscoll is still shaping up to fight as Ledoux moves to console him after the towel had been thrown in.**

Nel Tarleton

When he retired from the ring at the age of 39, Nel (short for Nelson) Tarleton (1906–1956) was undefeated British featherweight champion, a title he had won three times. He had taken part in ten title fights and won two Lonsdale Belts outright. He had also twice fought for the world championship, losing on close margins, and had fought in Australia and America. He had taken part in 145 bouts, winning 116, losing 21 with eight drawn. He had never been stopped.

He owed his success to a great extent to his tall frame for a nine-stone man, being nearly six feet in height and with a correspondingly long reach. To these physical advantages he added the development of a perfect straight left, plus the ability to weave in uncanny manner on the ropes, defying the most determined of his opponents to nail him with a damaging punch. His footwork, use of the ring, ability to draw an opponent into a punch, the avoidance of infighting by subtle clinching, enabled him to take on all comers.

Born at Liverpool, the eldest of eight children, 'Nella' began boxing as a schoolboy and soon showed such promise that at the age of 12 he was entered in the local boys' championships at three weights: 6 st 5 lb, 7 st 5 lb and 7 st 12 lb. He won his way into the final in all three classes, took two titles, but refused to compete in the third as it meant boxing his best friend. He took up professional boxing when he was close up to his 20th birthday, the majority of his bouts taking place in Liverpool Stadium where he remained a great favourite for the rest of his life.

Yet he was 24 before he secured his first crack at the featherweight title and could only succeed in forcing a draw with champion Johnny Cuthbert. Eleven months later he outpointed Cuthbert to gain his first notch on a Lonsdale Belt. He lost the title and regained it from Seaman Tom Watson; defeated challenger Dave Crowley at Wembley Arena, and outpointed the bantam champion Johnny King, who was trying to win a second crown. The championship was lost to Johnny McGrory but regained from Johnny

Cusick and defended against Tom Smith. All his championship fights went the full distance of 15 rounds, as did his two attempts to win the world title from Freddie Miller, that talented American southpaw, both taking place in the open air at Liverpool before enormous crowds. Although Miller took a close decision the first time, the second was a disputed verdict, Tarleton having learnt how to deal with his opponent's right-foot-forward stance. Nella was nine days past his 39th birthday when he brilliantly outpointed Al Phillips, the famous 'Aldgate Tiger', a stronger, much younger challenger. It was his final bow and he made it a fitting occasion. When Tarleton died two days before his 50th birthday, he just missed being the first boxer to receive the pound a week pension that goes to outright Lonsdale Belt winners when they reach the half-century mark.

Tarleton on the ropes as challenger Crowley comes in to attack.

Featherweight
Willie Pep

Apart from his great boxing skill, it was an indomitable fighting spirit both in and out of the ring that enabled Willie Pep to last as long as he did and to pile up such an astonishing record. In January 1947, when he was the reigning world's featherweight champion, he was involved in an air crash. When the ambulance man pulled him out of the wreckage and asked his name, one of them said: 'That's tough luck, Willie, I guess you'll never fight again. You've got multiple injuries.' But Pep did fight again. In six months he was back in the ring and continued to fight regularly for the next ten years. He also made a comeback at the ripe old age of 43.

Born at Middletown in Connecticut in 1922, real name William Guiglermo Papaleo, he was a tiny boy who used to run for his life when the others ganged up on him to administer a little mild torture. Then his mother suggested that he went to the local gymnasium to learn how to look after himself and he did just that, showing a remarkable aptitude for boxing and developing a zest for it. At 16 he won the State amateur flyweight title and a year later, the bantam championship, and before he was 18 had decided that it would give him even more pleasure if he was paid for it.

After 54 bouts in two and a half years he was unbeaten, so they matched him with Chalky Wright, a crafty experienced champion, ten years senior to Pep. They fought in Madison Square Garden in New York and the fans gasped as the youngster raced to a points victory, showing such dazzling speed of foot and rapid punching that he was immediately named 'Willie the Wisp'. Victory made him the youngest boxer in 40 years to win a world title. His status as champion was not recognized by the National Boxing Association, so Pep took on Sal Bartolo, the pretender to his throne, and ran away with another brilliant display of speedy boxing. Up to that time he had suffered but one defeat, losing to the lightweight champion, hard-hitting Sammy Angott, in a non-title bout. There wasn't a lot of stopping power in Pep's punches; he never gave himself time for that. But his long record of 241 bouts shows him

winning 229, of which 65 ended inside the distance. Some of these were clear-cut knockouts, but many of the others came when his opponents dropped from sheer fatigue, unable to keep up the amazing pace at which Willie conducted his bouts. After his remarkable recovery from the plane disaster, Pep made two successful title defences and then came up against Sandy Saddler, a lean and lanky Negro, three inches taller than Pep at 5 ft 8½ in with a reach of 70 inches of which he knew how to make best use, both as a striking weapon at long range or for entangling an opponent in the clinches, leaving his right hand free to work havoc on the body. He was to prove the bane of Pep's fighting life.

They were to meet four times, on each occasion in New York, and all were contests that sizzled with the 'needle' element. In the first meeting Willie wasn't prepared for the style of fight Saddler put up and was twice put down in the third round, the second time with a left hook that almost tore his head off. He just managed to beat the count, but in the next round, while

still recovering from that fearful punch, he stopped a right to the chin that sent him rolling and the referee counted him out. Less than four months later they had a return fight that most of Pep's friends and all the critics thought he was mad to go into. But the astonishing Willie fought the fight of his career, bedazzling Saddler with his fast, brilliant boxing and winning the unanimous decision of the referee and both judges. Although the winner, Willie suffered severe damage from the cruel-hitting champion, receiving cuts under and over his eyes that required 11 stitches before he could leave the dressing-room for home.

However, he was champion once again and made three winning title defences, beating Eddie Compo in seven rounds, Charley Riley in five, and high-ranking Ray Famechon, of France, on a points verdict. Then came the eagerly awaited 'rubber' match with Saddler. Pep was 28 now with 155 contests behind him, older than Sandy by four years and a lot more war-worn, it being said that the scar tissue around his eyes looked like the weaving tracks at a railway junction. They fought a grim battle, Pep being dropped for a count in the third with a left hook to the chin, but it was a series of savage rights to the kidneys that forced the champion to retire in his corner at the end of the eighth round. Even then he had not had enough and a year later met Sandy once more. This time it was such a savage brawl, with both on the canvas along with the referee on one occasion, that afterwards they were suspended by the New York Boxing Commission. Pep came off worse, suffering a lacerated right eye that eventually compelled him to give up after nine rounds. That should have been the end, but Willie's whole life was boxing and he went on and on, his opponents becoming lower down the scale as the years went by. When he finally retired for the second time, he had little to show for his fistic efforts, in spite of the fact that for his third bout with Saddler he received 92,889 dollars, the biggest cheque ever picked up by a boxer below the lightweight class. Pep keeps contact with the Fight Game, occupying himself as a referee and columnist for sporting magazines.

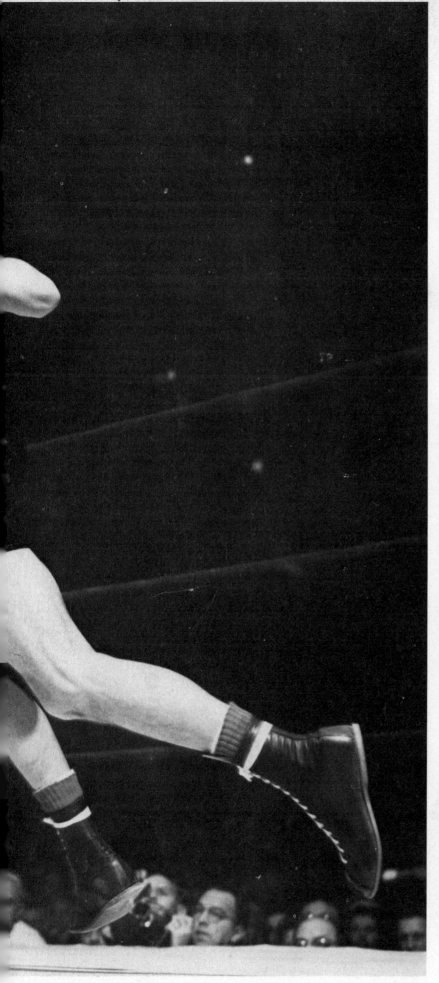

Above: Pep gets a right to Saddler's mouth in his victory in their second meeting. *Right:* Pep connects with Ray Famechon's jaw in a successful title defence.

Previous pages: Pep versus Saddler. In the big picture Pep connects with a left in the second fight. *Top:* The referee sorts out a tangle in the third fight. *Centre:* Another mix-up in the fourth fight. *Bottom:* The third fight and Pep down in the third round.

Sandy Saddler

Because of his extra physical endowments which he put to the fullest possible use in the ring, Joe (Sandy) Saddler, rates as one of the hardest-hitting featherweights of all time, his total of 103 wins inside the distance, out of a total of 162 bouts, being practical proof of this claim. He stood 5 ft 8½ in, his long skinny arms giving him the great advantage of a 70 inches reach. His punches played havoc on an opponent's features, but it was his long slashes to the body and his vicious uppercuts that made him such a dangerous man to meet.

Born at Boston in Massachusetts in 1926, his West Indian father moved to New York's coloured district of Harlem, where Sandy took up amateur boxing, liked it and did so well, that at 17 he became a professional, winning his first bout, but being stopped in his second inside three rounds. It was the only contest he was ever to lose inside the scheduled course, except for the time when he was accused of fouling and was ruled out in round four. Saddler really got on the title trail when he teamed up with Charley Johnston, who asked the fighter his real name. 'It's Benjamin Sandy Saddler,' he was told and was shown a birth certificate to prove it. The manager took his boy to a theatrical outfitters, rigged him up in Highland costume, had him photographed, and sent out pictures to all the promoters, advertising Saddler as the 'Harlem Scotsman'. Any annoyance they may have had at the deception disappeared once they saw Sandy in action.

It took them 100 contests and four and a half years of fighting to get Willie Pep to accept Saddler as a challenger and then they had to guarantee the champion 25,000 dollars to secure the fight. Sandy was fighting for little more than his training expenses, but he startled Pep and the fistic world by winning on a clean-cut knockout in round four. He lost the title temporarily back to Pep four months later on a unanimous points defeat, but regained it 19 months afterwards when he battered Pep into submission in eight rounds. In just over a year they met for the fourth time sand it was not a nice fight to watch. Pep had built up a

resentment against Saddler, whose methods did not encourage a good sporting contest. There was a lot more wrestling than boxing, but Saddler out-roughed his smaller opponent who retired in his corner after the ninth round owing to a severe eye wound.

Sandy did not get a chance to gain much from his title as he was inducted into the US Army, his championship being 'frozen' for two years. When he returned he outpointed the 'interim' champion, Teddy 'Redtop' Davis and stopped Gabriel Elorde, of the Philippines, in 13 rounds. He was then 30 and his career came to an abrupt halt the following year when he suffered a bad eye injury in a car smash that prevented any further thought of fighting.

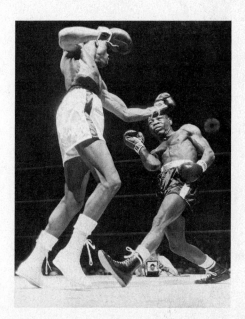

Below: The referee pulls apart Saddler and Pep in their fourth fight. Pep's cut eye is clearly visible.

Above: Saddler (white trunks) throws a left at Teddy 'Redtop' Davis when retaining his championship, 1955.

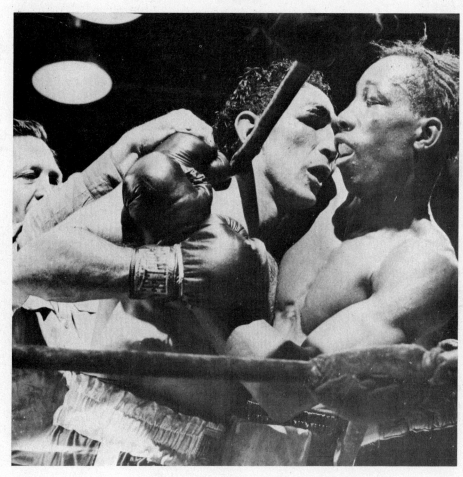

Hogan Bassey

Hogan Bassey came to England in 1952, at a time when there was a growing shortage of boxers and West African fighters could be sure of getting plenty of work. He had that extra bit of class that eventually made him the best featherweight in the world. Stockily built, with fine shoulders and well-developed arms, he was a demon close-quarter warrior, with a knockout punch in each hand that enabled him to win 20 of his 68 contests inside the distance.

Born at Calabar in Nigeria in 1932, real name Okon Bassey Asuguo, he began boxing from schooldays. At 18 he won the Nigerian bantam title with a ten-round knockout and the following year was acclaimed West African champion at that weight. Soon afterwards he took a boat to Liverpool where he settled and became a very popular performer in north country rings, especially on Merseyside.

He made his début as a bantam, by knocking out Ray Hillyard in four rounds to become a star overnight. After an eighth-round knockout win over Luis Romero, former European champion, Bassey concentrated on the featherweight division.

After 41 bouts in Great Britain he went to Belfast and outpointed Billy Kelly to become Empire featherweight champion, a title he defended against Percy Lewis, of Jamaica. Then he made a quick trip to America where he caused considerable eyebrow-raising as he pounded out a 12-round victory over Miguel Berrios, of Puerto Rico, who had won an elimination bout to find a successor to Sandy Saddler. The American and European Boxing Commissions then agreed to recognize the winner of a contest between Bassey and Cherif Hamia, of France, as undisputed featherweight champion, and Hogan went to Paris to batter the Algerian into helplessness in ten rounds, the French fans gazing in amazement as their favourite wilted under the Nigerian's determined attack.

Ten months later Bassey took his world title to Los Angeles where he laid

Bassey (left) gets a left to the face of Sammy McCarthy and went on to outpoint him in 1953.

it on the line against the Mexican sensation, Ricardo Moreno, winner of 29 inside-the-distance bouts in a total of 33 contests. It seemed as though Hogan was going into the lion's den, but he took the Mexican kayo king's best punch and hit back even harder. In the second round he swamped his challenger with paralysing hooks and uppercuts, knocking him out in the next round with a sizzling right to the chin. Bassey beat Willie Pep in Boston, Carmelo Costa in New York and Ernesto Parra in Hollywood. Next in line was Davey Moore whom Bassey met in Los Angeles in March 1959. The Nigerian was favoured to win, but had to retire at the end of the 13th round with severe cuts over both eyes when he was falling behind on points. A return contest in Los Angeles ended surprisingly after the tenth round when Bassey's manager called over the referee and intimated that Hogan could not continue. Up to that point he had been holding his own, but an eye injury again caused him to give up. On his return to Nigeria he announced his retirement from professional boxing and was appointed a director of physical education. He had already been awarded an MBE for his services to sport.

Vicente Saldivar

In modern boxing it is not a rarity for a one-time champion of the world to regain his title, more often than not, from the man to whom he lost it. Vicente Saldivar did something of greater significance than that. He resigned the featherweight championship of the world in October 1967, stayed away from the ring for 21 months, then recaptured his discarded crown in May 1970 – a very creditable performance. A fierce-attacking southpaw with damaging punching power, Saldivar's ten-year span of pro fighting, less those two and a half years in voluntary retirement, contained only 38 bouts. He won all but two of these and 25 of his victories were gained inside the scheduled number of rounds. Right-foot-forward fighters usually carry their heaviest punch in their left glove, but Saldivar could punch just as hard with his right, a leading, jarring delivery that often rolled an opponent into a following left hook or swing that spelt trouble.

Born in 1943 at Oaxaca, the slum area of Mexico City, one of a family of eight, he had a tough upbringing that stood him in good stead during boyhood. His street slugging brought complaints from other parents, but instead of reproving his belligerent son, Papa Saldivar told him that if the desire to fight was so strong that he couldn't give it up, then he should make up his mind to make a vocation of it. The boy nodded and followed this advice so well that at the age of 16 he became Golden Gloves champion and the following year was sent to the Rome Olympics with the Mexican team. He was outpointed by a Swiss featherweight with a neat left jab.

It was a sad homecoming, but he practised hard to learn the way to get past an educated left hand, and early the following year he climbed into the ring for his first paid bout. It ended triumphantly in the third round and the still 17-year-old Vicente realized that it was the easiest and quickest way he had ever earned money. His 16th fight which he lost on an alleged foul to Baby Luis, was his first pro set-back, but he got full revenge six months later when he won over the same opponent inside eight rounds. He was to remain unbeaten until his very last contest.

Winning the Mexican featherweight title and successfully defending it, Saldivar was given a title fight in the bull-ring at Mexico City against Urtiminio (Sugar) Ramos, the Cuban holder of the world championship.

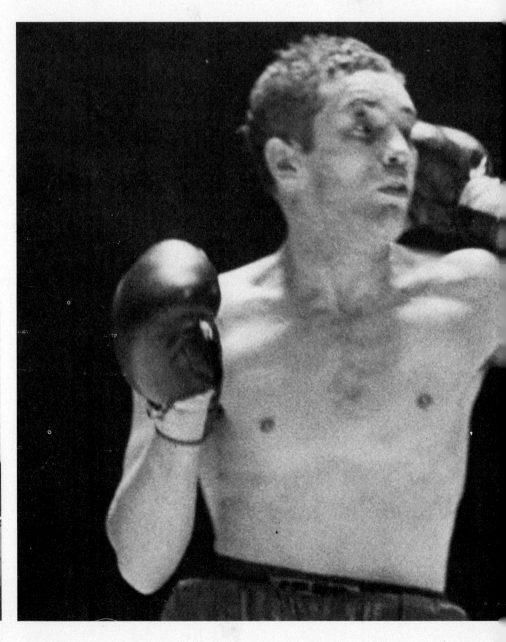

Ramos had stopped Davey Moore and mauled him so badly that he had died two days afterwards. Since then he had successfully defended his crown against Rafiu King right there in Mexico City; stopped Mitsunori Seki in six rounds in Tokyo; and beaten Floyd Robertson in Accra, Ghana.

So Sugar Ramos was a formidable proposition for anyone to tackle, but Saldivar set about it in such determined and confident fashion that the championship changed hands, the tough Cuban failing to answer the bell for the 12th round after having been floored in the tenth and then punched into helplessness by the blazing blows from the Mexican challenger. Up to the time he dropped Ramos, giving him the first knockdown of his triumphant career, Saldivar had outgunned the champion in a sustained bruising battle that was testimony to the physical fitness of both

Saldivar was not the sort to keep his title in cotton wool. In the next year he defended it eight times, taking on all comers and not denying any challenger a chance. He had a hard battle in Los Angeles against Raul Rojas, a rugged Californian, but stopped him in the 15th and final round, coming out of the ring with severe facial cuts. But he was ready four months later to accommodate Howard Winstone, the British champion, in London, who stayed the full distance to lose by a close margin of points. Floyd Robertson and Mitsunori Seki (twice) were beaten in Mexico City, then came a return bout with Winstone in Cardiff, with Saldivar again a points winner, but by an even narrower margin this time. The talented Welshman was still unsatisfied, so a third meeting was arranged, this time in Mexico City, with the challenger being forced to retire in the 12th round after having been put down and in a helpless state with bad cuts about the eyes.

To the amazement of everyone, the victorious champion announced his immediate retirement from the ring. This left the title vacant and it ultimately passed into the hands of Johnny Famechon. Saldivar now decided to return to the ring and after giving himself a trial bout when outpointing Jose Legra, took on the Australian in Rome and astonished the fistic world by winning a handsome 15-round points verdict to once again rule as feather-weight champion of the world. Unfortunately, not for long. Seven months later, in the first defence of his regained crown, he was stopped in 13 rounds with severe eye injuries by Kuniaki Shibata of Japan, after which Saldivar again retired – this time for good.

Saldivar (*right*) gets a right to the face of Howard Winstone in their first title fight.

Howard Winstone

To lose the tops of three fingers of your right hand in a machine accident must be very demoralizing to a youngster bent on making a career of boxing. It was a restricting handicap for an orthodox-stance fighter because the right hand is reckoned to carry the most power. Automatically it reduced young Howard Winstone to a one-handed boxer, therefore he developed his left until it was the best anyone had seen since the days of his fellow-countryman, 'Peerless' Jim Driscoll. It was so good it saw him victorious in 61 of his 67 bouts, its potency being enough to cause 28 of his victims to be stopped inside the distance.

Born at Merthyr Tydfil, South Wales, in 1939, Winstone became a brilliant amateur, ending his career as ABA bantamweight champion and Commonwealth Games gold medallist in 1958. He turned professional the following year and became British featherweight champion in his 25th contest by stopping talented Terry Spinks in ten rounds at Wembley Arena. It was a title for which he was never beaten and he defended it on six occasions during the next five years to win outright two Lonsdale Belts. The way Winstone used his left was not as just a straight lead or jab, but like an immaculate piston that had wearing-down qualities of great effectiveness. Once he had got it going it was a well-oiled machine behind which his sharp brain dictated its speed and accuracy.

Winstone became European featherweight champion by stopping Alberto Serti in 14 rounds at Cardiff; he stopped Lino Mastellaro in eight rounds at Wembley in its defence, and outpointed Yves Desmarets in Rome. Twice more he put it at stake successfully, stopping Andrea Silanos at Sardinia in the final round, and putting paid to Jean de Keers in three rounds in London. Winstone was never defeated for this title, but was made to forfeit it when he went after the world crown.

No man, apart from Jersey Joe Walcott, had a longer or more discouraging chase after a world title. When he first fought Vincente Saldivar in London in September 1965, he made the mistake of trying to outpunch the

aggressive Mexican and came off worst to lose on points after suffering a battering in the final rounds. At Cardiff in June 1967, he boxed beautifully to lose by the narrow margin of half a point, and in their third meeting the gallant Welshman was forced to retire at the end of the 12th round with an eye injury. Finally, in January 1958, he realized his life's ambition and became world champion by stopping Mitsunori Seki, of Japan, in nine rounds for the title left vacant by Saldivar's premature retirement. Winstone's reign was not long. Against Jose Legra, the Cuban, in Porthcawl just seven months later, he was caught by a bolo right uppercut in the opening round that put him down and also closed his left eye completely. The champion fought back until the fifth round when he was being freely punished and the referee rightly called a halt. It was Winstone's last contest.

Winstone (*right*) misses with a swinging right to Saldivar near the end of their first fight.

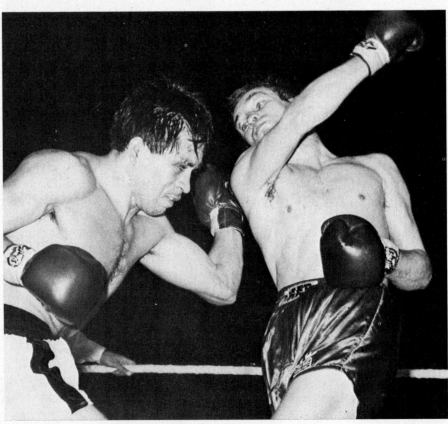

Johnny Famechon

Boxing is so cosmopolitan, otherwise how could an Australian, born in France, come to be fighting a Cuban in Great Britain for the featherweight championship of the world? No one could have had a better boxing background than Johnny Famechon. His father had been lightweight champion of France, his uncle Emile had been flyweight king, while Uncle Raymond had made it a hat-trick of French titles and come close to winning the world title. There were two other uncles who enjoyed swapping punches, but Johnny, son of André, did not begin his career in France. It started in Australia where he had been taken to live at the age of five. Yet his father did not want Johnny to take up a boxing career at the age of 16. He told him that he hadn't the physique or stamina that glove-fighting demands, but the eager son pleaded to be given his chance and did so well that in his 21st contest he won the Australian featherweight championship, a title he defended three times.

Famechon did not carry a real knockdown punch, although 21 of his 57 wins failed to go the scheduled course. He relied on fast and clever footwork and the speedy use of an accurate left jab that he could land with effect while on the move. In addition, he knew all the moves, possessed a sound defence and was blessed with a fighting brain. He lost only five points verdicts.

Winning the British Empire title by stopping John O'Brien, of Scotland in 11 rounds, and defending it by beating Billy McGrandle of Canada in 12, he was matched to fight Jose Legra, the Spanish-based Cuban, who had destroyed Howard Winstone in five rounds to become world titleholder. Famechon met him at London's Royal Albert Hall and the fans watched a breathless, scintillating battle between the young Australian's clever boxing and the whirlwind aggression of the champion. At the finish of one of the fastest 15-rounders ever fought, Famechon was declared the winner by $74\frac{1}{2}$ points to Legra's $73\frac{1}{4}$ and Johnny went back to Australia as a national hero two months before his 24th birthday.

Six months after becoming world titleholder, Johnny put his crown at stake in Melbourne against Fighting Harada, of Japan, former fly and bantamweight champion of the world, who gave the young Australian the fight of his life, putting him down three times, but not being able to keep him there or prevent him from retaining the championship by a full point. Harada clamoured for a return which he got five months afterwards, but wished he hadn't as Johnny knocked him through the ropes and out for the count in the 14th round, this time in Tokyo.

At 25 Famechon looked like remaining as champion for many years and was favoured to beat Saldivar when they were matched to fight for the title in Rome. It was thought that his speed would be too much for the former champion, but all his brilliant left-hand work, speed and boxing know-how, was not quite good enough against the Mexican's tempestuous aggression and at the finish Famechon had not only lost his cherished title, but also his zest for fighting, for the next day he announced his retirement from the ring.

Famechon (*right*) swaps punches with British junior lightweight champion Jimmy Anderson. Famechon won on points.

Al Brown

Something of a physical freak, Alphonse Theodore Brown (1902–1951) was the tallest of the world bantamweight champions, standing six feet and with correspondingly long, skinny arms that were capable of stunning an opponent with uppercuts he could bring from his shoe-tops, or wrapping up a rival with them to prevent any close-quarter work on his sparse mid-section. With his 76-inch reach, Brown could jab a man back on his heels before he was within striking distance, or slam him on the chin with a telling right at long range. His record of 156 contests shows that 58 of these were stoppages. In all he won 123 bouts, and the fact that he drew 12 and lost 19 was because he became lackadaisical at times, especially towards the end of his career, when winning or losing did not seem to matter as long as he was well paid.

Coloured Panama Al Brown as he became known, was born in the Canal Zone and picked up his boxing, along with dozens of other local boys by performing in an arena set up to entertain the American community there. By the time he was 20 he was the flyweight champion of the Isthmus and attracted the attention of Dave Lumiansky, a fight manager, who promptly took Brown to New York where he stayed for over three years and became a star performer. He then had a year in France where he was the delight of Paris fans, went back to New York for six winning bouts, returned to Europe for another long stay because of the demand for his services, and then

fought Vidal Gregorio for the world bantam title in Madison Square Garden, winning on points.

He took his title round the world, defending it successfully against Knud Larsen in Copenhagen, Eugene Huat in Paris, Pete Sanstol and Eugene Huat in Montreal, Kid Francis in Marseilles, Emile Pladner in Toronto, Dominico Bernasconi in Milan, Johnny King in Manchester and Young Perez in Paris. All this occupied five years and there were many non-title contests, mainly against featherweights. There was a riot when he fought at Marseilles when one of the judges favoured his challenger, and a rowdy rumpus in Milan, when owing to confusion the title contest was stopped and then restarted. But

Panama Al took it all in his long stride until he encountered Baltazar Sangchilli at Valencia when to his mortification the decision went against him and he had lost his lucrative crown.

Now he began to go home by stages. There were more fights in Paris, then some in America and finally he was back in Panama where he fought a 15-round draw for the local featherweight title. He was 39 then and although there were a few more ring appearances, the curtain was finally brought down in 1944. When he died seven years later in New York from tuberculosis, he was penniless.

Al Brown (*left*) beating Sangchilli in 1938. Sangchilli took his title from him in an earlier fight.

Manuel Ortiz

Manuel Ortiz deserves his place in boxing's Hall of Fame, not only because he was twice bantamweight champion of the world, but also for the fact that he defended his crown 21 times, a record number for the 8 st 6 lb division, second, in fact, to Joe Louis's tally of 25 title defences. Tough, fast and two-fisted, he swarmed over his opponents, his hard hitting enabling him to chalk up 45 inside-the-distance wins. In a total of 122 bouts, he lost 27 times, but mostly when he went out of his class and took on men a lot bigger and heavier than himself. His two reigns as world champion covered eight years.

Born of a Mexican family at Corona in California in 1916, Ortiz had not the usual incentive of poverty for taking up a fighting career. He boxed as a hobby, purely for the love of it, and had no ideas about competitive fighting until a member of his club's boxing team failed to pass a medical examination and Ortiz volunteered to take his place. Winning his bout, he was encouraged to enter the State amateur championships and became Golden Gloves flyweight champion at the age of 21.

The following year he turned

professional and made such steady progress that he beat Tony Olivera in Hollywood in a bout recognized by the National Boxing Association as involving the world bantam title. It was not until he had outpointed Lou Salica, who was recognized in New York as champion, that Ortiz received general acceptance as world champion, and he then proceeded to put his claim beyond any shadow of doubt by meeting anyone who fancied his chance. Fifteen

challengers were safely taken care of, some of them getting more than one opportunity of winning the title, then after he had been champion for five years, he dropped the championship to coloured Harold Dade in San Francisco, only to regain it in a return title bout two months later.

Ortiz continued to take on contenders with success, twice going to Honolulu, where he defeated David Kui Kong Young and Dado Marino; to Manila in the Philippines, where he beat Tirso del Rosario, and Mexicali, where he knocked out Memo Valero in eight rounds. Still taking his title on a world tour he arrived in South Africa where his long reign as bantam champion came to an end. Ortiz was fast coming up to 34 then and the well-used fighting machine was beginning to run down. Opposed to Vic Toweel, 13 years his junior, he fought desperately to keep his crown, but running out of steam in the latter half of the contest, he left his championship in Johannesburg.

Ortiz (left) has Theo Medina in trouble whilst outpointing him in Paris in 1949.

Vic Toweel

Jimmy Carruthers

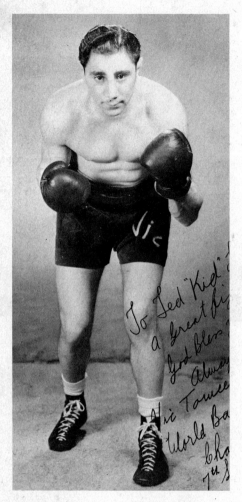

Of the five fighting Toweel brothers, Victor, the second son, gained the highest honours, becoming the first South African boxer to win a world championship. His rise to fame as a professional was rapid, his descent even swifter, but he made his presence felt unmistakably by winning four championships in 24 contests, half of which ended within the scheduled limit. Toweel was a tearaway fighter, who took the war into the enemy camp and stayed there, punching away until the battle was over. Up to the time of losing his world title, he was unbeaten.

Second son of a Lebanese ex-fighter, Vic was born at Benoni, outside Johannesburg in 1928. His father encouraged all his sons to become amateur boxers with the exception of one who had been born crippled. It was soon evident that Vic was the best at his weight, in fact, he was such a holy terror in the ring that few could stand up to

him. When he was chosen to represent South Africa in the London Olympics of 1948, he had won all but two of his 190 bouts, 160 on the intervention of the referee or by knockouts. It was fully expected that he would bring gold back to his country, but he was the victim of a very unpopular decision in his first bout, and came home a disillusioned youngster. Straightaway the family decided that he should turn pro.

In his fourth fight he won the South African bantam title, in his ninth he took the featherweight crown. In his 11th he beat Stan Rowan, the British champion, for the Empire championship, which he defended successfully against Fernando Gagnon of Canada. He did not have to go out of Johannesburg for any of these contests, nor did he when Manuel Ortiz, the veteran champion from California, put his title on the line against the far less experienced but 13-years-younger Benoni boy. For 15 rounds they fought practically toe-to-toe with Ortiz forced to give ground step by step against the non-stop attack set up by the challenger. At the finish of a bruising bout, Toweel had won on points in only his 14th professional contest.

Danny O'Sullivan, the British champion, was his first challenger, but was stopped in ten rounds after being put down no less than 14 times. Luis Romero, tough Spanish southpaw and former European champion, was next, but suffered a points defeat as did Peter Keenan, the reigning British and European champion. The fourth challenger Jimmy Carruthers, came from Australia, a tall southpaw of limited experience, who looked too frail to stand up to the rumbustious South African. It was all over in 2 min 19 sec of the first round, with Toweel, bewildered by the Australian's rapid long-range punching, being knocked out of the ring and finally counted out. His defeat was inexplicable, for he had fought several southpaws prior to this. A return fight was demanded and Carruthers came again to Johannesburg to administer a second defeat on the local idol, this time in ten rounds. It spelt finish for Vic's career and after an abortive trip to America, he announced his retirement at the age of 25.

When Jimmy Carruthers read in the newspapers that Vic Toweel had won the bantamweight championship of the world, he immediately resolved to become a professional fighter. As a member of the Australian Olympics Game team of 1948, he had sat at the Wembley ringside and watched the South African being outpointed in the first bout of the bantam series and decided that he could beat him if they were called upon to clash. Toweel's defeat made that an impossibility, but now it could be brought to reality. Straightaway he went to see Bill McConnell, trainer at his amateur club, and asked him to manage him through a paid career. With the aid of Dr John McGirr, who had great faith in Carruthers, they formed a team that was to produce highly satisfactory results.

Born at Paddington in New South Wales in 1929, Carruthers was tall for a bantam at 5 ft 6½ in, with powerful shoulders and a skinny body perched on spindly legs. A natural southpaw, he carried a terrific dig in his left fist. A fast mover, making full use of every inch of the ring, he was able to keep comparatively free from punishment. In his first eight pro bouts he was taken the distance only once and when he challenged Elley Bennett, a talented Aborigine, for the Australian title, he romped home a clear-cut points winner. Five more spectacular wins followed, then a challenge was sent to Toweel to fight for the world crown.

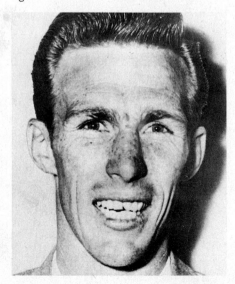

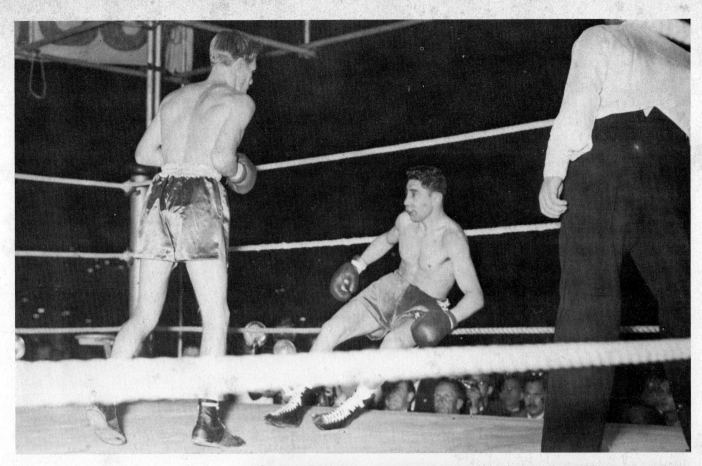

Two views of Jimmy Carruthers knocking out Vic Toweel, a feat he performed in two world title fights.

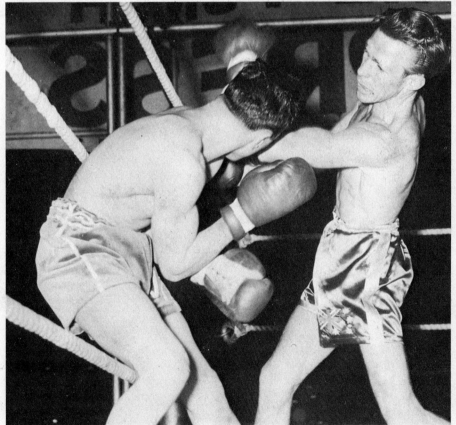

It meant boxing in the high altitude of Johannesburg, so Jimmy decided to get it over as quickly as possible and set off at a fast pace, spraying the champion with crisp punches about the head to have him dazed, knocked through the ropes and counted out with 41 seconds of the first round still remaining. The South Africans could not believe that their idol had been demolished so quickly by such a frail-looking fighter. Immediate plans were made for a return title contest, again in Johannesburg, four months later. But Carruthers had the psychological advantage over Toweel, who put up resistance for the best part of ten rounds until he succumbed to the Australian's sharper hitting and took the full count in the tenth round – 32,000 fans saw the fight and paid £40,000 for the privilege.

There were two more title defences. In the first Carruthers took on the American champion, Henry (Pappy) Gault, and outpointed him over 15 fast rounds. At Jimmy's insistence the bout was staged on behalf of the Wooloomooloo Police Boys' Club where he had learnt his boxing, the gate-money reaching the gratifying sum of £40,000 Australian, of which the club received 51 per cent. Six months later Carruthers went to Bangkok to outpoint Thailander Chamren Songkitrat in torrential rain, both men fighting best part of the time in their bare feet owing to the slippery canvas. It was a great victory for Jimmy, yet a fortnight later he announced his retirement from the ring. After an absence of seven years he made a comeback, but it proved a disaster and after six contests, with only two wins, he left the fighting to others.

Eder Jofre

When Eder Jofre was a small boy he accompanied his father to a slaughter-house where the sight of blood so sickened him that he could never eat meat and became a strict vegetarian. When at the age of 21 he became a professional fighter, his blazing fists caused the blood to flow from many an opponent – but that was different. One of the most destructive bantams ever to win the world title, he punched like a small edition of Joe Louis and boxed with the grace of Ray Robinson. His right hand carried dynamite as his record of 41 wins inside the distance out of 62 bouts amply proves.

Born at São Paulo in Brazil, he knew all about boxing from boyhood, his father and his uncles all being fighters. At full maturity he stood only 5 ft 4 in, but every inch and ounce of him was full of power and precision as his opponents were to learn to their cost. He was never knocked out or stopped and the only two occasions when he was outpointed were when he lost and failed to regain his world title.

In his third year as a paid fighter he won the South American title, adding the NBA world crown with a sensational right to the jaw of Eloy Sanchez in round six, a blow that dropped the Mexican on his face to roll over and be counted out. Then came a fantastic run of 12 kayo wins in succession, eight of these being in defence of his

championship. The most impressive of these had been scored over the brilliant Irishman, Johnny Caldwell, who in addition to being British flyweight king was also a strong claimant to the world bantam crown, having beaten Alphonse Halimi, of France, in a European version of the world title. They met at São Paulo to settle who was the rightful champion and Eder outpunched the game Belfast boy, whose seconds threw in the towel during the tenth round.

Herman Marques, of Mexico, lasted ten rounds; Joe Medel, another Mexican, stayed six. In Tokyo, Katsutoshi Aoki, was belted out in three rounds, while Johnny Jamito was put away in 12 at Manila. At Bogota in Columbia, Bernando Caraballo was stopped in seven, and for the ninth defence of his

world crown Jofre went back to Japan to face Masahiko (Fighting) Harada, who previously had been world flyweight king. Unbeaten in 51 bouts, even the Japanese made Jofre favourite to win, but he was harassed from start to finish by Harada, who maintained a non-stop attack, mainly to the body, that kept the titleholder with his back to the ropes, unable to land his big punches on the bobbing and weaving challenger. At the finish Jofre, the first Brazilian ever to hold a world title, was no longer champion and in a return fight in Tokyo a year later, he was again outpointed. That was in June 1966 when Eder was 30 and he retired from boxing forthwith. He was back again, however, three years later, to box successfully as a featherweight, becoming world champion in 1973.

A terrific left from Jofre to the stomach of Aoki gives him a knockout victory in the third round.

Fighting Harada

Only two fighters, Bob Fitzsimmons and Henry Armstrong, have won three world championships. Ray Robinson came close to doing it and so did Masahiko (Fighting) Harada, the best fighter ever to come out of Japan. In a meritorious ten-year career, he won and lost the world flyweight title, won and lost the world bantam crown after five defences, and came within a single point of gaining the world featherweight championship.

Son of a gardener, Harada was born in Tokyo in 1943. Although keen on boxing in his youth, he did not join an amateur club, but trained at home for two years before embarking on a professional career two months before his 17th birthday. His great asset was his speed, his non-stop whirling punches, and his continually bobbing head that kept him out of trouble. He went 25 bouts without defeat, starting with four-rounders and working up to ten. He had never been matched over 15 rounds until, at the age of 19, he challenged Pone Kingpetch, of Thailand, for the world's flyweight title and before 12,000 hysterical Japanese fans, punched the titleholder into submission in 11 rounds. At no time did he allow the champion to get into his stride and hammered him so severely that it needed 11 stitches to repair the

Thailander's face at the finish.

There was a return contest in Bangkok three months later. Now it was a different situation, with 15,000 locals cheering every punch that Kingpetch launched and barely a sound to encourage Harada in his efforts. They set a whirlwind pace and the Japanese fighter looked like keeping his crown when he dropped the challenger in the eighth round with a fine right to the chin. But the Thailander got up to bring his better boxing into play and was declared the winner, the referee and one judge voting for Kingpetch, with the other judge making it a 'draw'.

That looked like being the extent of Harada's title ambitions. He gave up the flyweight class and took on the bantams, causing a sensation by taking a split decision over hitherto unbeaten Eder Jofre, of Brazil, to become world's bantam champion. He was to keep his second big title a lot longer than he had the first. Alan Rudkin, the British champion, was outpointed in a thriller that went the full distance in Tokyo, and in the same ring Jofre was again beaten on points. Joe Medel, who had given Harada his solitary inside-the-distance defeat, was awarded a crack at the championship, but he, too, was outpointed, while Bernardo Caraballo was another challenger to suffer defeat.

But the Australian Aborigine, Lionel Rose, outpointed Harada after a gruelling Tokyo battle, and once again it seemed that it was the end of the road for Japan's great hero.

Nothing of the sort, for in July 1969, at the age of 26, Harada was still full of fight and took Johnny Famechon to a close decision for the world featherweight title, referee Willie Pep first calling it a 'draw' before recasting his score-card to make the Australian a winner by one point. Harada had been forced to go to Sydney for that one, but he begged the Tokyo promoters to induce Famechon to defend his title in Japan so that he could make one further attempt to win a third world crown. Alas, he met a champion in ultra-top form, who wore him down for 13 rounds and then bundled him through the ropes in the next to win by a knockout. Harada retired the next day with a lot of fistic glory to reflect upon.

Harada poking a left into the face of Jofre on his way to a points win in their second fight.

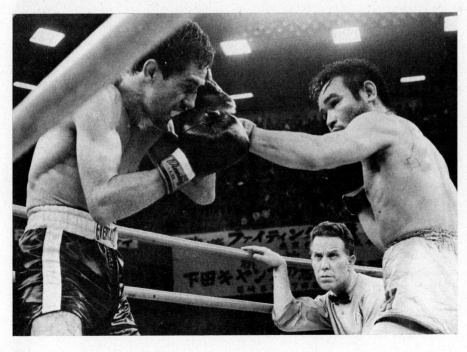

Lionel Rose

Australian Aborigines have produced a number of excellent boxers, but the first to attain world status was Lionel Rose. A free-hitting, natural fighter, he combined sound boxing with colourful aggression that made him a great favourite with the fans. Born in the small country town of Drouin, 60 miles from Melbourne, in 1948, the first child in a family of nine, his father was a fairground fighter who taught his eldest son the rudiments of boxing almost as soon as he could toddle.

Rose was made a member of an amateur club at the age of 12. Three years later, as a flyweight, he became one of the youngest ever to win a national title and when he grew into a bantam, was selected to box in the 1964 Olympic Games trials, but lost his bout by one point after flooring his opponent. In September the same year he became a pro at the tender age of 16. In his 20th paid bout he won the Australian bantamweight title, successfully defended it and then challenged Japan's Fighting Harada for the world title. At that time he was four months short of his 20th birthday.

The champion was five years older and correspondingly more experienced, having been world flyweight king before winning the bantam crown. Rose was a 4 to 1 outsider when he climbed into the ring, but he boxed brilliantly against a difficult opponent to earn a unanimous points decision, even the Japanese judge voting in his favour, the fact that he dropped the champion with a superb right cross in the ninth round for a count of 'eight', no doubt influencing the officials. In April 1969 Lionel was awarded the MBE for his contribution to Australian boxing.

A busy champion, Rose went back to Tokyo for a successful title defence against Takao Sakurai, and before the year was out had gone to Los Angeles where he outpointed Chucho Castillo, of Mexico, to keep his crown. His only championship defence in Australia came next when he faced British champion, Alan Rudkin at Melbourne. Again he had to go the distance to gain victory, but he was making hay while the sun shone and three months later was in Honolulu boxing a ten-round non-title bout with Ernie Cruz who was beaten on points.

Apart from two points losses in his early days, Rose was enjoying an unbeaten run of 22 victories, including four world title bouts. He had just turned 21 and the world was at his feet. But in Mexico they had a knockout king in Ruben Olivares, who was unbeaten with 53 wins inside the distance. They offered Rose 10,000 dollars to defend his championship in Los Angeles and the Australian did not hesitate about accepting, even though he was beginning to find it hard to make the bantam limit. His boxing skill proved no match for the Mexican's blazing fists and after being put down three times, Rose took the full count in the fifth round.

Undaunted, he turned his attention to the featherweights, but his performances were up and down and he called it a day to become a pop singer.

Lionel Rose (*left*) taking the title on points from Harada.

Ruben Olivares

Pound for pound the stocky bantams have provided some of the greatest punchers in the world; their compactness seems to give them the maximum power to put behind their blows. Perhaps the hardest hitter of them all has been Ruben Olivares who, up to the end of 1972, had piled up 63 inside-the-distance wins in a total of 72 bouts. In this time he had won the world's bantamweight title, defended it successfully on two occasions, lost it, regained it, kept it against two further challengers and finally dropped it again. Each time he was defeated for his crown he was stopped, these being the only two blemishes on his astonishing record.

Born at Mexico City in 1947, Olivares enjoyed amateur boxing so much, he decided to go in among the paid boys when he ran out of vested opponents. He was 18 then and a married man working as a wood-carver at 30 pesos a week. To say that he did the right thing in pinning his faith in his busy fists is an understatement. At the end of two years of ring activity he had chalked up 22 victories in an aggregate of 85 rounds, i.e. less than four rounds apiece with none of them going the distance. In the next three years he scored 29 more wins, only two bouts going the full ten rounds, one being a 'draw'.

George Parnassus, a Los Angeles promoter, then made a tempting offer to Lionel Rose to come to California and defend his world crown against the Mexican firebrand, and Olivares caused a major upset by stopping the classy Australian Aborigine in five tempestuous rounds. Olivares was paid 30,000 dollars for that brief spell of fighting, half of which he handed over to his father to settle expenses and to invest. The other half he spent on buying several cars, a great many suits and a row of houses.

Despite being world champion Ruben continued to box at frequent intervals and continued to win just as quickly. He disposed of British champion, Alan Rudkin, in a title defence that lasted only two rounds, but was taken the distance by fellow-countryman Chucho Castillo, who then caused the upset of the year when he halted Ruben in the 14th round of a return title bout, the

The fatal fifth round for Rose down and out against Olivares.

champion suffering a severe eye wound that necessitated the referee's intervention. In the 'rubber' match five months later, Olivares regained his crown, but was again forced to go the distance and he wound up 1971 by stopping Jesus Pimental, a Californian challenger, in 11 rounds.

Olivares was 24 then and seemed set to stay champion for some years to come, but like most boxers who start young, he was putting on weight and finding it increasingly difficult to get down to the bantam limit. Before his own fans in Mexico City he was far below his usual form and after being punished and cut by determined Rafael Herrera, another Mexican, he went down in the eighth round to the first and only knockout defeat of his career. After that he said goodbye to the bantams and turned his attention to the featherweight class.

Alan Rudkin

No man tried harder than Alan Rudkin to win a world's title and no one failed more gallantly. He was in turn British, Empire and European bantam king, yet the biggest prize of all evaded him, although he went all over the globe in his three vain attempts. A strong attacking fighter with two busy fists, Alan could box with the best. He had tremendous courage and tons of endurance, and it took a very good man to beat him. He won a Lonsdale Belt outright and scored two notches on a second. When he retired at 30 he had won 42 of his 50 bouts and had been stopped only twice, the first time in his second pro contest because of an eye injury, and the other occasion when he was beaten in two rounds when making his final assault on the world crown.

Born at Cowen in North Wales, where his family had been evacuated during the war, Rudkin returned to Liverpool to join the Florence Institute, a boys' club with a strong boxing section. Quickly he developed into a class amateur. Twice he was an ABA finalist, in one quarter-final boxing a brilliant bout with Walter McGowan, who he was to meet twice in historic contests as a pro. In May 1962, six months after his 20th birthday, he started to fight for pay, becoming British champion in his 21st bout by stopping Johnny Caldwell in ten rounds. Four fights later he was in Tokyo to give Fighting Harada a stern battle for the world crown, but losing on points.

It looked as though Rudkin had slipped back when he lost his title on a very close verdict to Walter McGowan, but he convincingly won the return battle two years later and subsequently stopped Evan Armstrong in 11 rounds to make the Lonsdale Belt his own property. Rudkin's first assault on the European title saw him lose on points to Ben Ali in Barcelona, but four years later he stopped Franco Zurlo in 11 rounds to take the EBU crown. He dropped this title to Agustin Senin on an adverse points verdict in Bilbao.

A left from Rudkin jolts Nigerian title-holder Karin Young. The referee stopped the fight in the first round.

Alan's next try to win the world title came nearly four years after his first attempt. It meant going to Australia to meet the formidable Lionel Rose in Melbourne, and after 15 exciting rounds, when it seemed that at any moment the determined Britisher might win, he was adjudged the loser on a split decision, one judge voting for Rudkin, with the referee and the other judge going for Rose, the latter official producing a ridiculous score-card that did not credit Rudkin with a single round, whereas it was generally agreed that he had won at least five. Nine months later Alan was in Los Angeles to meet the Mexican with the terrifying kayo record, Ruben Olivares. Rudkin wilted speedily under the champion's blazing fists and was stopped in the second round.

He came home to gain first notch on a second Lonsdale Belt by outclassing Johnny Clark, the referee calling a halt in round 12, then Alan went after the British featherweight title, but could not give reach and weight to Jimmy Revie, who won on points. So back to the bantams went Alan and in his final contest again defeated Clark, this time on points and being given a much harder struggle. He was turned 30 now and it came as no surprise when a few months later he retired from ring activity to become a boxers' manager among other things.

Jimmy Wilde

It is no exaggeration to say that little Jimmy Wilde (1892–1969) was the greatest flyweight of all time and it is doubtful whether there will ever be another like him, because apart from being a physical freak, he was also a phenomenal fighter. Never weighing more than 7 st 10 lb, i.e. 4 lb below the flyweight limit, he stood a mere 5 ft 2½ in and with his pipe-stem arms and skinny legs, looked far too frail to be allowed to enter a boxing ring. Yet he won 77 of his recorded 140 battles inside the distance, lost only one decision and although stopped on three occasions, two of these set-backs came at the tail end of his astonishing career.

Born at Quaker's Yard, near Merthyr Tydfil, he came of mining stock at a time when working in the pits was poorly paid for the hazardous work and hard labour involved. From school-leaving age (14) he was up at the coal face lying in seams too small for most men, hacking away to develop those amazing back and shoulder muscles that were to give him the punching power to knock out opponents stones heavier than himself. To augment his earnings he boxed for pennies among his work-mates and did well enough to chance his arm in the boxing booths that regularly visited the town.

His vigorous aggression made him very popular and gained him many victories. Always on the attack, gloves held at hip level, body swaying, head moving, he was a difficult target to pinpoint with a decisive punch, while his own blows came from all angles and with unexpected explosive power. He delighted in trapping an opponent on the ropes or in a corner when he would release a bombardment of shock punches without fear of return as the other man would be too busy defending himself. Jimmy kept fit by fighting in the early days of his career, boxing 30 times in 1913 without taking too much out of himself, because so few of his fights went the allotted distance.

Having become established as the master of all men who would meet him in Wales and the northern cities of England, Wilde descended on London being engaged to box at the famous 'Ring' at Blackfriars against a promising lad known as 'Matt Wells's Nipper'.

When she saw him, Mrs Bella Burge, wife of the proprietor, told her husband that he ought to be ashamed of himself for engaging the services of such a 'child'. 'But I'm a married man, mum,' exclaimed little Jimmy. 'I work in the pits, I've had hundreds of fights. I can look after myself.' He could, too, winning by a knockout half-way through the first round.

At the National Sporting Club in Covent Garden, Wilde proved a great favourite with the members who could not see enough of him. But when he was selected to box Tancy Lee for the Lonsdale Belt, he expended his efforts in trying to knock out his cagey, ten-years-older opponent and was himself stopped in the 17th round. In the dressing-room afterwards he was furious with his manager for throwing in the towel. 'Don't ever do that again,' he commanded. It was an order that almost cost him his life in his last battle.

A year after losing to Lee, Wilde became British flyweight king by stopping Joe Symonds in 12 rounds. He defended the title against his former conqueror, Tancy Lee, who was unable to go on after the 11th, defeated Johnny Hughes by a knockout in ten rounds and stopped George Clark in four. In between, however, he had laid claim to the world title when knocking out Johnny Rosner of America in 11 rounds at Liverpool. The same year he went a step nearer in establishing himself as the best flyweight in the world by scoring a kayo win in 11 rounds over the Young Zulu Kid, an American challenger, who made the trip to London fully confident of success.

One of Wilde's outstanding wins was against Joe Conn, the challenger for the featherweight title. They met on the Chelsea Football Club's ground at Stamford Bridge, the tournament being staged in aid of war charities. It was asking a lot of Jimmy to face a much taller man with a weight advantage of over a stone and a class boxer into the bargain, but Wilde swarmed over his man from start to finish and gave him such a going-over that the one-sided affair was halted in the 11th round. Because he was serving in the British Army as a sergeant instructor, Wilde

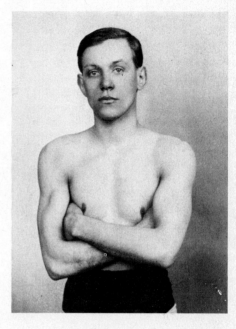

could not accept payment for the fight, but his wife received a present of a package of diamonds valued at £3,000, which would have been his purse had it not been for the war.

Joe Lynch and Pal Moore, two leading American bantams, were beaten in turn by Wilde's brilliant if unorthodox methods, then to add to his world supremacy, Jimmy went to the United States where he stayed for six months, engaging in 12 contests without defeat, five of his wins being by knockouts. Home again he eagerly agreed to fight Pete Herman, American holder of the world's bantam title at the Albert Hall, confident that he would win another championship. But the promoters were slack in their organization and when Herman arrived he had conveniently lost his world title to Joe Lynch three weeks earlier. With Herman refusing to weigh-in before the fight, Wilde refused to come out of his dressing-room until he did and it looked as though the contest would not materialize. Then someone told Jimmy that the Prince of Wales was in a ringside seat, whereupon he got to his feet saying: 'I can't keep *him* waiting,' and went out to meet his doom. Outweighed by nearly two stone, Wilde put up a courageous battle against one of the best bantams ever to hold the world title and was beaten down in the 17th round. Three times the game Welshman got off the canvas, then the referee put his arm round his waist and took him to his corner, saying: 'It's the best thing, Jimmy. I can't let you take any more.'

Wilde retired after that. He was 29 and there were no challengers for his flyweight crown. But two and a half years later, his admirers were startled to find him willing to go to New York to defend his world crown against Pancho Villa, a young and dangerous Philippino. Neither his wife nor his manager wanted Jimmy to accept Tex Rickard's offer, but Jimmy was adamant. 'I'm world champion and it's up to me to defend my title,' he told them – and off he went. They fought in the Polo Grounds before a crowd of 23,000, most of whom had come to see the famous Welshman. For a time he held his own with the demon-like Villa, who outspeeded the veteran and at 22 was his junior by nine years. Bravely Wilde tried to box off his aggressive challenger, but was severely punished and cut about, until it became a question of how much longer he could last.

When the bell sounded to end the sixth round, Jimmy dropped his hands and turned to go to his corner, but Villa landed a vicious blow to the champion's chin that dropped him in a heap. They wanted to retire him in the interval, but dare not, knowing that if he was going to be beaten he would go down fighting. Wilde came out on tottering legs and fought with amazing fury until his strength deserted him and Villa pounced on his prey. Blows to the head from both hands came at great speed until Jimmy fell at his challenger's feet completely unconscious. It took a long time to bring him round and it was a week before he was fit enough to go home. His retirement from boxing was automatic, but he kept in the fight game for many years as a boxing columnist, manager and referee, delighting in visiting tournaments to show his Lonsdale Belt, of which he was immensely proud, and to re-count stories of his many great victories.

Wilde training in 1918, below skipping, and right with his wife as pace-maker. *Below left:* **Wilde (***left***) moving in against Tancy Lee.** *Below right:* **The scene in the ring after Wilde had beaten American bantamweight Pal Moore.** *Opposite:* **Wilde (***left***) versus Pal Moore in 1919. Wilde won on points after 20 rounds.**

Jackie Brown

The hey-day of boxing in Manchester was in the 1930s when, apart from a host of fine boxers at all weights, there was that great triumvirate of champions, Jackie Brown, Johnny King and Jock McAvoy. All three reigned for long spells, but whereas Johnny and Jock had to be content with British titles, little Jackie got the jackpot, being flyweight champion of the world as well as British and European champion. Quick-witted and slick out of the ring, he was a fast and brainy fighter inside it, with a lot of sting in his gloves rather than power, although he scored more than a quarter of his 97 wins in 129 contests inside the distance.

Born in the Ancoats district of 'Cottonopolis', in a street of terraced houses, Brown (1909–1971) was boxing professionally at 16, after picking up the rudiments of the game in combat with other youngsters and seizing every opportunity to take part in booth-fighting. Rapidly he went to the front and after becoming Northern Area flyweight champion, he was matched to fight Bert Kirby for the right to challenge Johnny Hill for the British crown. Quite suddenly the champion fell ill and died, so the Brown versus Kirby fight became a title affair. It was fought on a Sunday in Birmingham amidst scenes of intense drama with hundreds unable to gain admission, there being a near riot when Brown produced a right-hand punch to the chin that knocked Kirby out. Five months later an over-confident Brown was himself knocked out in three rounds by Kirby, but when they met for the third time, the Mancunian gained a narrow points win. He went on to win the European title by beating Emile Degand, of France, kept it against Vincenzo Savo, of Italy, and won the Lonsdale Belt outright by defeating the Scottish champion, Jim Maharg, in eight rounds.

Brown's great triumph came when he fought Young Perez, French holder of the world crown, at Manchester's Belle Vue in July 1933. The locals who packed the hall to capacity fully expected Jackie to win a points victory with his speedy boxing, but he had them going berserk when he knocked out the champion with a perfect combination of jaw punches in the 13th round. Twice he successfully defended his title against strong opposition provided by Valentin Angelmann, of France, and he brought off another great victory when he retained his titles against the younger Ginger Foran, the pride of Merseyside.

When challenged by Benny Lynch, Brown was overwhelmed from the start by the aggressive Scotsman and was put down ten times before the towel was thrown in from his corner, getting up with great courage to face his rival's blazing fists until beaten into helplessness. Defeat stripped Jackie of all his hard-won titles, but he remained a top-of-the-bill fighter for four more years until he joined the Army at the age of 30. He made one bid to win the British bantam title, but was knocked out in the 13th round of a thriller by his fellow-townsman, Johnny King.

Brown (*right*) in his world title defence against Frenchman Valentin Angelmann.

Benny Lynch

Many people rate Benny Lynch (1913–1946) as close up to Jimmy Wilde as the greatest of world flyweight champions. A perfect boxer, the little Scot had outstanding punching power, especially in the latter half of his fighting career when the majority of his wins were gained inside the scheduled course. A calculating attacking boxer, Lynch also developed a sound defence and was never stopped, except in the last bout of his career when he was but a shell of his former brilliant self. Benny did not go all out for a quick kayo win, but weakened his rivals with carefully placed punches to all the vulnerable points of the body above the belt-line, before putting over the one punch that paid for all.

Born in the impoverished Gorbals district of Glasgow, Lynch spent his boyhood on the streets, selling newspapers out of school hours. His first introduction to boxing came when his father took him to the local fairground on a Saturday night to watch the booth-fighters, encouraging the lad to box other boys for a shilling or two. Benny joined an amateur club and was a highly successful member, winning all but two of his 37 bouts, and he spent the summers touring with a booth through the northern counties.

By the time he was 18 and devoting his whole time to pro fighting, he was a seasoned campaigner. His advance was meteoric and when he became Scottish flyweight champion, his manager George Dingley, who had ambitions towards promoting, induced Jackie Brown, the world flyweight king, to

visit Glasgow and meet Lynch in a non-title bout over 12 rounds. At that time Brown was streets ahead of any other flyweight in the country, but Lynch surprised even his own ardent followers, by holding the champion to a draw and learnt enough from the experience to stop Brown in two rounds six months later to win three titles at one fell swoop.

In gaining victory Lynch produced a degree of hard punching seldom seen among flyweights, and when he defended his trio of championships against the highly fancied Pat Palmer from London and won by a knockout in eight rounds, it was a superb performance that prompted Arthur Elvin to stage an international world title bout at Wembley Arena, between Lynch and the American claimant to the title, Small Montana from the Philippines. Their 15-round bout was a model of the art of self-defence, with barely a foot or a glove put out of place on either side, but with Lynch emphasizing his superiority with dazzling footwork and crisp and accurate hitting. It was a contest that should have been filmed for the benefit of all budding boxers and at

Lynch has Brown down for the first time in winning the title.

the finish the packed arena rose to Lynch as he was acclaimed a worthy points winner.

He was now undisputed world champion and he kept his crown against young Peter Kane nine months later when 40,000 excited fans at Shawfield Park, Glasgow, saw a thrilling bout that went into the 13th round before Benny produced the knockout punch that put paid to Kane's ambitions. Tragically that was the last that was seen of the mighty Lynch. Matched to defend his world crown against Jackie Jurich, of America, Benny was six and a half pounds overweight and had to forfeit all his titles. He knocked out Jurich in 12 rounds to avenge his losses, but now went all to pieces. Excessive weight-making had turned him into a drunkard and weighing more like a lightweight than a fly. Three months after the Jurich débacle he was knocked out by Aurel Toma, whom he would have outclassed when in his prime, and eight years later he was dead due to debilitation at the age of 33.

Peter Kane

The astonishing thing about Peter Kane was his ability to make a successful comeback after his career had been rudely interrupted by the war, during which he suffered an accident to an eye that caused him a lot of trouble in the second half of his fighting life. Born at Golborne in Lancashire in 1918, he was employed as an apprentice by the local blacksmith and built up the muscular development and hitting power that was to make him a great box-office attraction and the winner of 51 bouts inside the distance from a total of 95 contests. Having sampled his punches in amateur bouts the local boys were delighted when he announced his intention of turning professional. His request for a contest was turned down by Johnny Best, manager of the Liverpool Stadium, because of his extreme youth, but persistence paid and he was given a trial bout, although he was still only 16.

In a year Peter had proved himself the idol of Merseyside with 13 knockouts that occupied only 37 rounds, and he went on winning until he was unbeaten in 41 contests and, as Northern Area champion, was entitled to a crack at Benny Lynch for the world title. It was a severe test for a 19-year-old lad and many thought it was a mis-match. They seemed right when the champion dropped his young challenger with a magnificent dexter punch to the jaw. But Kane struggled up to carry the fight to the champion and trade punches enthusiastically until he ran out of gas in the 13th, was caught again and this time failed to beat the count.

Peter forced a draw with Lynch in an overweight match at Liverpool and when Benny forfeited his title because of being overweight for a match with Jackie Jurich, the Golborne blacksmith defeated the American to become world flyweight king. He was 20 years old. The war prevented all the lucrative matches that were Peter's due, and he joined the Royal Air Force. There were only 17 bouts in the next four years, then he boiled himself down to make the weight for Jackie Paterson and as a result was put down and out in 61 seconds.

Sadly it seemed the end of Kane, although he was only 25. But he took a rest, then returned to action as a bantam with renewed vigour. Winning

14 bouts on the trot, he challenged Theo Medina, of France, for the European title and beat him on points. In his next contest he outpointed challenger Joe Cornelis, of Belgium, but lost to Guido Ferracin, a talented Italian. Striving to regain his championship, Peter was forced to retire after five rounds suffering from cuts over both eyes, the result of a collision of heads. When he was outpointed by Stan Rowan in his next bout, Kane decided to retire from the ring. He was 30 then, had held a world title and a European championship, yet had never been a champion of his own country.

Above: **Kane (*right*) becomes world champion by beating Jurich on points. *Below:* Kane (*right*) avoids a left from Pierre Louis on** his way to a win. *Opposite:* **Two views of Kane's successful European title defence against balding Cornelis.**

Jackie Paterson

Although a southpaw, Jackie Paterson (1920–1966) could hit equally hard with both hands as his tally of 41 inside-the-distance wins in a total of 91 professional bouts makes clear. An excellent boxer, smooth and speedy, he was a menace to flys and bantams alike while in his prime. It was when he was fighting a losing battle with the scales that he was toppled from his high estate. Blessed with a long reach, he could time his punches to a nicety and always hit with the knuckle part of the glove. Perhaps the most sensational of his 63 wins was when he fought Danny O'Sullivan, one of his leading contenders. The Londoner had been pressing the bantam king for the best part of eight rounds while keeping a watchful eye on Paterson's deadly left hook. Suddenly Jackie was backed into a corner and seemed to be in trouble, but as O'Sullivan came in to punish him with a blistering two-handed attack, Paterson picked him off with a neat but decisive punch from his right hand that knocked Danny down and out.

Born at Springfield in Ayrshire, Scotland, Jackie was taken to America by his parents at the age of eight. When they returned five years later, he joined the Anderston Club in Glasgow, but became a professional at the age of 17 and soon showed that he had all the makings of a champion. In his 19th bout he won the vacant British flyweight crown by knocking out Paddy Ryan in 13 rounds, added the Empire title with a

points victory over Kid Tanner, then took the world crown from Peter Kane with a dramatic one-round win. He was thus a triple flyweight champion and he remained such for nine years, during which he put up a brilliant display in defending his laurels against clever Joe Curran, of Liverpool, and also competed for and won the British, Empire and European bantamweight titles.

It was a great misfortune for this talented boxer to lose his world title because of weight-making. Matched to defend it against Dado Marino of Hawaii, he could not attend the weigh-in ceremony and was stripped of his title by the British Boxing Board of Control. Later he crucified himself to make eight stone for Rinty Monaghan, who knocked him out in seven rounds at Belfast.

Jackie had similar troubles as a bantam. He first won the Empire title after two tries against Jim Brady, then won the European crown on a foul over Theo Medina, the Parisian hairdresser, but lost it in a return contest by being knocked out in four rounds. He regained prestige by the masterful way in which he took the British title from veteran Johnny King, and caused a great surprise when he knocked out in five rounds a more youthful and dangerous challenger in Norman Lewis of Wales. He was in his 29th year when he was finally rendered titleless by Stan Rowan, who relieved him of his British and Empire bantam crowns on a close points decision. There were five more bouts, of which he lost four, then Jackie hung up his gloves for good. In spite of his large earnings during 13 years of scrapping he had little to show for it when he retired. He went to South Africa to live and in 1966, at the age of 46, was killed in a public-house brawl.

Paterson knocking out Kane in the first round to win the world flyweight title.

Rinty Monaghan

John Joseph Monaghan, otherwise 'Rinty', was named after the famous film dog of the silent days because of his speed as a youngster. Fleet-footed both at running and football, it came as a great asset when he turned to boxing at the tender age of 14. His long arms gave him a reach advantage over most and his punches carried plenty of sting. His career covered 15 years, but because of the war, it was severely curtailed and produced only 51 bouts, of which he lost eight. If the truth is known the best of Monaghan was never seen, except at the start when, of course, he was not fully mature.

Born in a poor district of Belfast in 1920, it was a great boon to boys with boxing ability to be able to secure fights at the local Ulster Hall, even if they were underpaid for their services. Rinty scored a knockout on his first appearance and was a regular performer thereafter. In fact, all but one of his first 24 bouts took place in Belfast, the exception being when he was offered a fight in Liverpool which he won. A long winning run was broken by Jackie Paterson, whose southpaw style proved too great a problem for the Irishman and he was stopped in the fifth round. He was to gain a double revenge for this defeat in later years.

Monaghan had five nice wins in 1939, then the war intervened and in the next four years he could manage only three contests, all of which he lost to make him almost a forgotten man. With the war over, he came back quietly, including a six-round victory over Paterson, who by now was the holder of five titles. This caught the notice of a London promoter who engaged Rinty to tackle the up-and-coming Terry Allen, who was five years younger. Those who thought the Irishman might prove a stepping-stone for the Islington youth were shocked when Monaghan won by a knockout in the opening round, and when he defeated Emile Famechon, of France, he appeared as the leading challenger to the world title.

He had to wait because Paterson was booked to defend his crown against Dado Marino, from Honolulu, but when the Scot failed to make the weight, Monaghan came in as a very late substitute, only to be ruled out in round nine for 'holding'. He was then matched with the Hawaiian in a 'vacant' championship fight in London and defeated Marino on points. Paterson claimed that he was still titleholder, so they met in Belfast for the third time with Rinty winning over a weight-making weakened Scot who took the full count sitting on the canvas utterly beaten in round seven.

Monaghan made two defences of his world crown, outpointing Maurice Sandeyron, of France, to take his European championship, then boxing a draw with Terry Allen. This latter verdict caused a disturbance and Rinty quelled a threatened riot by taking the microphone from the announcer and singing an Irish ballad which soon had the fans joining in. Monaghan was approaching 30 then; even so it was something of a surprise when he decided to retire without again defending his titles.

Yoshio Shirai

To Yoshio Shirai goes the distinction of being the first Japanese boxer to win a world title. It is also noteworthy to add that he was turned 29 when he gained the championship. It took the war and the subsequent occupation by American troops to bring boxing into Japan. Most of the eager young scrappers slugged it out with very little science, but Shirai was lucky to be taken in hand by Dr A. R. Cann, a botany professor from the University of Illinois, who was attached to the Natural Resources Division of the occupying forces. He was a boxing follower and seeing Shirai punching a bag with method and a variety of moves, he gradually developed him into a boxer of considerable merit.

Born in the Oji district of Tokyo in 1923, Shirai had a darker skin than the average Japanese and was also tall for a flyweight. He used his physical endowments to advantage and became both flyweight and bantamweight champion of his country. Eleven days after his 28th birthday he had his first contest outside Japan, going to Honolulu to meet Dado Marino, the world flyweight champion, in a non-title bout, and causing an upset by flooring the local idol six times before Marino's manager tossed in the towel in round seven.

That entitled Shirai to a crack at the championship and four months later, in Tokyo, the title passed into Japanese hands as he won an undisputed points victory over his seven-years-older opponent. It was the first time Shirai had fought over 15 rounds, but he paced himself well and when they had a return contest six months later, he gained an

Shirai has Dado Marino down. He won the title on points.

even more conclusive victory on points.

Following a successful title defence against Tanny Campo of the Philippines, Shirai accepted a challenge from Terry Allen, who was anxious to win back the world championship he had lost to Marino three years earlier. In an outdoor stadium, 30,000 fans, including hundreds of American soldiers and Prince Yoshi, youngest son of Emperor Hirohito, huddled in overcoats on a chilly wind-swept night to watch the champion come close to defeat by the aggressive determined Briton on several occasions. But a late rally saved the day for Yoshio by a close points margin. The gate was £25,000 with another £5,000 from radio and television receipts. It was the first fight ever televised in Japan.

Shirai remained champion for another year, then he lost his crown to Pascual Perez, a tiny tearaway fighter from the Argentine, who swarmed over him, put him down in the 12th and was a unanimous points winner at the finish. Six months later they met in a return title fight and this time Shirai was given a fearful battering that ended with him taking the full count in the fifth round. Immediately after he had been helped to his corner his retirement from boxing was announced. He was 32.

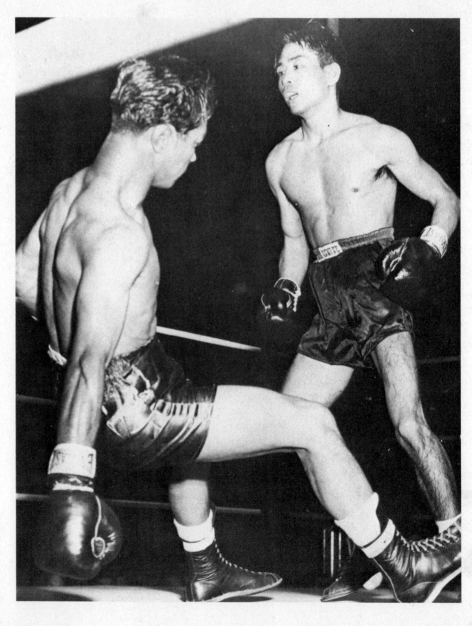

Pascual Perez

At 4 ft 11 in and weighing 7 st 7 lb,
Pascual Perez of the Argentine was the
smallest man to win the world's
flyweight title and also the most
dynamic. Difficult to hit because of his
short stature, he could dive under an
opponent's defence to set up a blistering
and sustained attack that gave him 83
wins (56 inside the distance) in 91
contests. Two of his bouts were drawn.
His record is all the more amazing when
it is realized that he was 26 before he
became a professional, won the world
crown two years later, defended it 14
times, was champion for six years and
was still fighting at the age of 37.

Born at Tupungate near Mendoza in
Argentina in 1926, he lacked schooling
because he came from a poor family of
nine which required the working
services of all to make both ends meet.
From an early age he became a vineyard
worker, and although on the tiny side,
was blessed with a strong physique and
an abundance of stamina. When he was
18 he became an amateur boxer against
his parents' wishes, but did so well that
he won the Latin-American title in
Chile, repeated it the following year in
Brazil and was then chosen to
represent the Argentine at the 1948
Olympic Games in London, returning
home with the gold medal for the
flyweight class.

When he was given a job as a janitor
in the civil service at Mendoza, his father
induced him to give up boxing, but he
continued to box under the assumed
name of Pablo and when this was
discovered he turned pro, and proved
his point by winning his first 50 contests.
In Buenos Aires he boxed a ten-round
draw with Yoshio Shirai, the world
champion, and was so convinced that he
could beat him that he ventured to
Tokyo to win the title on points after
hammering his taller opponent all over
the ring. In a return title bout Perez
stopped the Japanese boxer in five
rounds and ended his career.

Now came that long list of
championship defences in which he met
and defeated Mexicans, Spaniards,
Japanese, Argentinians, Philippinos and
other South American challengers,
beating the majority inside the distance.
Dai Dower, the British champion, lasted
exactly 90 seconds against the ferocity

**Perez bores in to battered
challenger Leo Espinosa of the
Philippines.** *Right:* **Perez after
winning the title from Shirai.**

and punching power of little Perez.

Eventually, he tripped off to Bangkok
and lost on points to Pone Kingpetch,
flyweight champion of the Orient and
ten years his junior. A return match at
Los Angeles five months later saw Perez
stopped for the first time in his life,
being rescued by the referee when he
was out on his feet in the eighth round.
But Pascual was not finished and
continued to box for three more years,
winning the majority of his 33 bouts,
until two successive inside-the-distance
defeats made him realize that the time
had come to retire.

Pone Kingpetch

When he first took up sport, Pone Kingpetch used his feet as weapons in true Thailander style, but when he realized that he could never become world champion at it, he switched to boxing, learning the rudiments of fist-fighting from a book written by an American instructor who was employed by the Thailand Government to teach the art of self-defence to the Bangkok youngsters. Kingpetch proved an enthusiastic pupil and was soon good enough to take part in amateur bouts. After three of them, of which he lost one, he decided that if he was going to be punched he might as well be paid for it, so at the age of 18 he turned professional. Real name Nana Seadoaghob, it is easy to understand why he changed it.

Born at Hua Hin, a seaport province of North Thailand, he was the seventh child in a family of nine, five boys, four girls. His mother was anxious that he should become a Buddhist priest, it being a Thailand belief that if a son serves in a temple one is relieved of all sins.

When she realized that his heart was set on a boxing career she gave in. Tall for a flyweight at 5 ft 7 in he proved an excellent long-range boxer and used his smart footwork to keep himself away from infighting. He followed the winning of his native championship by becoming the Orient titleholder. Then he suffered a fractured jaw as the result of a car smash and was out of action for nearly a year.

During this time he found employment at a pharmaceutical laboratory, the owner of which, Thong Thos Indradat, became his sponsor and put up the money to tempt Pascual Perez to come to Bangkok and defend his world crown against Kingpetch. Pone had a rough time coping with his small, aggressive rival, but he stuck to his boxing and emerged a points winner on a split verdict. There was a return match in Los Angeles, but now Kingpetch had got the Argentine's measure and cut him to ribbons in eight rounds to retain his crown. In the next two years he went thrice to Tokyo to face Japanese

contenders and on the last occasion came away without his title, having been outpointed by Fighting Harada. He won it back from this boxer three months later, but on again visiting Japan was sensationally beaten in the first round by Hiroyuki Ebihara, a southpaw, who swung a left to the Thailander's chin to drop him for 'eight' and then finished him off in 2 min 7 sec.

That seemed the end for Kingpetch, but his backer still had faith in him and invited the Japanese champion to see if he could do it again in Bangkok. He couldn't, Pone putting up the best fight of his life to recapture the flyweight title for the second time, the only man ever to win the eight-stone championship three times. In 1965 at the age of 29 he dropped the crown to Salvatore Burruni, of Italy and retired from boxing the following year.

Kingpetch (*right*) successfully defending his title against a game Mitsunori Seki of Japan who went the distance in Tokyo, 1961.

Walter McGowan

Fistic fathers do not always produce fighting sons, but the sire of Walter McGowan, who had fought with a great deal of success under the name of Joe Gans, his boxing idol, began teaching his boy the rituals of self-defence at a very early age so that at ten he was ready to participate in his first contest. Walter had all the moves, the punching power and the cool temperament to make him the complete boxer. But for a tendency to cut easily around the eyes, he might have become more famous than he did.

As an amateur he won all but two of his 124 bouts, gained several Scottish titles, represented his country in a number of international matches and crowned his unpaid career by becoming ABA flyweight champion in 1961. He was then 18, having been born at Burnbank in Lanarkshire in October 1942. His professional career was confined to only 40 bouts, but in the short time of eight years he won three titles at his weight, his greatest success being to bring the world flyweight crown back to Great Britain after an absence of 16 years. He also went out of his class, poundage-wise, to take the British and Empire bantam titles.

A smart left jabber, a crisp right-hand hitter and a sound combination puncher, McGowan won the British eight-stone title in his tenth professional fight, knocking out Jackie Brown in the 12th round. Four months later he stopped Kid Solomon in nine rounds to add the Empire championship to his holdings, but was adjudged to have lost on points to Salvatore Burruni when he went to Rome to try to win European honours. The following year he again visited Italy when attempting to win the EBU bantam title from Tommaso Galli. This time he secured a 'draw' although in the opinion of many ringside critics, he deserved the full verdict.

McGowan became world champion by brilliantly outpointing the tough Burruni at Wembley Arena after 15 rousing rounds, most of which the little Scot fought under the handicap of a ravaged right eye caused by an accidental butt. He was, however, the first Britisher to hold the world title since Terry Allen's short tenure in 1950, and that in itself was a satisfying achievement. Three months later he

reached his peak of achievement by outpointing Alan Rudkin for the British and Empire bantam titles, yet within 20 months he was completely titleless.

Defending the world flyweight crown against Thailander Chartchai Chionoi, at Bangkok, he was forced to retire with a severe nose injury in the ninth round and in a return match at Wembley he was stopped with a ghastly left-eye injury in round seven. Rudkin regained his bantam honours and McGowan had already been forced to surrender his flyweight titles because of a Board of Control ruling that a boxer may not hold championships at two weights. Walter's

Top: **McGowan (*left*) had two exciting battles with Rudkin, winning and losing the British and Empire bantam titles.** *Below:* **McGowan (*left*) avoids a right swing from Burruni when taking his world flyweight championship.**

short career came to an end with his retirement two years later, but he had two permanent mementoes of his fistic achievements – a Lonsdale Belt that became his own property when he had been without a challenger for three years, and the MBE awarded in the 1967 Queen's Birthday Honours List.

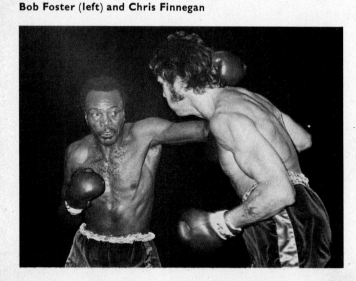

Bob Foster (left) and Chris Finnegan

Lionel Rose (left) and Alan Rudkin

Sugar Ray Robinson (left) beating Jake LaMotta

**Barney Ross (left) and
Jimmy McLarnin**

Pete Herman knocks out Jim Higgins

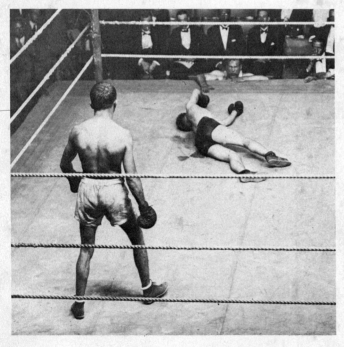